Banking Law and Practice

Banking Law and Practice

The Hong Kong Institute of Bankers

WILEY

John Wiley & Sons Singapore Pte. Ltd.

Published in 2013 by John Wiley & Sons Singapore Pte. Ltd.
1 Fusionopolis Walk, #07-01, Solaris South
Tower, Singapore 138628

Other Wiley Editorial Offices
John Wiley & Sons, 111 River Street, Hoboken, NJ 07030, USA
John Wiley & Sons, The Atrium, Southern Gate, Chichester, West Sussex, P019 8SQ, United Kingdom
John Wiley & Sons (Canada) Ltd., 5353 Dundas Street West, Suite 400, Toronto, Ontario, M9B 6HB, Canada
John Wiley & Sons Australia Ltd., 42 McDougall Street, Milton, Queensland 4064, Australia
Wiley-VCH, Boschstrasse 12, D-69469 Weinheim, Germany

ISBN 978-0-470-82761-1 (Paperback)
ISBN 978-0-470-82763-5 (ePDF)
ISBN 978-0-470-82762-8 (Mobi)
ISBN 978-0-470-82764-2 (ePub)

Typeset in 11/14pt. ArnoPro Regular by MPS Limited, Chennai, India.
Printed in Singapore by 1010 Printing Group Limited.

10 9 8 7 6 5 4 3 2 1

Contents

Preface

Because of its sensitivity and importance to the public at large, banking is a heavily regulated industry. This book continues along the path started by the first two in this series by discussing bank operations. It takes a new tack, however, by looking at how banks operate in a legal and regulatory light and delves deep into laws and regulations and how banks can shape their practices to meet all the necessary legal and regulatory requirements.

This book is divided into four parts and nine chapters, each looking at a separate issue at considerable depth. Further reading is encouraged and suggestions are provided at the end of each chapter. Every effort has been made to ensure that the laws and regulations referred to in this book are up to date and the most current in use as of November 2011. Updates will be made for later laws and regulations in future editions.

The first part of this book starts with a discussion of the laws and regulations that determine and impact the relationship between a bank and its customers including Hong Kong legislation, Hong Kong Monetary Authority guidelines, and privacy and confidentiality requirements. It includes a look at account handling, the many documents involved in a bank's external operations, and the different types of customers.

The second part of this book begins in Chapter 3 with an examination of the legal issues that govern negotiable instruments, in particular bills of exchange and promissory notes. The part continues with a look at other types of services and delivery platforms. Prominent among these are credit cards, investment advice, direct debiting, and automated banking.

Part 3, which begins in Chapter 5, begins with a look at security, security held by banks against a loan or credit. The first chapter in this part looks at guarantees, the most common form of security used by banks and other creditors. Chapter 6 looks at mortgages, which are a more popular type of security. Chapter 7 closes off this part with an examination of the laws and regulations governing the use of other types of security like company charge, stocks or bonds, or physical goods.

The last part of this book encompasses the last two chapters. Chapter 8 looks at insolvency and the legal issues that emerge in bankruptcy, when a client cannot pay debts to a bank. Chapter 9 looks at the process of winding up and the legal issues that emerge that involve a bank.

This book includes detailed explanations, summaries, tables, and charts to help industry professionals develop sound theoretical frameworks for their work in the field. Both students and working professional can benefit from this detailed work, produced in collaboration with some of Hong Kong's most prominent professionals. Aimed at banking practitioners and designed as an essential tool to achieve learning outcomes, this book includes recommendations for additional readings. A list of further readings at the end of each chapter will help readers expand their knowledge of each subject, while supplementary readings can help dig deeper into specific areas. Essential readings will occasionally be highlighted and these are important for students preparing for the Associates Examination of the Hong Kong Institute of Bankers (AHKIB).

Above all, it is most important to acknowledge Mr. Simon B. C. Chan, whose decades of experience and encyclopaedic knowledge of laws and regulations have been invaluable for the development of banking in Hong Kong. His book *Hong Kong Banking Law and Practice* (Vol. 1 & 2), published by the Hong Kong Institute of Bankers, has long been the go-to legal reference for the industry. While Mr. Chan was not directly involved in the writing or editing of this book, we are thankful for his support in permitting his work (1st edition) to be used as an important reference and source of information.

There are others whose contributions have been of particular significance in the preparation of this essential reference for banking professionals. Among them are Mr. Steve Lau, Mr. Eddie W. K. Leung, Dr. Luk Kwai Wing, Mr. Antony M.H. Sin, Dr. Alex Wong, and representatives from the Hong Kong Monetary Authority.

The preparation would not have been possible without the help, advice, support and encouragement of all these people and dozens more. We would like to extend our warm thanks to them all.

The Hong Kong Institute of Bankers

PART 1

1

BANK-CUSTOMER RELATIONSHIP AND ACCOUNT OPENING

CHAPTER 1

1

Contractual Relationships in Law and Practice

Learning objectives

After studying this chapter, you should be able to:

1. Describe the nature of the relationship between banker and customer and the key legal and regulatory issues relating to the terms of the contract between them

2. Understand the legal issues around the operation of bank accounts, including mandates, power of attorney, limitation of actions, appropriation of payments, set-off, and banker's lien

3. Explain the concept of banker's duty of secrecy and how it relates to the provisions of the Personal Data (Privacy) Ordinance, including the six principles of data protection

4. Discuss recommended bank practices related to a statement of account or passbook, wrongful dishonour of cheques, and exemption clauses

Introduction

Many legal issues arise in the course of day-to-day banking operations. Bankers, therefore, need to learn about these issues and be guided by them in order to protect their companies and themselves from liability. In this chapter, we provide an overview of the relationship between a bank and its customers from a legal and regulatory perspective. We discuss the implied terms of the banker and customer relationship relating to a banker's duty of secrecy, and explain specific legal issues relating to the terms of the contract and the respective rights and duties of the bank and the customer.

References are made to common law, legislation in Hong Kong, guidelines of the Hong Kong Monetary Authority and the Code of Banking Practice. We also discuss the relevance of the Personal Data (Privacy) Ordinance and the six data protection principles in protecting, and providing for the proper use of, the personal data of customers in the course of day-to-day banking operations. We conclude the discussion with an analysis of a number of issues commonly affecting the operation of bank accounts.

Definition of 'Customer'

There is actually no statutory definition in Hong Kong of who a customer of a bank is, so we have to refer to the decisions of the courts in order to discover the principles which determine whether or not a person is a customer.

In common law, which is a body of law developed through court decisions rather than bills passed by the legislature, a customer is a person who maintains an account with the bank. "There must be some sort of account, either a deposit or a current account or similar relation, to make a man a customer of a banker," a British court held in the case of *Great Western Railway Co. v. London & Country Banking Co.* The judge ruled that though a person may habitually deal with a bank, for example, to buy gift cheques, this does not make the person a customer of that bank.

Common law also holds that a relationship between a banker and customer does not come into existence unless and until both parties intend to enter into it. However, the relationship can be deemed to have started even before an account has been actually opened. In *Ladbroke & Co. v. Todd*, the court held that it was not necessary that a person "should have drawn any money or even that he should be in position to draw money" before he could become a customer. A banker-customer relationship is immediately established upon the bank's acceptance of a person's offer to open an account in that bank.

Why does a banking professional need to know who is a customer and who is not, legally speaking? One reason is to avoid contractual liability, which can arise when giving off-the-cuff investment advice, for example, in the belief that no contractual relationship exists. If there is an intention on both sides to enter into a relationship, that person can be considered already a customer and therefore could theoretically sue the banker for giving negligent advice.

Another reason is to be protected by Section 86 of the Bills of Exchange Ordinance, which provides that bankers who receive a payment for a customer or credit a customer account will not be treated as having been negligent if the customer turns out to have no title or a defective title to that payment. If the banker receives a payment or performs a remittance funded by a cheque, to give two examples, for someone who is, legally speaking, not a customer, then he is not protected by Section 86.

Nature of the Banker-Customer Relationship

In legal terms, the relationship between banker and customer is essentially a contractual one, meaning that each side has explicit and implicit obligations. Breaching those obligations could be grounds for litigation. The nature of the relationship can take several forms, arising from the types of services rendered by the bank:

- Banker and customer;
- Debtor and creditor;
- Principal and agent;
- Bailor and bailee.

Banker and Customer

In recent years, many banks have tried to set out the terms of the contract between banker and customer as comprehensively as possible in written form. Customers are provided with a set of standalone consolidated terms and conditions and are asked to sign an application for account opening, which includes a reference to the terms and conditions and an acknowledgment of acceptance. The application normally takes the form of the customer's mandate to the bank and the terms and conditions are incorporated by reference in the application.

However, in most cases, there is no formal agreement which provides that a banker must maintain strict secrecy concerning his customers' accounts or that the customer must exercise care when drawing cheques to prevent the amounts from being fraudulently altered.

Of course, when most accounts are opened, such as current and savings accounts, a mandate is executed, which gives the bank express instructions and/or authorities concerning the operation of the account. However, even in those cases, no attempt is made to prepare a comprehensive list of the respective rights and duties of banker and customer.

This may be because it is impossible to list all the terms contemplated and banks also consider the impact on bank marketing.

The contractual relationship between banker and customer is founded on the customs and trade usages of bankers. To the extent that the customs and trade usages have been recognised by the courts of Hong Kong, they must be regarded as implied terms of contract between banker and customer. Therefore, the implied terms are of vital importance in banking law and practice.

The Code of Banking Practice requires banks to make readily available to customers, or prospective customers, written terms and conditions of each banking product or banking service and to advise customers to read and understand them. The terms and conditions should meet the following criteria:

- Provide a fair and balanced description of the relationship between bank and customer;
- Generally available in both Chinese and English;
- Use plain language and avoid legal and technical language unless it is necessary;
- Highlight any fees, charges, penalties, and the relevant interest rates (or the basis for determining the interest rates), and the customer's liabilities and obligations in using the service;
- Consistency with the provisions of the Code, and be kept under review to ensure such consistency;
- Have due regard to applicable laws in Hong Kong, in particular prevailing consumer protection legislation.

Debtor and Creditor

The deposit of money into a bank renders the bank a debtor and the depositor a creditor. The bank is therefore obliged to repay any sum deposited to the depositor (except in certain defined circumstances such as banker's right and set-off). These roles are reversed when a bank lends money to a customer.

It was settled in *Foley v. Hill* that the established debtor and creditor relationship excludes any element or suggestion of trusteeship or fiduciary relation with the banker with regard to a current account. The House of Lords held that the relation between a banker and his customer, who pays money into the bank, is the ordinary relation of debtor and creditor, with an additional obligation arising out of the custom of bankers to honour the customer's cheques.

Principal and Agent

When a banker is performing certain duties, he frequently acts as an agent. For example, the banker often collects the proceeds of cheques as an agent for his customers. In drawing and paying cheques, the relationship between customer and banker is that of principal and agent. Further, the banker acts as an agent when accepting customers' instructions in regards to the purchase and sale of the stocks and shares.

However, when a banker is instructed by the customer to place an order with a broker for the purchase of shares on the customer's behalf, the relationship of principal and agent arises between the customer and the broker when the broker accepts the order; no such relationship arises between the customer and the banker.

Bailor and Bailee

When articles are delivered to a bank for safe custody, the contract between the bank (as bailee) and the customer (as bailor) is one of bailment, which involves the transfer of possession, not ownership. The bank is not entitled to use the articles whilst they are in its possession. The customer can demand the return of the articles at any reasonable time.

Safekeeping of title deeds after the mortgage loan of a customer is paid off is an example of custody service.

Laws and Practice

In Hong Kong, the sources of the laws and practice that govern the bank-customer relationship include the following:

- Common law
- Legislative sources
- Non-statutory rules
- Code of Banking Practice

Common Law

Although China has resumed sovereignty, Hong Kong still follows the English legal system of Common law. As laid down by the Basic Law of the Hong Kong Special Administrative Region, laws previously in force in Hong Kong (Common law), rules of equity, ordinance, subordinate legislation, and customary law shall be maintained except for any that contravenes the Basic Law. However, Common law is subject to amendment by the Hong Kong legislature, which has begun passing measures that diverge from it.

The doctrine of legal precedent has also been preserved in Hong Kong, although the court of final adjudication is the Court of Final Appeal in Hong Kong instead of the Privy Council in England. All decided cases in Commonwealth countries would be considered in equal standing by the court of Hong Kong, which may also refer to precedents of other common law jurisdictions. The same is applicable to Banking Law.

Legislative Sources

The two most important legislative sources in Hong Kong are the Banking Ordinance (Cap. 155) and the Bills of Exchange Ordinance (Cap. 19).

The Banking Ordinance is a statute providing for the regulation of banking business and the business of taking deposits in Hong Kong. It defines the term "banking business" and refers to the three-tier financial system in which licensed banks, restricted licence banks, and deposit-taking companies are collectively referred to as "authorised institutions." The Bills of Exchange Ordinance, on the other hand, deals with the law relating to negotiable instruments, including bills of exchange, cheques, and promissory notes.

The Hong Kong Association of Banks Ordinance (Cap. 364), the Exchange Fund Ordinance (Cap. 66) and the Protection of Investors Ordinance (Cap. 335) are other important sources of banking law. The Companies Ordinance (Cap. 32), the Partnership Ordinance (Cap. 38), the Bankruptcy Ordinance (Cap. 6) and the Conveyancing and Property Ordinance (Cap. 219) have a bearing on banking as well.

Subsidiary legislation made by virtue of the Banking Ordinance and the above-mentioned ordinances are also important and bankers must take note of such legislation.

Given the growing significance of securities related services among banks' core business, the Securities and Futures Ordinance (Cap. 571) is also an important legislative source.

The Anti-Money Laundering and Counter-Terrorist Financing (Financial Institutions) Ordinance (Cap. 615), which codifies customer due diligence and record-keeping requirements for financial institutions and provides for supervisory and criminal sanctions for contravention of the statutory requirements, was enacted in June 2011 with effect from 1 April 2012.

Statutory and Non-statutory Guidelines

The Banking Ordinance empowers the Hong Kong Monetary Authority (HKMA) to issue guidelines relating to the internal workings of authorised institutions to ensure that proper banking standards are maintained. There are two broad categories of guidelines: statutory and non-statutory.

The HKMA's statutory guidelines are issued under the Banking Ordinance, which set out the minimum standards with which authorized institutions are expected to comply to satisfy the requirements of the Banking Ordinance. Statutory guidelines do not have the force of law. Non-statutory guidelines are typically issued to set out the HKMA's recommendations to AIs in respect of the standards they should aim to achieve, or for the purpose of clarifying the HKMA's interpretation of regulatory and reporting matters. Any failure to adhere to any of these guidelines, whether statutory or non-statutory, may call into question whether the AI concerned continues to satisfy the minimum criteria for authorization under the Banking Ordinance. In addition, where such failure is in respect of any of the statutory guidelines, it may constitute a contravention of the relevant provisions or requirements of the Banking Ordinance.

Code of Banking Practice

The Code of Banking Practice is issued jointly by the Hong Kong Association of Banks (HKAB) and the DTC Association (the industry group for restricted licence banks and deposit-taking companies), and is endorsed by the HKMA. Whilst it specifically covers banking services such as current accounts, savings and other deposit accounts, loans and overdrafts, and card services, its principles apply to the overall relationship between institutions and their customers. The Code does not apply retrospectively to transactions completed before its issuance.

The recommendations do not supplant any relevant legislation, codes, guidelines, or rules applicable to institutions authorised under the Banking Ordinance. However, the HKMA expects all authorised institutions to comply with the Code and will monitor compliance as part of its regular supervision. Authorised institutions may be challenged for any non-adherence to the Code.

The Code applies to cases where an institution is dealing with a personal customer. A personal customer is defined as a private individual who (i) maintains an account in Hong Kong with or receives services from an institution; or (ii) acts as guarantor or provider of third party security for a borrower (who may or may not be an individual).

Mandates

A mandate is a written instruction from a customer to a bank to do certain acts on the customer's behalf. In practice, it is a standard printed form drafted by the bank for customers' use on the opening of new accounts or when customers change the ways accounts are to be operated. The printed forms typically refer to a booklet that includes the terms and conditions of the mandate.

Through these documents the customer typically declares that, until he gives written notice to the contrary, a named person (whose signature appears on the mandate) is authorised to draw and endorse cheques on his behalf, notwithstanding that the debiting of any such instruments to his account may cause the account to be overdrawn. This latter provision is important because, in common law, the authority to draw cheques does not necessarily confer power to overdraw the account.

In a mandate, most terms are compulsory, that is, customers must accept them if they wish to open and maintain an account with a bank. However, there may be a number of optional clauses, one or more of which may be deleted in order to meet the wishes of the customer.

Most banks have two types of mandates:

- **Mandates for opening new accounts**, which are individual, joint, sole proprietorship, partnership, limited companies, clubs, unincorporated associations, and society; and
- **Mandates allowing third parties to operate the account**, which would confer power upon the agent:

i. to receive cheques, statements, and other vouchers relating to the account;
ii. to draw, accept, make, and endorse bills of exchange and promissory notes on behalf of the customer;
iii. to withdraw from the bank securities or other property belonging to the customer;
iv. to negotiate advances whether by way of loan, overdraft, discount, or otherwise; and
v. to pledge or deposit with the bank types of security for repayment for such advances.

These types of authority will not enable any agent to execute a deed on behalf of the customer, and the agent will not be able to create a legal charge by way of security.

In a strict legal sense, mandates are only instructions from customers to banks and not an agreement made between bankers and customers. In practice, however, most banks have incorporated many contractual clauses into a mandate. In other words, a mandate has become in practice a binding contract between the bankers and customers in most aspects of the terms of contract between them. For instance, the mandates of the banks would stipulate that both joint account holders would accept and limit the joint and several liabilities in respect of or arising out of the operation of the joint account maintained with the banks.

A bank should exercise reasonable care and skill when considering which clauses should be incorporated into a mandate. The clauses may not be enforceable if they are not in accordance with usual banking practice in Hong Kong.

Furthermore, any exemption clauses in a mandate, if any, are subject to the test of reasonableness under the Control of Exemption Clauses Ordinance (Cap. 71). Whether the clauses are reasonable will be determined in accordance with usual normal banking practice.

Because a mandate in practice has become a contract between bankers and customers, banks should not accept a mandate drafted by the customer, except for an account opened only for very special purposes and for a very valuable customer. In this special case, the bank must seek legal opinion on the contents of such special mandates, which should be approved by top executives.

In practice, banks would not open an account for any customer, including a valuable customer, if the customer requests to amend or vary the terms stated in the mandate. Only in a very special case would the bank allow any amendment or variation to the mandate. In those cases, the bank must seek legal opinion on any proposed amendment or variation.

Power of Attorney

Sometimes a customer may wish to authorise a third party to operate his account. He may do so by signing the bank's third-party mandate or executing a power of attorney. In this connection, it is important to distinguish between a mandate and a power of attorney.

A power of attorney is a document, usually executed under seal, which authorises one person (called the attorney, donee, or grantee) to act on behalf of another person (called donor, principal, or grantor).

The following differences between the two types of documents should be noted:

- A power of attorney is usually addressed to the world at large. A customer who wants the appointment of an attorney to be known to several parties could just execute one document instead of several. A mandate is usually addressed to one particular person, for example, a particular bank.
- In general, the donor of a power of attorney cannot notify his decision to revoke the power of attorney to everyone who might rely on it. The law makes special provision in favour of persons who rely upon a power in the honest belief that it has not been revoked. By contrast, a person who has signed a form of mandate may easily inform the person to whom it was addressed (the bank) that the authority of the agent has been cancelled.
- The general rule of law is that where an agent is authorised to execute a deed on behalf of his principal, his authority must be given by an instrument under seal. Therefore, an attorney under a power may be empowered to execute deeds, for example, legal charge. In contrast, an agent whose appointment is set out in a mandate cannot do so.

Types of Power of Attorney

There are two main types of powers of attorney: special/specific and general. A **special power** is one given for a specific purpose, for example, the attorney may be empowered to execute a legal charge only or to operate the accounts. An example would be an attorney being empowered to execute a mortgage.

A **general power** usually confers very extensive powers upon the donee. Both types (special and general) are usually executed under seal (signed, sealed, and delivered), thus enabling the donee to execute deeds on behalf of the donor.

Regardless of type, the power is revoked upon the death, winding up, bankruptcy, mental incapacity of, or expressed revocation by the donor. If a person without knowledge of the revocation deals with the donee, the transaction between them will be as valid as if the power is in existence.

Rules in the Use of Power of Attorney

The general rules in the use of the power of attorney include the following:

- Any person having power to contract may appoint an attorney.
- A corporation may appoint an attorney to complete *intra vires* (within the authority) acts.
- The attorney need not have contractual powers.
- The attorney cannot delegate his powers except under clear authority.
- A power given to two or more trustees jointly may be exercised by the survivors of those trustees.

The banker should make sure that:

- The power is operated exactly within the specific objects laid down.
- The power is still in force.
- The identity of the attorney is verified.
- The power is under seal.
- A certified copy of the power of attorney is obtained.

Revocable and Irrevocable

The banker may regard all powers of attorney as revocable, meaning that they can be revoked any time, even if expressly stated otherwise.

The only exception is under Section 4 of the Powers of Attorney Ordinance, which provides that the power of attorney is irrevocable if the power is expressed to be irrevocable and is given to secure a proprietary interest of the donee of the power or the performance of an obligation owed to the donee.

So long as the donee has that interest or the obligation remains undischarged, the power will not be revoked unless consented to by the donee or upon the death, bankruptcy, liquidation, and so on of the donor. As an example, the banker as mortgagee is always granted an irrevocable power of sale of the mortgaged property as an attorney of the mortgagor.

Enduring Power of Attorney

The Enduring Powers of Attorney Ordinance enacted in 1997 established a procedure for appointing an attorney who can manage a person's affairs after that person has become mentally incapable.

Practical Considerations for Banks

When a banker is given a general power of attorney under the Powers of Attorney Ordinance, there will be no problem ascertaining the scope of the attorney's power or authority. He will have power to do anything on behalf of the customer which the customer can lawfully do. But when a banker is given a special power of attorney, he would face the onerous task of finding out exactly what power has been conferred.

To operate an account under a power of attorney, the bank will need the original sealed power of attorney. If a bank is furnished with a power of attorney which is not in a form set out under Section 7 of the Powers of Attorney Ordinance, the banker has to ascertain the nature and extent of the power. Reading the document as a whole is a must.

Any exercise of the power by the attorney must be in accordance with the purpose for which the power was given. If the purpose of the power is unclear to the banker or the banker is not sure whether the actions of the donee will benefit the donor, a prudent banker should ask the donor of the power directly so as to confirm the actions of his attorney. In such cases, the banker should seek legal opinions from the bank's legal advisers.

When a power of attorney or a certified true copy (certified by the donor or a solicitor) executed by a customer is exhibited to the customer's bankers, the bankers must satisfy themselves that the following requirements have been complied with:

- The power must appear to have been validly executed. In some cases, difficulties arise if the customer is verging on senility, for example. In practice, it is prudent to have the power witnessed by the customer's doctor (a registered medical practitioner), who should certify that the said customer understands the nature and effect of the document being executed. However, the power may be revoked by the subsequent mental incapacity of the customer. The Enduring Powers of Attorney Ordinance establishes a procedure for appointing an attorney who can manage a person's affairs after that person has become mentally incapable.
- A true copy of the instrument creating the power of attorney must be supplied to the bank, preferably supplied directly from the donor (the customer) or his solicitors.
- The person claiming to be the attorney or donor must in fact be the person named in the power. In practice, the banker has to check and/or verify the identity of such person.
- The powers conferred upon the attorney must cover the transaction(s) which the donor wishes to enter into. This occasionally gives rise to difficulty because powers are strictly construed by the courts. The banker should request the customer to execute the bank's standard mandate, which is specially adapted to banking transactions. Alternatively, the customer may execute a general power of attorney. The signing of a

third-party mandate is a must whenever a bank is asked to operate an account by an appointed attorney.

Limitation of Actions

Lapse of time does not generally put an end to a contract or other liability, although it has been part of the public policy of Hong Kong law to prevent enforcement by legal action of long-dormant claims. The legislature has laid down certain periods of limitation after the expiry of which no action can be maintained. The statute of such law is the Limitation Ordinance (Cap. 347).

Two-year Limit

A two-year time limit applies in respect of actions to recover a penalty or forfeiture recoverable under any ordinance and to actions to recover a contribution pursuant to the Civil Liability (Contribution) Ordinance (Cap. 377). However, this does not apply to any action or arbitration for which a period of limitation is prescribed by another enactment.

Three-year Limit

The three-year time limit applies in actions for negligence, nuisance, or breach of duty, where the damages claimed by the plaintiff include damages in respect of personal injuries and to actions under the Fatal Accidents Ordinance (Cap. 22).

Six-year Limit

The six-year time limit applies to:

- Actions in respect of or arising out of simple contract or tort;
- Actions to enforce a recognizance;
- An award (where the submission is not by an instrument under seal);
- Actions to recover any sums recoverable under any ordinance;
- Actions for an account;
- Actions in respect of successive conversion of chattels;
- Actions to recover rent;
- Actions to recover arrears of interest payable in respect of money secured by a mortgage; or charge or in respect of a legacy;
- Certain actions by beneficiaries against trustees.

Twelve-year Limit

The 12-year time limit applies to:

- Actions upon specialities;
- Actions upon any judgement (save and except in respect of arrears in interest in respect of any judgement debt for which the period of limitation is six years);
- Actions to recover land, including foreclosure actions;
- Actions to redeem land;
- Actions to recover the principal monies secured by a mortgage or to foreclose a mortgage of personality;
- Actions claiming the personal estate of deceased persons.

No Limit

There is no period of limitation applicable to an action by a beneficiary, against a trustee, in respect of the trustee's fraud or fraudulent breach of trust or to recover trust property in the possession of the trustee or converted by him.

Extension of Period of Limitation

Part II of the Limitation Ordinance provides for the extension of the period of limitation as follows:

- In cases where the plaintiff was under a disability at the time when the cause of action accrued;
- In cases of an acknowledgement of the cause of action in writing or part payment by the defendant or his predecessor or agent;
- In cases where the action is based on fraud, the right of action was fraudulently concealed, or where the action is for relief from the consequences of a mistake.

The court also has the discretion to override the time limit for actions in respect of personal injuries, where the court considers that it would be equitable to allow the action to proceed.

Appropriation of Payments

Appropriation of payments is the right of a customer or a bank to apply a specified deposit to meet a specified debt. If the right of appropriation devolves on the creditor, the creditor may appropriate to a debt which is statute-barred, although such appropriation will not revive or acknowledge the debt. However, he may not appropriate to an illegal debt.

In *Canton Trust and Commercial Bank Ltd. v. Ho Pui Shue*, it was held that, in the absence of any instructions from the customer, the bank was entitled to appropriate any account. In this Hong Kong case, the court ruled that the bank acted properly in applying the payments to the current account and not to the trust account.

The creditor need not exercise his right of appropriation at the time of payment. It was held in *Seymour v. Pickett* that the creditor may make an appropriation when he is being examined as a witness in a legal action by him against the debtor. However, once a creditor has made an appropriation, "it is made once and for all, and it does not lie in the mouth of the creditor afterwards to seek to vary that appropriation."

The common law principles regarding the appropriation of payments are as follows:

- The party who makes a payment has the right to apply that payment in whichever way he deems fit. For example, if the payer owes more than one debt, he is entitled to specify which debt is to be discharged by his payment. The payer's intention may be inferred from the course of dealings or other circumstances. Money deposited into a bank account to pay a bill or cheque cannot be applied in any other way.
- If the payer does not specify the manner of application of funds at the time of payment, the right to apply the funds will generally pass to the recipient of the payment.
- If there is no specific appropriation by the parties in relation to current accounts where payments into and out of the account continue to be made, it is presumed that the first sum paid in is first drawn out, and the first debit item is discharged or reduced by the first sum paid. This is the rule established in *Devaynes v Noble, Clayton's Case* (commonly referred to as the rule in Clayton's Case). However, Clayton's rule is a presumption in law only and may be rebutted by evidence indicating it was not the intention of the parties to apply the rule.

Rule in Clayton's Case

The rule may operate against a bank in certain circumstances where the current account is overdrawn and subsequent payments into the account operate to reduce the overdraft, to the prejudice of the bank's interests. The following are two examples:

- The bank extends an overdraft facility to the customer, which is secured by a mortgage. Clayton's rule would operate such that any payments into the account will reduce overdrawn amounts which are secured, whilst payments out will constitute fresh advances, which are not covered by the security. To overcome this, bank security documents typically contain a clause providing that the security shall be a continuing security that extends to cover any sums constituting the balance due for the time being.
- Where an overdraft is guaranteed by a third party and the guarantee is for any reason terminated, the rule in Clayton's case would operate such that payments into the account after termination will reduce or even discharge the principal debtor's liability, whilst payments out will constitute fresh advances made after termination for which the guarantor will not be liable.

- To overcome this, guarantees now typically provide that in case of termination, the bank may continue the account with the principal debtor, and the guarantor's liability for the debtor's debt as at the date of termination will remain intact, notwithstanding any subsequent payments into or out of the debtor's account.

Appropriation of payments is very important in banking practice. Apart from the rule in Clayton's case, the following illustrations are given in order to show how the rules relating to appropriation of payments affect the banks, their customers, and third parties in modern banking practice.

- If a customer who maintains two or more accounts at the same bank makes a payment to credit, he has the right to appropriate the money to whichever account he may choose. If he fails to choose, then in theory the bank may appropriate, but in practice the bank would inquire which account is to be credited.
- A customer does not have any available credit balance in his current account. He informs the bank that he has issued two cheques, each for HK$1,000, in favour of, let us say, Chan and Lee, respectively. But the customer pays in only HK$1,000, and instructs the bank that only the cheque in favour of Chan should be paid.

If the bank wrongfully pays the cheque in favour of Lee and returns the cheque in favour of Chan, the customer will be entitled to sue the bank for damages for wrongful dishonour. Chan cannot sue the bank in this regard because there is no contract between him and the bank. However, if the bank had received notice of a specific appropriation and of an equitable assignment of the proceeds, the bank may be sued by the third party.

Set-off

Set-off arises when a debtor or his creditor wishes to arrive at the net figure owing between them when separate accounts or debts are involved. For example, if Peter owes his friend Thomas HK$20,000 for monies lent, and then later Thomas buys Peter's car for HK$10,000, Thomas could refuse to pay Peter the HK$10,000. He can set off this sum against the loan due and simply settle the net figure of HK$10,000.

Set-off is also referred to as 'consolidation' or 'combination' of accounts. It is a general principle of dealing between debtor and creditor, and therefore applicable to the relationship between banker and customer.

There are three requirements before a right of set-off can be exercised, although these can be varied by special agreement between the parties. The three requirements are:

- The sum involved must be certain and clearly ascertained;
- They must be due between the same parties; and
- They must be due in the same right.

In the context of banker and customer, if a customer has more than one account at a bank, the bank has the right to set off the customer's credit balance on one account against the same customer's debit balance on another account in order to ascertain the net amount owing to or by the customer. Such right may be exercised if both credit and debit balances are:

- Of ascertained amounts, and not mere claims of uncertain amounts;
- Owed between the same parties in the same capacity, meaning that a bank may not set off a customer's debts against monies in an account held by the customer as trustee, for example; and
- Already due, meaning that a bank may not set off its immediate liabilities to the customer (for example, deposits in a savings account) against sums which are to become due from the customer at a future time (known as unmatured or contingent liabilities, an example being future instalments of a mortgage loan).

The exceptions to this rule are:

- Where there is express agreement between the bank and the customer allowing set-off for unmatured or contingent liabilities; and
- Where the customer becomes insolvent, in which case the legislation allows all debts and liabilities, whether present or future, actual or contingent, to be the subject of set-off.

The banker's right of set-off is automatically exercisable in situations such as the customer's death, mental incapacity or insolvency, when accounts are normally estopped and a prudent banker would attempt to consolidate the position of the bank. In the case of insolvency (i.e., the bankruptcy of an individual, or winding-up of a company), the Bankruptcy Ordinance (Cap. 6) expressly provides for a right of set-off for creditors of a bankrupt individual.

The same rule applies to companies in a winding up under the Companies Ordinance (Cap. 32). This statutory right overrides any agreement between the parties to the contrary, which means that any agreement between banker and customer to exclude or restrict the bank's right of set-off is invalid in an insolvency situation.

If a customer has more than one account maintained with the same bank in Hong Kong (irrespective of the branches where the accounts are kept), the question may arise whether the bank has the right to set off what is due to the customer on one account against what is due from him on another account, and to have regard only to the ultimate or net balance when deciding what sum is available to the customer for drawing purposes.

One basic principle supporting the doctrine that in certain situations the bank is entitled to set-off or to combine the accounts of one customer, is that the customer's underlying contractual relationship is with the bank, and not with the branch at which the account is maintained. Further, the basic relationship of a banker and customer governs all the accounts of a customer regardless of their type. As there is only one contract between banker and customer, there is room for the argument that when the bank becomes the customer's creditor, it can exercise a right of set-off regarding mutual dealings with him.

No Right of Set-off

In general, a bank is not entitled to right of set-off in the following cases.

- **Express or implied agreement.** Both banker and customer are free to agree that there is no right of set-off at all. For example, a customer has a loan account and a current account and the agreement is that the customer is to be allowed to draw upon his credit balance on a current account without reference to his loan account. It is clear that, in such a case, there will be no right of set-off. However, in practice, most banks are reluctant to agree to such express terms, except when the particular customer has strong bargaining power.

  It is recognised by the court that it is an implied term in the contract between the bank and its customer that the right of set-off is not available to a bank if the customer maintains a loan account and current account in credit with a bank.
- **Contingent liabilities.** In *Jeffryes v. Agra and Masterman's Bank Ltd.*, the court observed that "you cannot retain a sum of money which is actually due against a sum of money which is only to become due at a future time." For example, a bank accepts a foreign currency deposit from another bank for a fixed period, and subsequently makes a loan in the same currency and to the same bank, but for a different period. If the deposit is due to be repaid on say, 15 January, the bank holding the deposit is not entitled to retain it against a loan which is due to be repaid on, say, 31 January.

  Likewise, in the absence of some special arrangement, a bank is not entitled to retain its customer's credit balance to secure the bank's interest against a contingent liability on bills which it has discounted for the customer. However, if the customer is bankrupt the position is different. The rule in bankruptcy is that all debts and liabilities, present or future, certain or contingent, may be the subject of set-off.
- **Account contains trust funds.** In some cases, the title of an account indicates that it contains money belonging to other people, for example, Charles Chan, 'AA Football Club Account,' or Chan & Partners, 'Clients' Account.' A bank is not entitled to set-off a credit balance on such accounts against a debit balance on the customer's private account.

  Similarly, professionals often maintain separate banking accounts for clients' moneys. Where it is known to a bank that a particular account is used for this purpose, no right of set-off can arise. There are statutory provisions that compel a solicitor to keep a separate banking account for the money of his clients and the word 'client' must appear in the title of the account. A bank cannot have any recourse or right, whether by way of set-off or otherwise, against moneys standing to the credit of such accounts.

- **Accounts of different customers.** In *Uttamchandami v. Central Bank of India*, the defendant bank sought to set-off accounts held in different names on the grounds that in each case the accounts were 'nominee' accounts, and that in each case the customer was in reality a Mr. Vaswani. The English Court of Appeal held that the bank had no such right.

Code of Banking Practice

For personal customers, Section 17 and 18 of the Code provides that:

- Institutions should make readily available to customers general descriptive information about the operation of their accounts, including any rights of se-off claimed by the institution. Such information should include clear and prominent notice of any rights of set-off claimed by the institution over credit and debit balances in different accounts of the customer.
- In particular, it should be made clear to customers of a joint account whether the institution claims the right to set off the credit balance in that account against the debit balance in other accounts, which may be held by one or more of the holders of the joint account.
- Institutions should set out the terms and conditions and the circumstances under which they will exercise their right of set-off.
- Institutions should inform the customer promptly after exercising any rights of set-off.

Banker's Lien

A lien is a right to retain possession of a debtor's goods until the debt is paid. In addition to any security it may have taken and to its right to combine or consolidate its customers' accounts, a bank in general law has a lien over securities deposited by the customer with the bank to the extent of the customer's indebtedness to the bank.

The banker's lien (or bank's lien) extends to cheques and bills collected by the bank on behalf of the customer. The Bills of Exchange Ordinance (Cap. 19) provides that where the holder of a bill has a lien on it, arising from either contract or by implication of law, he is deemed to be a holder of value to the extent of the sum for which he has a lien.

In practice, if the banker allows a customer to withdraw funds exceeding the credit limit of overdraft facilities temporarily or allows his account to be overdrawn temporarily, then the banker may hold the funds of his savings or time deposit account(s) as the banker's lien.

Rights of Bank Asserting lien

The bank has an implied power to sell the asset subject to the lien if the debtor defaults in repayment, after giving notice to the debtor of its intention to sell. Where the lien is asserted on instruments deposited with the bank for collection or presentment, the bank is not relieved of its duty to collect or make presentment, hence there is no need for the bank to rely on a power of sale. The bank cannot use the asset under lien unless the debtor has defaulted and the bank seeks to enforce its lien.

However, a banker's lien can only be exercised in relation to an actual liability. It is doubtful whether a mere contingent liability can support a banker's lien.

It is now the practice of banks to either obtain a letter of lien from customers that expressly sets out the rights of the bank in relation to assets subject to the lien, or to incorporate a provision to such effect in its general agreement for lending customers. A genuine lien coupled with a contractual power of sale is not a charge.

The following are the types of assets that may be subject to a banker's lien:

- Share certificates;
- Negotiable instruments;
- Insurance policies;
- Credit balances in bank accounts (which strictly should be subject to the banker's right of set-off);
- Other documents such as bonds, coupons, deposit receipts, etc.

Matters Excluding Lien

Banker's lien is subject to the following limitations:

- It does not attach to assets deposited for safe custody only.
- It does not attach to securities known by the bank not to be the property of the customer at the date when they are first received by the bank.
- It is displaced by any contrary agreement between the parties. The bankers should not enter into such agreement.
- It does not attach to securities deposited by the customer which the bank knows to be subject to a trust in favour of a third party.

The lien is also excluded if, at the time the assets are deposited with the bank, the bank is aware that they belong to a third party, for example, if they are held by the customer on trust for a third party. However, if the bank receives the assets in good faith and without notice that they belong to a third party, the lien is not excluded.

Banker's Duty of Secrecy

Whilst the main relationship between a bank and its customer is that of debtor and creditor, there are other relationships and duties which do not normally exist between such parties. The most important of these is the duty of secrecy and it is one which every customer expects his bank to maintain at all times.

Under common law, this duty is implied when the account is opened and extends not only to the account itself and the information that could be gained from it, but also to any other particulars of the customer's affairs which come to the bank's knowledge from conducting the account or in carrying out any other transactions or financial dealings on behalf of the customer. The duty must be maintained both whilst the account is open and even subsequently after it has been closed. Most banks ask their employees to sign a declaration that they will not disclose any matters concerning the customers' affairs to any outside party.

In practice, it would be impossible to conduct the bank's business unless some disclosure was made to outside parties, and whilst one may start with the basic concept it will soon be realised that this duty of secrecy is a qualified duty and not an absolute one.

Common Law Principle

It is a long established general principle of common law that a bank is under a legal obligation to keep its customer's affairs secret. In the leading case of *Tournier v. National Provincial and Union Bank of England*, the English Court of Appeals held that:

- A bank owes an implied duty of secrecy to its customers.
- The duty not only covers knowledge derived by the bank whilst it maintains a contractual relationship with the customer, but also extends to:

    i. Knowledge acquired by the bank before the relationship was in contemplation, or after its termination; and
    ii. Knowledge derived by the bank from sources other than the customer's accounts but still in relation to its dealings with the customer, for example, information obtained from a third party that would help the bank decide how it should treat the customer.

Exceptions to Duty of Secrecy

The Tournier case also established four exceptions to the banker's duty of secrecy:

- Disclosure under compulsion by law;
- Disclosure as a duty to the public;
- Disclosure in the bank's interest;
- Disclosure by express or implied consent of the customer.

Disclosure Under Compulsion by Law

There are two main scenarios where this exception may be invoked: obligation to make disclosure under legislation and obligation to make disclosure under court order.

- **Obligation to make disclosure under legislation.** The following are among those most commonly encountered by authorised institutions:
  i. The Inland Revenue Ordinance (Cap. 112) empowers the Inland Revenue Department to require any person in possession of information or documents relevant to any matter affecting a taxpayer's liability to furnish or produce such information or documents within a reasonable period. A bank may be obliged to provide copies of statements of accounts in a customer's name.
  ii. The Prevention of Bribery Ordinance (Cap. 201) empowers the Commissioner for the Independent Commission Against Corruption to require a bank to produce for inspection, and provide copies of, statements and other records of a customer's account that are likely to be relevant to an ICAC investigation.
  iii. The Police Force Ordinance (Cap. 232) specifically empowers the Commissioner of Police to require information from banks and deposit-taking companies for investigation of an indictable offence or apprehension of an offender. Such information includes whether a named individual has an account with a bank or deposit-taking company, and whether a bank provides a safe deposit box or holds property in its custody for the individual.
  iv. The Drug Trafficking (Recovery of Proceeds) Ordinance (Cap. 405), the Organized and Serious Crimes Ordinance (Cap. 455), and the United Nations (Anti-Terrorism) Measures Ordinance (Cap. 575) oblige banks to report suspicious transactions or activities of customers to the authorities for investigation of suspected money laundering or terrorist activities or commission of serious crimes.

  Failure to comply with the authorities' request is a criminal offence. However, care should be taken where the authorities in a foreign country (for example, the U.S. Inland Revenue Service) request disclosure of information of a customer from a bank located in Hong Kong. Such requests have no legal basis under the laws of Hong Kong and a bank would breach its duty of secrecy if it complied with such a request.
- **Obligation to make disclosure under court order.** A bank may be compelled by an order of the court to disclose information relating to a customer's affairs. Non-compliance constitutes contempt of court, which is a criminal offence. Some common examples are the following:
  i. Subpoena: A bank employee may be served with a writ of subpoena (being a summons issued by the court) ordering him to attend court and to bring records and documents relating to a customer's affairs in the bank's possession. This may occur, for example, where the customer's affairs with the bank are relevant to the subject of litigation involving the customer.
  ii. Order for discovery or disclosure: In *Norwich Pharmacal Co. v. Customs & Excise Commissioners*, the English House of Lords held that if an innocent person becomes caught up in another's wrongful acts through no fault of his own and thus inadvertently facilitated the wrongdoing, he does not incur personal liability, but the court

may order him to assist the victim by disclosing the identity of the wrongdoers and providing full information. In *Bankers Trust Co. v. Shapira*, it was established that not only could the court order disclosure of the fraudster's identity, but discovery could also be ordered of a bank's books and records in aid of a tracing claim.

iii. Garnishee order: The bank is normally requested by the creditor of a customer to disclose the amount of credit balances held available for attachment. If the garnishee order does not also compel disclosure of information by the bank, the bank should take care not to reveal any information until the order is made absolute. In practice, banks normally will only disclose to the creditor the availability of credit balances for attachment. It is normal practice for banks to inform customers of the service of a garnishee order and its effect on the operation of the customer's accounts.

Care should be taken where a court order granted by a foreign court is served on a bank's offices in Hong Kong, or in that foreign jurisdiction requiring production of confidential information relating to a customer's accounts maintained with the Hong Kong branch of the bank. The foreign court order has no effect in Hong Kong. If the Hong Kong branch of the bank were to produce the information to the foreign court directly or through the bank's offices in the foreign jurisdiction, it would be in breach of its duty of secrecy.

Duty to the Public to Disclose

The majority of the scenarios in which this duty would have arisen are already provided for by legislation empowering authorities to compel disclosure of otherwise confidential information by banks. However, problems occasionally arise where there is yet insufficient grounds to invoke the statutory powers of ordering disclosure unless confidential information is first obtained.

For example, the police may be in the early stages of investigating a suspected crime and merely suspect, but do not yet have proof, that a customer of the bank is implicated in the crime. If the police make an informal request to the bank for information relating to the customer's affairs to assist in its investigation, the bank may find it difficult to decide whether its duty to the public overrides its duty to the customer.

In practice, banks will insist on the police certifying that the information is necessary for the prevention or detection of crime before agreeing to release the data, pursuant to an exception under the Personal Data (Privacy) Ordinance (Cap. 486) that applies to personal customers. For non-personal customers such as corporates, banks will normally resist such informal requests and insist that the police invoke their statutory powers.

Disclosure in the Bank's Interest

There are a number of obvious instances where the bank's interests will require disclosure.

- Where there is litigation between the bank and the customer. For example, where the bank sues the customer for recovery of debt due, the court papers must set out the amount claimed and particulars of the underlying transaction giving rise to the debt.

- Where there is litigation between the bank and a third party in relation to matters arising from the bank's dealings with the customer. For example, if the bank sues a guarantor of the customer's liabilities, the court papers must set out the relevant information.

Disclosure with Customer's Consent

The customer's consent to make a disclosure may be express or implied:

- **Express consent.** A customer may expressly authorise his banker to make disclosure to a third party. For example, a customer may specifically request the bank to provide a banker's reference on the customer's relationship with the bank to a third party.

  The Personal Data (Privacy) Ordinance obliges banks, as a data user in relation to personal customers, to inform customers of the classes of persons to whom the customer's personal data may be transferred. The Code of Banking Practice further requires banks to be as specific as possible in their notification to customers of these classes of persons, which include debt collection agencies, computer firms to which processing of personal data may be outsourced, credit reference agencies, and related companies of the bank within the same group to whom customers' names and addresses may be disclosed for marketing purposes.

  Whilst the Ordinance and the Code contemplate the giving of a notice to customers in respect of disclosure of personal data to the above classes of persons, it is the practice of most banks to either incorporate this part of the notice by reference, or duplicate it in their account terms and conditions such that the customer expressly consents to disclosure to the named classes of persons.

  The Code also requires banks to obtain customers' express consent for giving bankers' references to another financial institution in respect of a customer, and for disclosure of customers' names and addresses to unrelated companies for marketing purposes. Although it is not a statutory or regulatory requirement, most banks now extend the practice of including an express disclosure clause to non-personal customers.
- **Implied consent.** In the case of *Sunderland v. Barclays Bank Limited,* the court accepted that the customer, by drawing a third party into her conversation with the bank, had given implied consent for the bank to reveal her affairs with the bank to that third party. However, it is never easy for a bank to ascertain in the first place, or establish when challenged, a customer's intentions.

  In the modern era, in particular with the enactment of data protection legislation, it is no longer prudent for a bank to rely on implied consent in disclosing customers' information to third parties other than under compulsion of law or for the protection of the bank's interest.

  For example, with regard to the provision of bankers' references or status opinions about a customer by one bank to another, banks had previously relied on customers' implied consent to what they contended was an established practice. However, the English court rejected this argument in the case of *Turner v. Royal Bank of Scotland plc* and held that the provision of bank references cannot be based on implied consent as the practice is not sufficiently notorious to constitute an implied contractual term. In Hong Kong, it is now a requirement of the Code of Banking Practice that banks obtain customers' express consent to the provision of bankers' references.

Banker's Opinion

Whilst a banker has a duty to keep his customers' affairs secret, one of the exceptions is where the customer has given his consent. In the case of a banker replying to a status enquiry, the practice is so well established that the customer is presumed to have given his implied consent when he opened the account. If he expressly told the bank not to answer any status enquiries made about him, the implied consent would be revoked. However, the circumstances would be very unusual, and the bank might wonder about the advisability of conducting the account at all.

Businessmen and others value the status enquiry system, which is usually a free service, and there is no doubt that it is of considerable help in day-to-day commerce when dealing with an unknown or even a regular customer. The enquirer must approach his own branch as bankers will only give opinions to other bankers, and opinions will not be given directly to an individual. An exception to the latter rule, however, would be where the customer making the enquiry banks with the same bank and branch as the subject of the research, in which event the banker has in effect two roles.

The enquiries made should always be for genuine trade or financial transactions, and the answer is usually given also in brief terms. Over the years, certain phrases have come into general use between banks and their meaning is usually clear to the recipient banker or to an experienced trader.

Thus, in response to an enquiry as to whether a customer is good for $100,000 trade credit, an answer might be given to the effect that he is considered "Undoubted" or "A respectable customer who maintains a satisfactory account. We regret however that we have insufficient knowledge of his affairs to speak for your figure ($100,000 trade credit)."

It is usual for the bank to keep a record of all opinions given. This helps ensure that a consistent view is taken. Also, when a customer's financial position changes, it is then easier for the bank to decide how it should shade or improve its answer as against former expressions of opinion. A record will also help the account-holding bank to see if a customer is apparently attempting to raise too much by way of credit finance.

Disclaimer

In practice, banker's opinions are not signed and the standard printing form used by the bank will bear a disclaimer clause which might read "Confidential, and for your private use and without responsibility on the part of the bank or its officials."

However, since the Control of Exemption Clauses Ordinance (Cap. 71) came into force, it has been felt that such a disclaimer clause would not protect the bank if the recipient relied on the answer and suffered loss, where the answer would not meet the test of "reasonableness" as described in the Ordinance.

When preparing his answer, the banker should give consideration to all matters relating to the customer's financial and business affairs that are known to him. There is no onus on the banker to make outside enquiries as to the customer's solvency or otherwise. All that is required is an honest opinion, which should give no details of the actual bank account or the security lodged. Where the bank holds a debenture from a limited-company customer, it is invariably the practice to disclose that fact, the nature of the security being so all-embracing that the bank's special position is perhaps material to the enquirer.

Duty to Enquirer

The bank might have a duty to the enquirer because he might suffer a loss in acting on the opinion given. The drafting of a suitable reply can be particularly difficult where the customer is known to have financial problems. Clearly, in such circumstances, a favourable reply cannot be given but, equally, to infer that the customer's business is about to collapse could cause that very event. The bank must be neither too optimistic nor too pessimistic in its reply.

The leading case which examined these matters is *Hedley Byrne & Co. Ltd. v. Heller & Partners Ltd.* Hedley Byrne enquired to the respectability and standing of Easipower, whose account was with Heller & Partners to the extent of £100,000 per annum. The answer given was that Easipower was "considered good for its ordinary business engagements." Relying on the banker's opinion, Hedley Byrne entered into a contract with Easipower, but lost £17,000 when that company went into liquidation. They then sued Heller & Partners on the grounds that the opinion had been given negligently and in breach of a duty owed to them to exercise care.

The judge held that there was no contract between Heller & Partners and Hedley Byrne, and thus there could be no duty of care and therefore no breach. Moreover, there was no fiduciary relationship between the enquirer and the bank giving the opinion. The plaintiffs appealed, but the judgment was affirmed. Hedley Byrne went to the House of Lords, where the decision was still in favour of the bankers, although for different reasons. Here, it was felt that if it could be shown that the circumstances whereby information and/or opinions were given established a form of relationship, which was equivalent to, but did not actually constitute a contract, then a banker's opinion could well fall in that category.

However, the decision in favour of the bank was made because the bank had included a disclaimer clause in its answer, declining at the outset to accept any responsibility and, therefore, had never established such a special relationship. It can be seen from this decision that the use of standard forms, with the disclaimer clause, is most important. Where opinions are given orally (a practice which is unusual and which requires special care), the giver of the opinion should always preface his remarks with the disclaimer.

As we have noted, however, the passing of the Control of Exemption Clauses Ordinance has thrown some doubt upon the worth of this practice in Hong Kong. It may be that a court in the future will take a different view. Bankers should continue to maintain the disclaimer clause in their answers to status opinions, but it is now necessary to exercise even greater care in framing the answer.

Personal Data and Consumer Credit Data

Since the Personal Data (Privacy) Ordinance (Cap. 486) came into force in Hong Kong in 1996, no consideration of the banker's duty of secrecy would now be complete without an understanding of this legislation and its implications for bankers. The Ordinance is an additional requirement to the banker's duty of secrecy.

The Ordinance aims to protect the privacy of living individuals in relation to their personal data. It aims to regulate the activities of all data users, such as banks, including the collection, holding, processing or use of personal data. It also contributes to Hong Kong's continued economic well-being by safeguarding the free flow of personal data to Hong Kong from restrictions imposed by countries that already have data protection laws.

What is Personal Data?

The Personal Data (Privacy) Ordinance defines 'personal data' as information that is recorded in a document in writing and stored on paper or electronically, or stored in a disc, film, tape, or other devices on which data (including visual images) are stored in such a way that they can be reproduced. This means that a tape recording of a telephone conversation between a bank employee and a customer of the bank is personal data and covered by the ordinance.

However, information transmitted verbally does not constitute personal data, unless it is recorded in writing. Data relating to deceased persons are also not covered by the ordinance; only personal data relating to living individuals are covered, and only those from which it is reasonably practicable to identify the individual.

Personal data thus includes any representation of information, opinion, and "personal identifier," including date of birth, personal or banking reference from other sources, family or education background information, account statements or deposit ticket and so on. A "personal identifier" means any numbers or documents that can identify an individual, such as a bank account number, ATM personal identification number, and copies of identity documents.

Collection of Data

When a bank first collects personal data from its customer, it has to give that customer a copy of its data policy. The customer must agree to accept the bank's data policy before or at the same time as data is first collected. A data policy clause is therefore usually incorporated into the bank's account opening or service application forms.

The purpose and manner of data collection must comply with the following requirements:

- **Data can only be collected for a lawful purpose.** For example, data should not be collected to facilitate criminal activities. Only data necessary for or directly related to the purpose should be collected; the volume of data should be adequate, not excessive.
- **Data should be collected by fair and lawful means.** In assessing fairness, consideration should be given as to whether less intrusive means will achieve the same result. An example is the tape recording of clients' instructions by banks or securities firms. This is justified by the need to obtain a record of the instructions for use in case a dispute arises. Any alternative means of obtaining such record before execution of the instructions, for example, by obtaining each client's signature to a written record of the instructions, is impractical.
- **Certain information should be provided to the data subject.** He or she must be told at the time of data collection:
    - i. Whether it is compulsory that he or she supply the data, and if so, what are the consequences of failure to do so;
    - ii. The purpose for which the data is to be used
    - iii. The classes of persons to whom the data may be transferred
    - iv. The data subject's right to request access to or correction of the data, and the name and address of the individual to whom such request may be made.

The Privacy Commissioner has recommended that data users prepare and make available to data subjects a Personal Information Collection Statement (PICS). Most banks have adopted a PICS form, developed by the Hong Kong Association of Banks, as a notice to customers and other individuals relating to the Personal Data (Privacy) Ordinance's requirement on the use of a Data Privacy Notice.

Data Protection Principles

The Ordinance establishes six data protection principles, with which all data users must comply.

- **Data Protection Principle 1: Purpose and manner of collection of personal data.** This provides for the lawful and fair collection of personal data, and sets out the information a data user must give to a data subject when collecting personal data from that subject. The banks' use of a Data Privacy Notice complies with this principle, but it is impractical to give customers a copy of the notice every time new data is collected because, for a bank, every new instruction from and transaction with a customer constitutes the collection of new data.

The Ordinance provides for this situation by allowing data users to give a Data Privacy Notice once every 12 months, in cases where personal data is repeatedly collected under the same circumstances, such that there is no material difference in the notification. Typically, banks mail a copy of the Data Privacy Notice annually to customers along with the monthly statement of accounts or promotional materials, or include a reminder in the monthly statements of the availability of the Data Privacy Notice at the bank's branches or on its website.

- **Data Protection Principle 2: Accuracy and duration of retention of personal data.** This provides that personal data should be accurate, up-to-date, and kept no longer than necessary. Data users are obliged to take all practicable steps to ensure that inaccurate data is not used until its accuracy is validated or rectified. Wrong data should be erased.

  Banks should establish procedures for updating customers' personal data to ensure their accuracy, including internal procedures for the prompt processing of customers' notification of personal data changes.

  Banks are required under the Inland Revenue Ordinance to retain business records for a minimum of seven years. Since the Personal Data (Privacy) Ordinance does not have the effect of overriding other legislation, seven years is a valid period for which a bank may retain records of its dealings with customers, including the personal data of those who have terminated their relationship with the bank.

  Where an individual applies for facilities with a bank but is rejected or withdraws the application, the question arises as to whether the bank is entitled to retain the applicant's personal data and, if so, for how long. It seems justifiable for banks to retain the data collected in such circumstances for a short period, so they can answer any subsequent queries from the applicant.

  Some banks have argued for a longer retention period in case the bank decides to consider the applicant for another type of facility in respect of which he or he is likely to meet the approval criteria. To comply with Data Protection Principle 2, it is important that banks establish a clear policy covering this type of situation and make it known to applicants for their services.

- **Data Protection Principle 3: Use of personal data.** This provides that unless the data subject agrees otherwise, personal data should only be used for the purposes for which they were collected or for another but directly related purpose. If a bank wishes to use customers' data for a purpose not specified in the Data Privacy Notice, it will not be practicable to obtain express consent from all customers. Banks normally would notify customers of the intended use and rely on the customer's acceptance by his or her conduct of continuing to use the bank's services after the effective date of the change in data usage.

However, if a bank intends to transfer customers' data to an unrelated company for marketing purposes, for example, in a joint promotion scheme, the Code of Banking Practice specifically obliges banks to obtain customers' express consent. It should be noted that the code prohibits banks from terminating the basic banking relationship with a customer who objects such data transfer.

- **Data Protection Principle 4: Security of personal data.** This requires the application of appropriate security measures to personal data (including data in a form in which access to or processing of is not practicable). A data user should take all practicable steps to ensure that personal data held are protected against unauthorised or accidental access, processing, erasure, or other use. The greater the sensitivity of the data and the harm likely to be caused by unauthorised access or leakage, the higher the level of security should be.

  Data users should take the following into account:
  i. location of the data, for example, in a restricted area
  ii. security measures incorporated into equipment storing the data, for example, computer passwords
  iii. measures for ensuring the integrity, prudence, and competence of persons having access to the data
  iv. measures for ensuring secure transmission of the data.

  Banks should have tight procedures to safeguard its systems and records containing customers' personal data, restrict access only to authorised staff who need to access the data in order to perform their duties, and establish adequate guidelines for staff in handling personal data.

  Where banks transfer personal data to a third party service provider, for example, as part of an outsourcing arrangement, the Code of Banking Practice requires them to take steps to ensure that the personal data will be treated as confidential and adequately safeguarded by the service provider.

  Normally, the service contract between the bank and the service provider will include the service provider's confidentiality undertaken and obligation to establish and abide by adequate procedures for safeguarding the personal data, and the right of the bank to conduct audits on the service provider's observance of its secrecy obligations. The Code also requires banks to remain accountable to customers for any complaints arising from the service providers' handling of personal data. Banks should not disclaim responsibility to customers for breach of customer confidentiality by service providers.

- **Data Protection Principle 5: Information to be generally available.** This provides for openness by data users about the kinds of personal data they hold and the main purposes for which personal data is used. A data user must take all practicable steps to ensure that a data subject can ascertain the data user's policies and practices in relation to its collection, holding, and use of personal data.

  In addition to the use of PICS, as previously mentioned, the Privacy Commissioner recommends that data users prepare and make available to data subjects a Privacy Policy Statement (PPS) to explain the data user's policies and practices. The statement should be given to data subjects at the time of data collection, together with the Data Privacy Notice.

The Privacy Commissioner has also published guidelines on "Preparing Online PPS and PICS." These are meant to provide guidance to data users that collect personal data online from individuals, for example, in an online application or registration form or without the individuals being aware of the data collection through, for example, the use of 'cookies.' It is recommended that a data user provide prominent links to their PPS from its homepage as well as from each website form used to collect personal data.

- **Data Protection Principle 6: Access to personal data.** This provides for data subjects to have rights of access to and correction of their personal data. The Ordinance requires data users to comply with a request from a data subject for access to, or correction of, personal data within 40 days, and to give reasons if this cannot be complied with. Data users may charge a fee, which must not be excessive, for processing a data access request.

Use of Personal Data in Direct Marketing

The Personal Data (Privacy) Ordinance defines "direct marketing" as an offer or advertising of goods, services, or facilities by means of information or goods sent by mail, fax, e-mail, or similar means of communication, with the communication addressed to a specific person or persons by name.

Where personal data is used for direct marketing for the first time, the data user must inform the data subject that if the data subject so requests, the data user will, without any charge, cease to use his/her personal data for direct marketing. This is commonly called an 'opt-out clause.' The Code of Banking Practice requires banks to remind customers of their opt-out right at least once every year, or to do so by including a standard opt-out clause in all marketing and promotion materials.

For data users like banks that regularly engage in direct marketing, it is important to maintain a list of all individuals who have notified it that they wish to opt out from receiving further direct marketing, keep that list regularly updated, and ensure the list is promptly distributed among marketing staff as and when updated. The opt-out clause included in the account opening form or direct marketing materials should allow customers to choose which channel(s), such as direct mail, telephone, fax or email, they may or may not want to receive direct marketing information from.

Code of Practice on Consumer Credit Data

In the area of consumer credit, where credit is provided by a credit provider to and for the use of an individual, or to and for the use of another person for whom an individual acts as mortgagor or guarantor, the Privacy Commissioner issued a Code of Practice on

Consumer Credit Data (last updated in 2011), which requires credit providers such as banks to notify an applicant for credit facilities that his or her personal data may be supplied to a credit reference agency and, in case of loan default, to a debt collection agency.

The notification should also state that the applicant has the right to request the credit provider to inform him or her which items of data are routinely disclosed to the agency and to be provided with information (such as contact details of the agency) to enable the making of a data access or correction request to the agency.

For its part, the Hong Kong Monetary Authority has published a Supervisory Policy Manual on the sharing and use of consumer credit data through a credit reference agency. The guideline requires bank policies and procedures to be designed to ensure the security, confidentiality, and integrity of consumer credit data and to guard against unauthorised access to, or use of, such data that could result in a breach of the Code of Practice on Consumer Credit Data and the data protection principles and relevant provisions of the Personal Data (Privacy) Ordinance.

Statement of Account or Passbook

The modern practice is to issue computerised statements for current accounts and other tailored accounts, and passbooks for savings accounts and, occasionally, time deposit accounts. For a savings account, it is usual for the customer to retain the passbook and produce it during a withdrawal or deposit. Specimen signature(s) and other brief personal details usually will be encoded in the passbook. For time deposit accounts, the banks usually generate a receipt or advice to the customers as the evidence of such deposits.

Problems arise when errors occur in passbooks or statements which show the customer's account being either over-credited or over-debited. To address this and other areas of concern, the Code of Banking Practice requires banks:

- To provide customers with monthly statements of account, unless a passbook or other transaction records are provided, or there has been no transaction on the account since the last statement, or the bank has agreed otherwise with the customer;
- To advise customers to examine their statements of account and allow at least 90 days for customers to report unauthorised transactions;
- To warn customers that if they fail to report unauthorised transactions within the specified period, the bank reserves the right to regard the statement as conclusive. But banks should not exercise their reserved right to deny a customer's claim if the unauthorised transaction arises from a third-party fraud or forgery in relation to which the bank has failed to exercise reasonable care and skill; or arises from forgery or fraud by the bank's employee, or default or negligence of the bank or its employee.

The importance of complying with the Code's provision to advise customers to examine their statements is underlined by the ruling in *Tai Hing Cotton Mill Ltd. v. Liu Chong Hing Bank Ltd. and others*. In this case, the bank had paid out money on a cheque that was later discovered to be forged. It then moved to debit the customer's account to cover the amount of the cheque. The court held that the bank was not entitled to do so.

The reason was, firstly, that unless it was otherwise agreed between the banker and the customer, the duty of care owed by a customer to the bank in the operation of his current account is limited to (a) a duty to refrain from drawing a cheque in such a way as to mislead the bank or facilitate fraud or forgery, and (b) a duty to inform the bank of a forgery as soon as it is discovered. This means that unless the terms of the contract seek to impose an express obligation on the customer to examine monthly statements and make the statements unchallengeable after a specified period, the customer has no duty to examine the bank statements.

Secondly, with regard to such a provision in the contract, the court held that the burden of the obligation imposed on the customer and of the sanction imposed must be clearly brought home to the customer. The clause must be clear and unambiguous and satisfy the 'undoubtedly rigorous' test. In that particular case, the court held that the bank had failed to meet the test.

Wrongful Dishonour of Cheques

Article II

A bank must pay cheques drawn by the customer on presentation, so long as there are sufficient funds in the account or the cheques are within the limit of an agreed overdraft, and the bank is not legally restrained from making payment. If a bank wrongfully dishonours a cheque drawn by the customer, the customer may claim damages from the bank based on either breach of contract or libel.

Thus, before the bank dishonours a customer's cheque for shortage of funds, it should be absolutely sure that it is in order to do so. Substantial damages might be awarded against the bank if it wrongfully dishonours a cheque and thereby injures the customer's credit. Before actually returning a cheque, banks should also ensure as far as possible that a credit has not been misapplied to another account or that other cheques have not been paid which have been stopped or which are post-dated.

Practical Considerations for Banks

In computing the balance available in a customer's account, the bank need not take into consideration cheques paid that are still in the course of clearing (uncleared effects), unless in the past the bank has agreed specifically or by implication through its conduct to pay cheques so drawn. This implication could arise where previous cheques drawn against uncleared effects have always been paid and there has been no warning to the customer that he must in the future ensure that cleared covering funds are available.

If a bank has wrongly returned a cheque with the answer "Refer to drawer" and the mistake is then discovered, the banker should at once take all possible steps to correct matters. This practice is due to business considerations and also because, in so doing, the bank will help alleviate the extent of damages which might be awarded in any subsequent court action brought by the drawer. Steps to remedy the situation should include contacting the payee and the presenting banker as soon as possible, by phone initially, and then by letter in confirmation.

The message should state that the cheque should have been paid and that the fault lies wholly with the bank and that neither party should construe the events as being any reflection upon the creditworthiness of the drawer. The bank may prefer to obtain the customer's authority to disclose any details which are relevant and should, of course, remember that, in admitting the error, it will be unable to defend an action brought by the customer against it later. However, the court will take the bank's conduct into account in assessing the actual loss to the customer and so this action may limit any damages awarded.

Breach of Contract and Libel

The general rule is that the party which is in breach must pay the amount of damage, which flows directly and naturally from his failure to keep his contract, provided that such would reasonably have been within the contemplation of the parties at the time when they made contract. It is difficult to apply this rule to a contract to honour a customer's cheques. This is because it would only be on very rare occasions that a bank has any knowledge as to the circumstances under which the customer came to be drawing his cheque.

For instance, an importer lost a valuable contract through the wrongful dishonour of its cheques. Would the bank be liable for the loss of profits that would be earned under that contract? Substantial damages would be awarded in that case because the importer was a trader. In the case of a non-trader customer, the court may rule that only the nominal damages would be awarded, unless special damages were proved. The banker should note that the smaller the cheque, the greater might be the damage to the customer's credit.

As stated above, the customer may claim against the bank for breach of contract and libel in case of wrongful dishonour. In some suits, the two claims have been dealt with without differentiation, whilst in others, there have been different decisions. In *Flack v. London and South Western Bank Ltd.*, the court ruled that the words "Refer to drawer" amounted merely to a statement by the bank: "We are not paying; go back to the drawer and ask why," or else "Go back to the drawer and ask him to pay." The judge felt it was not possible to extract a libellous meaning from the words "Refer to drawer."

However, there is a tendency in more recent cases to regard the words "Refer to drawer" as being capable of a defamatory meaning. In one such case, the plaintiff carried on business as a manufacturer and retailer in ladies' clothes. She claimed damages from the bank for alleged breach of contract and for libel, after her bank wrongfully dishonoured two cheques drawn by her. The cheques bore the notation "Refer to drawer," which the plaintiff claimed lowered her reputation.

In defence, the bank maintained that its obligation to pay the cheques was only on condition that the limit of £500 was not exceeded and this would have been the case if the cheques in question had been paid. The plaintiff's case was that the bank had agreed to meet the two cheques against her undertaking that she would pay in £100 in the following week. In an action heard before the jury, the bank agreed in response to a specific question that the words "Refer to drawer" did lower the plaintiff's reputation in the minds of right-thinking people. However, when the words were written on the cheques, she would have exceeded her agreed limit of £500.

The claim against the bank therefore failed and the bank successfully defended itself when an appeal to the English Court of Appeal was made. However, the jury's view that the words "Refer to drawer" could be libellous or defamatory was important, as the words have come to be regarded by the ordinary person as meaning "no funds."

Exemption Clauses

In the section on "Banker's Lien," we discussed the disclaimer clause in a trade enquiry reply. This is an example of an exemption clause, which frequently appears on standard bank forms such as account opening forms and third-party mandates. Exemption clauses are often meant to serve as an outright exclusion of banks' liability, but they can also be couched in such a way that they impose obligations on customers.

For example, in order to exclude liabilities to customers for wrongful debits due to forged signatures on cheques, banks may include the following clause on their account opening forms:

> "The account holder agrees that the statement of account shall, as between the Bank and the account-holder, be conclusive evidence as to the balance shown therein and that the statement of account shall be binding upon the account-holder, who shall be deemed to have agreed to waive any rights to raise objections or pursue any remedies against the Bank in respect thereof unless the account-holder notifies the Bank in writing of any such errors within 90 days after posted … such statement of account."

The above clause, whose wording is suggested by the Hong Kong Association of Banks, imposes an obligation on account holders. However, in essence, it is an exemption clause which excludes banks' liabilities for wrongful debits. Bank exemption clauses, whether they are written in a negative way of excluding liabilities or in a positive way of imposing an obligation, are subject to the Control of Exemption Clauses Ordinance (Cap. 71).

Control of Exemption Clauses Ordinance

In order to claim protection under the Control of Exemption Clauses Ordinance, one party must have been dealing with the other as a consumer or using the bank's standard form. Article 4 of the Ordinance defines "dealing as a consumer" as someone who neither makes the contract in the course of a business nor holds himself out as doing so, whilst the other party does make the contract in the course of a business. An incorporated customer can also be dealing with a bank as a consumer.

Both private customers and incorporated customers are dealing with banks as consumers when the contracts are prepared by banks or a banks' standard forms are used. However, in special dealings when banks' special forms are not used *and* that contract is prepared jointly, such as in loan syndication, the Ordinance will not apply and the exemption clauses in the documentations are not controlled.

Furthermore, any exemption clauses in a mandate, if any, are subject to the test of reasonableness. If the clause cannot pass the said test, then it is not enforceable. Whether the clauses are reasonable will be determined in accordance with usual and normal banking practice. The Code of Banking Practice is one of the important references for such determination.

The "reasonableness" test is highly subjective. However, the Ordinance, having regard to the difficulties in applying the test, provides to the court or arbitrator some guidelines. In arriving to a decision that a clause is reasonable, and therefore should be upheld (or vice versa), the court or arbitrator should consider:

- The bargaining strength of both parties, taking into account alternative means by which the customer's requirements could have been met
- The inducement offered by the bank to the customer to agree to the term
- Customer's knowledge of the existence and extent of the term (having regard to the trade custom or previous dealings)
- Whether it was reasonable and practicable at the time

When an exemption clause fails the "reasonableness" test, it will be omitted from the bank-customer contract and the bank will be liable to the customer as though the term has never been inserted.

Summary

- Bankers need to understand the many legal issues that can arise in the course of day-to-day banking operations in order to protect their organisations and themselves from liability. One issue is the relationship between banker and customer, which can take several forms, such as banker and customer, debtor and creditor, principal and agent, and bailor and bailee.

- A mandate is a written instruction from a customer to a bank to do certain acts on the customer's behalf. In a strict legal sense, mandates are only instructions from customers to banks, but many banks have incorporated contractual clauses into a mandate. Some of those clauses may not be enforceable if they are not in accordance with usual banking practice.
- A power of attorney is a document that grants a third party the authority to operate a customer's account. A special/specific power of attorney gives the third party power for a specific purpose; a general power of attorney confers very extensive powers.
- Appropriation of payments is the right of a customer or a bank to apply a specified deposit to meet a specified debt. Set-off arises when a debtor or his creditor wishes to arrive at the net figure owing between them. If a customer has more than one account at a bank, the bank has the right to set off the customer's credit balance on one account against the same customer's debit balance.
- A lien is a right to retain possession of a debtor's goods until the debt is paid. In addition to any security it may have taken and to its right to combine or consolidate its customers' accounts, a bank in general law has a banker's lien over securities deposited by the customer to the extent of the customer's indebtedness to the bank.
- The banker's duty of secrecy is implied when the account is opened and extends not only to the account itself and the information that could be gained from it, but also to any other particulars of the customer's affairs, which come to the bank's knowledge from conducting the account or in carrying out any other transactions or financial dealings on behalf of the customer.
- The banker's duty of secrecy extends to the customer's personal data and consumer data. Banks must comply with the provisions of the Personal Data (Privacy) Ordinance and Code of Practice on Consumer Credit Data, respectively.
- The Code of Banking Practice requires banks to provide customers with monthly statements of account, advises them to examine them and allow at least 90 days to report unauthorised transactions, and compels them not to exercise their reserved right to deny a customer's claim if the unauthorised transaction arises from a third-party or bank employee fraud, forgery, or negligence.
- Substantial damages might be awarded against the bank if it wrongfully dishonours a cheque and thereby injures the customer's credit. The customer may claim damages from the bank based on either breach of contract or libel.

Key Terms

agent
bailee
bailor
banker's lien
breach of contract
Code of Banking Practice
Code of Practice on Consumer Credit Data
common law
consumer credit data

Control of Exemption Clauses Ordinance
creditor
customer
debtor
enduring power of attorney
exemption clauses
general power of attorney
libel
mandates
personal data
Personal Data (Privacy) Ordinance
power of attorney
principal
set-off
special/specific power of attorney
wrongful dishonour of cheques

Study Guide

1. Mr. A has opened two accounts in two different branches of the same bank. He is frequently overdrawn on one account and fails to correct the overdraft. However, his other account holds sufficient credit to cover his overdraft. Under these circumstances, what are the bank's legal options?
2. Investigators suspect Mr. M of certain financial irregularities and apply to his bank to look into his personal finances. Can they compel the bank to disclose such information? Under what circumstances can they compel the bank to disclose?
3. Mrs. M neglected to put sufficient funds in her current account to pay off her bills. She has sufficient funds in her personal account, but most of the funds are tied up in a time deposit. Can the bank use the funds in the time deposit account to offset the overdraft? Why or why not?
4. Explain when and how a banker and customer relationship begins.
5. Mr. A lost his high-salaried job and, as a consequence, has not been servicing a large overdraft with his bank. His bank plans to place a banker's lien on Mr. A's assets with it, which includes a time deposit that will mature in three months' time and a safe deposit box. Draft a plan of action for the execution of the lien, including an assessment of what assets can and cannot be included.

Further Reading

Chan Bo-ching, Simon. *Hong Kong Banking Law and Practice Volume 1*. First Edition. Hong Kong: Hong Kong Institute of Bankers, September 2000. Print.

Government of the Hong Kong Special Administrative Region. *Control of Exemption Clauses Ordinance*. Web. 14 April 2010 <http://www.hklii.org/hk/legis/en/ord/71/>

____________________ *Personal Data (Privacy) Ordinance*. Web. 14 April 2010 <http://www.pcpd.org.hk/english/files/ordinance/CCDCode_eng.pdf>

Hong Kong Monetary Authority. *Code of Banking Practice*. Web. 14 April 2010 <http://www.info.gov.hk/hkma/eng/consumer/code_eng.pdf>

Ko, Sai Hong. *Law and Practice of Banking Services in Hong Kong*. Hong Kong: City University Hong Kong Press, 1998. Print.

Office of the Privacy Commissioner for Personal Data. Code of Practice on Consumer Credit Data. Web. 14 April 2010. <http://www.pcpd.org.hk/english/files/ordinance/CCDCode_eng.pdf>

Privacy Commissioner for Hong Kong. Homepage. Web. 14 April 2010 <http://www.pcpd.org.hk/>

Opening and Conduct of Accounts

Learning objectives

After studying this chapter, you should be able to:

1. Describe certain legal issues commonly affecting the operation of different bank accounts
2. Outline procedures for opening of accounts for different types of clients as well as executing proper mandates for each
3. Determine the circumstances where the relationship between banker and customer may be terminated
4. Be alert to the different forms of money laundering activities and what to do to counteract such activities

Introduction

This chapter will discuss the opening and conduct of accounts as well as the different kinds of customers one encounters in a bank in Hong Kong. Contractual documents and mandates are daily features of banking procedures when opening a new account. As the world is turning more global and Hong Kong is an international financial hub, bank employees should be aware of the proper banking procedures as well as the dangers of money laundering and terrorist financing.

Opening of an Account

While all banks are anxious to increase their business, in particular deposit bases, it is necessary to exercise caution before opening an account and affording any banking facilities. No prudent banker would open an account immediately on the mere request of a stranger and/or without knowledge of the new customer, as there would be many risks in conducting an account for a rogue.

In the case of a deposit account, the bank may only require basic information from potential customers, that is, identity. Bank staff will ask for and check the identity card or passport of a new customer. If the amount of deposit is not very substantial, the banker will open an account as instructed by this customer. This is because time deposit accounts or savings mainly consist of cash credits, so there is little risk for the bank in agreeing to operate the account without a satisfactory introduction. In a case of substantial deposit, bankers should be alert to the possibility of money laundering and ask for more information about new customers.

There are procedures to follow to open an account for a new customer:

- The appropriate account mandate, which includes instructions and clauses of a contractual nature, should be executed.
- Written instructions from the customer in regards to the signing arrangements to operate the account should be received.
- Forward Terms & Conditions and Data Policy Notification (if any) should be given and explained to the customer.
- A specimen signature card or cards should be signed.

In the past, the most important requirement for opening a current bank account was a satisfactory introduction or "reference" from a new customer. An adequate reference is important. There have been cases in which actions have been brought against banks for conversion of cheques collected through a customer's account, which were subsequently found to belong to someone else.

However, in order to gain protection under the said Ordinance, the bank must act without a breach of duty to take care or "without negligence." The said breach can take place not only at the time when the cheque is presented for collection but can also date back to the time of account opening. That is called "antecedent negligence" and would include the omission to take a satisfactory reference.

Due to keen competition nowadays, many banks have decided to dispense with references and open current accounts for new customers, provided that the potential customer (actually a stranger) can provide proof of identity, that is, a Hong Kong Identity Card or passport, and the potential customers' names are not blacklisted. If banking facilities are to be granted or any credit facilities provided for other accounts, some banks may further engage credit reference agencies to carry out a credit reference bureau search. Those banks that have reduced their standard of care do so on the premise that easier requirements will attract more prospective customers. Some banks impose the minimum initial deposit for opening current accounts. No doubt those banks have examined claims and losses in past records and have calculated the risks.

In Hong Kong there is no decided case as yet to show whether it is sufficient to satisfy the court that banks act "without negligence" if the banks just check the identity of the new customer. Some leading banks still require new customers to provide a satisfactory reference for opening a current account.

According to the Code of Banking Practice issued by the industry associations in 2009, the authorised institutions should take the following steps when they open accounts for new customers. Section 15 of the Code provides that:

15.1 Institutions should satisfy themselves about the identity of a person seeking to open an account in order to protect their customers, the public, and themselves against misuse of the banking system.

15.2 Institutions should follow the customer identification procedures set out in the Hong Kong Monetary Authority's current Guidelines on Money Laundering. Those procedures include obtaining information on the customer's occupation or business activities and permanent address. Positive identification should be obtained from documents issued by official or other reputable sources, for example, passports or identity cards.

15.3 Institutions should provide to customers or prospective customers upon request general descriptive information about identification requirements.

It appears that if the bank does not fulfil the standard of the above Code, then it is highly probable that the court will rule that the bank has acted with negligence and the statutory protection may not be granted.

In the past, the courts (in particular in English cases) have always laid stress on the need for a satisfactory reference.

In *Guardians of St. John's Hampstead v. Barclays Bank Ltd.*, an account was opened for a stranger; a reference was received but from another stranger. It later came to be known that the new customer had in fact written a reference for himself; the bank was found to have been negligent as it failed to verify the facts provided. If the bank had attempted to verify the fictitious address given by their new customer or if it had made reasonable enquiries to prove his identity, the fraud would have been discovered earlier.

It is therefore a common practice that banks only accept the referees who are also existing customers. Some leading banks insist that the referees should be their existing customers for at least one year.

In *Lloyds Bank Ltd. v. E.B. Savory & Co.*, an account was opened for a married woman but the bank failed to take note of her husband's occupation and the name of his employers. Later, cheques were misappropriated from the husband's employer and were collected through the wife's account. The court held that the bank was guilty of conversion and could not claim that it had acted without negligence.

Prudent bankers therefore ask new customers for information about their spouse for anti-money laundering and "know your customer" provisions required by the HKMA.

It is also the banks' responsibility to keep themselves updated on the current banking practices. They should refer to the updated code of practice and the guidelines issued by the industry associations and the HKMA.

Conduct of Account

As mentioned earlier, banks must go through a prospective customer's credentials carefully before opening an account. Once the bank has opened an account for the new customer, it has several contractual obligations to its customer.

Monthly Statements

In Chapter 1, we discussed statements of accounts or customers' passbooks and the need of the banker to provide statements of account from time to time or when the customer requests such a statements.

The Code of Banking Practice states that banks should provide statements at monthly intervals unless a passbook (or similar record) is provided; there are no current transactions, or as otherwise agreed to with the customer.

Examination of Statements

Banks should advise customers to examine their statements and allow at least 90 days to report unauthorised transactions. Customers are warned that should they fail to report any unauthorised transactions within the specified period, the bank may regard the statement as conclusive.

Practice Duty of Secrecy and Personal Privacy

As was discussed earlier in Chapter 1, one of the most important relationships between a banker and customer is that of the duty of secrecy. This duty is expected upon the customer's opening an account and extends to the closure of the account.

Practice Duty of Care

At law, a bank owes a contractual duty to exercise reasonable care and skill in performing its duties arising out of its relationship with the customer.

Answering Banker's Reference

In certain circumstances, a duty of care may also arise in tort (a civil wrong for which the remedy is a common law action for unliquidated damages, and which is not a breach of duty arising out of a personal relation or contract), as was the principle established in the landmark case of *Hedley Bryne & Co. Ltd. v. Heller & Partners Ltd.*

In this case, an advertising agency requested a reference from a bank before placing a substantial order for a company, for which it would be responsible. The respondent was the bank that provided a satisfactory reference, even though it stipulated that the reference was "without responsibility." The court held that the reference could allow for an action and that the bank ought to have known that reliance was being placed on its skill and judgment.

Making Payments

Another example in which a bank has a duty to exercise care is in paying cheques or making payments.

The bank owes a duty of care not to pay cheques without enquiry, which would have led a reasonable banker to consider there is a serious or real possibility of fraud on the customer.

Investment Advice

Another common example where a bank owes a duty of care is where it gives financial and investment advice as part of its banking business.

A distinction may be drawn between the giving of information and provision of advice. In the case of *South Australian Asset Management Corp. v. York Montagne Ltd.*, the court drew the distinction as follows:

- Information is given to enable the recipient to decide on what course of action to take, and the giver of information is subject to the duty to ensure the information is accurate;

- Advice is given on what course of action to take, and the adviser is liable for all foreseeable consequences of the recipient acting in reliance on the advice.

In this case, a property valuer negligently over-valued a property that provided security for a mortgage loan. The court held that property valuation is an example of information given to enable the lender to decide on whether to approve the loan application. The valuer was held liable for the negligent over-valuation.

Where a bank assumes the role of a financial adviser, it has a duty to exercise reasonable care and skill in performing that role. In a lending situation, banks rarely assume such roles where they are held liable for giving negligent financial advice to a customer seeking a loan from the bank for investment purposes.

These issues are of increasing significance in the modern banking world, where wealth management services are a part of retail banking business. Typically, in a non-discretionary management situation, banks make recommendations to customers on the types of investments that suit their investment needs and match their risk tolerance profiles. It is a fine line to draw between merely providing information and recommendations for customers to make their own decisions, and giving advice, which give rise to different duties at law. Banks commonly seek to limit their duty of care by (i) refraining from giving advice in marketing materials and communication with customers, (ii) expressly stating that they merely provide recommendations, but not advice, to enable customers to make their own decisions, and therefore do not assume any responsibility for the consequences of the customer's decisions, and (iii) obtaining the customer's written acknowledgment of their own decision-making and the bank's disclaimer of responsibility. The validity of any disclaimer will be subject to the reasonableness test under the Unconscionable Contracts Ordinance.

Specific Issues Affecting the Operation of Accounts

Issues affecting the operation of accounts are:

- Title to moneys paid in;
- Powers of attorney for operating individual accounts;
- Garnishee order;
- Mareva injunction.

Title to Moneys Paid in

Title in money generally passes with possession. Monies paid into a bank account belong to the bank. For over-the-counter cash payments, so long as the monies are on the customer's side of the counter, title remains with the customer and the bank is not in any way responsible for the monies. Title does not pass to the bank until the monies are received on the bank's side of the counter and are checked and accepted by the teller who gives a receipt for them.

Powers of Attorney for Operating Individual Accounts

An individual customer may appoint a third party to operate a bank account on his/her behalf by:

- Authorization given in the account mandate by naming the third party an authorised signatory to the account. The agent's authority will be terminated upon the death, bankruptcy, or mental incapacity of the customer.
- Power of attorney;
  i. This is a document, executed under seal, whereby one person (the donor) authorises another (the donee or attorney) to act on behalf of the donor.
  ii. There are two types of powers of attorney: general and specific. A general power of attorney authorises the attorney to do anything that can be lawfully done on the donor's behalf. The Powers of Attorney Ordinance (Cap. 31) provides a form of general power of attorney (Schedule). A specific power of attorney is one that authorises the attorney to do only the acts specified in the document, for example, execution of a contract.
  iii. Where an individual seeks to operate a customer's accounts with the bank in reliance on a power of attorney, the bank should take the following precautions:
    a. In case of a specific power of attorney, ensure that it clearly authorises the attorney to operate the donor's bank accounts, and check for any limits on the attorney's authority, for example, any cap on the amount allowed to be withdrawn by the attorney;
    b. Execution of the document: verify the donor's signature against the bank's records, and ensure the document is under seal;
    c. Ensure the document is executed under seal, and is still in force;
    d. Verify the attorney's identity;
    e. Ensure the original document is produced.

  A power of attorney is revoked:
    a. On expiry of the validity period (if any) specified in the document;
    b. On revocation by the donor;
    c. On the death, bankruptcy, or mental incapacity of the donor;
    d. If the attorney renounces his powers by notice to the donor.

The Powers of Attorney Ordinance provides that if a power of attorney is revoked, subsequent transactions between the attorney and any third party dealing with the attorney (such as a bank) before they had notice of the revocation will remain valid as if the document was still in force. An attorney cannot delegate his power to another person, unless the power of attorney expressly authorises him to do so.

Garnishee Order

A garnishee order 'nisi' (formally known as an order to show cause) is a court order that is applied when a customer owes money to another and the creditor has obtained the court's judgment ordering the customer to repay the debt, but the debtor fails to do so. This attaches funds in the hands of a third party who owes money to the debtor, including the debtor's banker (known as the 'garnishee').

For example, D owes C money. C obtains judgment against D in respect of the debt. D fails to pay the judgment debt. D has a credit balance with his bank. C then obtains a garnishee order attaching D's credit balance at the bank. In that way, C will obtain payment of the judgment debt, either in whole or in part, as the case may be. Service of a garnishee order upon a bank may, therefore, determine—or at least suspend—the bank's duty to honour cheques drawn by the customer.

In effect, a garnishee order attaches, that is, freezes, debts due or accruing due (existing obligation but is future payment) by the garnishee to the judgment debtor, or so much thereof as is sufficient to satisfy the judgment and the costs of the garnishee proceedings. It has the effect of attaching the debtor's credit balances at the bank as at the time of service of the order and for which the customer can sue the bank at the time. The bank is restrained from subsequently allowing any payment from the attached balances, including the payment of cheques drawn before the service of the order. Payments into the account after service of the order are not subject to the order. When the garnishee order is made absolute, the bank will be ordered to pay so much of the credit balance to the creditor as will discharge the judgment debt and costs. The practice is for banks to notify the customer immediately when served with a garnishee order 'nisi'.

Enumerated below are circumstances where garnishee order may or may not be applied:

- Term deposit not yet matured is attachable: *Bagley v. Winsome & National Provincial Bank.*
- Money comes to a bank after receipt of order is not attachable. Bank should rule off the accounts of the judgment debtor upon receipt of the order.
- Money "gone out" before receipt of the order is not attachable. "Gone out": book entries passed and the transferee advised.
- A garnishee order will operate as a revocation of a transfer unless the transaction in question is not capable of being revoked.
- Uncleared outward clearing cheques are not attachable.
- Inward clearing cheques which have not been confirmed paid should be returned and the sum attachable.
- Money in a trust account is attached. The bank is required to inform the customer to enable him to take necessary action to protect the interest of the beneficiary of the trust. Also, inform the court of the trust: *Plunkett v Barclays Bank.*
- A bank invokes its right of set-off before arriving at the net balance to be attached.

- Garnishee To Show Cause (Nisi): requesting the bank to show cause for not complying with the order. The bank will inform the customer of the receipt of the order and choose not to attend court.
- If the order is for a limited amount, the amount involved plus charges can be transferred to a separate account pending payment. If it attaches all debts without limit, the account must be stopped.
- If the order is in a sole name, a joint account need not be attached.
- A partnership account need not be attached unless it is made against all partners, or the partnership.
- An account in foreign currency is attached: *Choice Investment Ltd v. Jeromnimon.*
- Money in overseas accounts is subject to garnishee proceeding in HK. But it can be argued that an overseas office of a bank in HK should be treated as a separate entity: *F D C Co Ltd v. Chase*—a case relating to duty of secrecy.
- A liquidator's account cannot be attached in respect of a debt owed by the company of which he is the liquidator.
- Garnishee Order Absolute: A request to the bank to pay over to court or to the judgment creditor.

Mareva Injunction

A bank's duty to obey its customer's instructions for the payment of money and for the transfer of funds has frequently been abrogated by Mareva injunctions, an order which has been given statutory recognition in section 21L of the High Court Ordinance, Cap. 4.

A Mareva injunction (named after a 1980 English case) is an order of the court restraining a defendant from disposing of his assets in or outside the jurisdiction of the court before judgment; and regardless of whether or not the party is domiciled, resident, or present within the jurisdiction.

It is, in effect, a freezing injunction. It is of significance to banks as it is commonly served on more than one bank. If the plaintiff is able to identify bank accounts maintained by the defendant, these are normally spelled out in the court order. Where, however, the plaintiff is unaware or uncertain of where the defendant maintains bank accounts, the practice is for the order to be served on all banks. This is tantamount to a request to the banks to search for accounts and assets in the defendant's name and to freeze them. A bank allowing any breach of the injunction in dealing with the defendant's assets (in the bank) will be liable for contempt of court.

The courts also grants worldwide Mareva injunctions which, when served on a bank's offices located within the court's jurisdiction, binds the bank's branches and offices worldwide. These have given rise to problems, as an order of the Hong Kong court does not have effect outside of Hong Kong and will not bind an overseas branch of a bank under the law of the foreign jurisdiction. The courts have, over the years, attempted to resolve this problem by the addition, where appropriate, of provisos to the terms of the court order, which state:

- That the order does not affect persons outside Hong Kong until it is declared enforceable by a court in the foreign country;
- Except for persons who have been given written notice of the order in Hong Kong and is able to prevent a breach of the order outside Hong Kong;
- For assets located outside Hong Kong, the order does not prevent the bank from complying with its contractual or other obligations under the law of the country in which the assets are located.

The sum effect of these provisos is that where a worldwide Mareva injunction is granted by the courts of Hong Kong, even though a bank with its headquarters in Hong Kong may be said to be able to prevent a breach of the order by its branch in, say, Singapore, by requiring its Singapore branch to freeze the defendant's assets, if this is in breach of the bank's contractual obligations under the laws of Singapore because the injunction is of no legal effect there, the bank would not be in contempt of court if its Singapore branch does not comply with the order.

The case *Z Ltd. v. A-Z and AA-LL* illustrates some key points of the Mareva injunction:

- Once a bank has notice, by whatever means, it must not dispose of any assets—otherwise it is guilty of contempt of court;
- Return cheque—'Refer to drawer—injunction in force';
- Credit account may be set off against debit account;
- A bank must freeze the account named, and the joint account too if the injunction is so worded;
- Items in safe custody that are covered by the terms of the injunction should be held pending;
- The injunction would not prevent payment under a L/C or bank guarantee; however funds received under L/C should be frozen;
- It would not affect honouring cheques drawn against a cheque card or credit card;
- banks are entitled to recover the related expenses, and be indemnified by the plaintiff in action, any liability that the bank may leave itself open to as a result of complying with the injunction;
- The injunction should clearly tell the bank what it could or could not do (bank account, branch should be identified); if the plaintiff could not do that, he could ask the bank to search (should undertake to pay all costs); if the bank finds an account or asset, it should freeze the assets discovered but should not tell the plaintiff;
- If the order specifies a sum to be used for "normal living expenses," the bank is not required to inquire how the money is used. It can open a special account for such a sum;
- The order should not apply to assets that come after the date served, unless they were specially referred to (take legal advice);
- Credit currency balance should be converted into local currency at the then buying rate;
- The customer should immediately be informed in writing of the receipt of the injunction.

Closing of Account

Accounts can be closed by either:

- Customer;
- Bank.

Closure of Account by Customer

For current accounts, whether in credit or overdrawn at the time of closure, it is always prudent for the bank to remind the customer to make provisions for the payment of any outstanding cheques already drawn. Banks typically will also ask the customer to hand in any unused cheques in the customer's possession.

For other deposit accounts, balances on savings accounts are generally repayable on demand, so customers may close such accounts without prior notice to the bank. For time deposits, the terms of the contract typically discourage premature uplifting, normally through forfeiture of any interest accrued up to the date of early termination by the customer. In this regard, the Code of Banking Practice requires banks to inform customers of the charges and/or forfeiture of interest that may arise from early or partial withdrawal of time deposits.

Closure of Account by Bank

At law, a bank that intends to close a customer's account or terminate its relationship with a customer must give the customer reasonable notice, the period of which should be long enough to enable the customer to make alternative arrangements. The exception is where the customer has been using the account for unlawful purposes. The Code of Banking Practice (section 16) echoes the legal requirement for reasonable notice to be given, unless it is a case of exceptional circumstances, such as where the account is being used for criminal activities.

In *Buckingham & Co. v. London and Midland Bank Ltd.*, the customer had both a loan account and a current account. While he had a credit balance of £160 in his current account the bank informed him that his account was closed and that the bank would not pay any more cheques or honour any more of his acceptances. On the following day, two cheques and two bills of the customer were presented and were dishonoured. The jury found that, in the course of dealing between the customer and the bank, the customer was entitled to draw on his current account without reference to his loan account, that he was entitled to reasonable notice discontinuing this course of business, and that no such notice had been given. The customer was awarded £500 in damages against the bank.

In *Joachimson v. Swiss Bank Corporation*, it was stated that one of the terms of the contract was that the banker would not cease to do business with a customer "except upon reasonable notice." Although the existence of this implied term is now well established, the practical difficulty is to know what length of notice would be regarded as reasonable in the particular circumstances of a given case. When a bank decides to cease providing banking facilities for a customer, it usually wants to end the relationship as speedily as possible. The customer, for his part, often wishes to continue the account for as long as possible, especially if he knows or thinks that other banks would not be prepared to open an account for him.

If, however, the customer is using his account for some unlawful purposes, the bank is under no obligation to give sufficient notice; either no period of notice at all, or a purely nominal period of 24 hours' notice, would suffice to put an end to the relationship of banker and customer.

Although a banker has a right to close an account that is in debit at any time, he may require further consideration. Depending upon the circumstances, a bank may be entitled to demand repayment of an overdraft forthwith, but this is very different from closing the account. It would be imprudent of the banker if he called in an overdraft to close an account and then, prior to the expiry of a proper period of notice, he dishonoured cheques which the customer was prepared to cover by paying in cash. It is one thing to call in an overdraft; it is quite another matter to withdraw banking facilities without giving the customer sufficient notice to enable him to make other arrangements.

Opening and Conduct of Accounts for Various Customers

A bank opens accounts for various types of customers:

- Personal customers;
- Joint customers;
- Minors;
- Executors and administrators;
- Trustees;
- Sole proprietors;
- Partnerships;
- Unincorporated associations, clubs, and societies;
- Solicitors;
- Incorporated companies.

Personal Customers

As the general principle and practice regarding the opening of a new account had been dealt with in Chapter 1, the following will be considered only for individual customers (normal adult):

- Four important matters for consideration;
- Authority to open an account;
- Customer's identity;
- Customer's integrity;
- Customer's employers;
- Customer Due Diligence (CDD) principle;
- Other questions to ask.

Four Important Matters for Consideration

When an individual adult makes an application to a bank to open an account in the name of a private individual, there are four important matters for consideration regarding this prospective new customer, namely (1) whether he has authorised the opening of an account in his name, (2) whether he can show that he is the person he claims to be, (3) whether he is a proper person to conduct a banking account, and (4) whether he is employed by someone else. In practice, most banks do not consider the last matter in regard to savings and/or time deposit accounts.

Authority to Open Account

In most cases, a prospective customer calls at the head office or the bank branch when he wishes to open an account. However, occasionally some third party may state that he has been authorised to open an account for the prospective customer, for example, the prospective customer is a public figure and/or a very rich person. In such cases, the request must be treated with extreme caution. *Robinson v. Midland Bank Ltd.* is a good reference. This case highlighted the danger of opening an account in the name of a new customer without meeting him.

In Robinson's case, a cheque for £150,000 was credited to open a current account by a dishonest solicitor's clerk, who later forged the signature of the account holder, "C. Robinson," and absconded with the money. Even though the real Mr. Robinson had not been entitled to the funds, upon learning what had happened, he later sued the bank for recovery of the monies said to have been lodged in his name and withdrawn without his authority. Although the bank succeeded in defeating the claim, this case is a warning that no current account should be opened without a satisfactory reference or enquiry; at the very least the bank should have required a meeting with the person.

Customer's Identity

There have been many cases in the past where a dishonest person has succeeded in opening an account under a fictitious name for the purpose of illegally obtaining money. Nowadays, it is the practice to verify the identity of a new customer if he wants to open any kind of account.

Banks should follow the customer identification procedures set out in the HKMA's Guideline on Anti-Money Laundering and Counter-Terrorist Financing, and the Code of

Practice on the Identity Card Number and other Personal Identities, issued by the Privacy Commissioner for Personal Data and the Anti-Money Laundering and Counter-Terrorist Financing (Financial Institutions) Ordinance, and ask for the following documents/ information:

- Copy of identity document(s). If there is doubt, the bank may call the Immigration Department to verify;
- Address (and proof of address where applicable);
- The customer's principal business or profession.

Customer's Integrity

For current accounts, the referee or person introducing the new customer should be in a position to identify him, at the very least to state that he is a fit and proper person to operate a current account. Should the bank become aware of any adverse comment, the bank should close the account.

For other deposit accounts, in practice the banks do not check the integrity of the new customers except for those who apply for credit facilities and when there is the possibility of money laundering.

Customer's Employers

The new customer for an account should be asked whether he is employed and, if so, the nature of the employment and the name of the employer. The reason for these enquiries is to protect the bank from the claim of conversion if, for example, the new customer should try to pay into his account cheques payable to his employers or cheques drawn by the employers in favour of a third party.

A banker must make careful enquiries if suspicious circumstances are observed. Although it is not common practice in Hong Kong to accept cheques payable to an employer when a customer opens an account, the case *Harding v. London Joint Stock Bank Ltd.* is a good illustration as to the dangers of this practice. In that case, a man named Francom, a cashier and bookkeeper of J. Bland, Smith-Harding and Co., opened an account based on an introduction by a bank's existing customer. When Francom opened the account, he wished to pay in a cheque payable to J. Bland, Smith-Harding and Co. The bank manager asked Francom to get written confirmation from that company that he was authorised to deal with said cheque. Francom wrote a letter in the name of his employers, stating that the cheque was all right and it referred to "our Francom." The plaintiff succeeded in his claim against the bank. The court decided that the bank had not taken the reasonable and proper precautions that they ought to have taken. It is suggested that the bank should not have accepted credit of the cheque in the first place. Even if the bank is willing to accept credit of the cheque and takes the risk (which does not comply with normal practice), the bank should have confirmed the authorisation directly with the customer's employers.

Customer Due Diligence (CDD) Principle

The identity of a person seeking to open an account should be satisfactorily ascertained and the CDD requirements set out in the HKMA's Guideline on Anti-Money Laundering and Counter-Terrorist Financing and the Anti-Money Laundering and Counter-Terrorist Financing (Financial Institutions) Ordinance should be followed. The Code of Banking Practices states that a bank should provide to a customer or prospective customer upon request general descriptive information about the identification requirements.

Other Questions to Ask

- What bank services will be requested? Large amount remittance/deposits?
- What activities generate the sources of the funds? (Is such amount consistent with the customer's business type?)
- Is the customer an individual who is (or has been) entrusted with prominent public functions (i.e., a politically exposed person) or an associate of such an individual?
- If the account to be opened is a trust account, what is the purpose of the trust? In which country is the trust established? Who are the beneficiaries and other co-trustees?

Joint Customers

An account opened in the name of two or more customers is known as a joint account. Further, these customers should be neither partners, executors, administrators, nor trustees. Husband and wife or fiancé and fiancée, frequently open a joint bank account. Joint accounts may be opened by others who may, or may not, be related to each other. Usually a joint account involves two or three account holders, although there is no restriction in law for the maximum number of account holders for a joint account. In practice, however, a bank usually does not allow a group of customers to open a joint account that has more than five account holders. In a joint account the owners, either jointly or severally, act on behalf of themselves. In law a joint account is simply a debt owed to the account holders jointly.

When application is made to a bank to open a joint account, the same four important matters for consideration as for an individual customer are required, that is, customers' authority, identity, integrity, and employment.

Mandate

Before a joint account is opened, it is usual for the bank to provide the prospective customers with a printed standard mandate form for completion. This form will embody the instructions of the account holders to the bank and is referred to as a "Mandate for Joint

Accounts." It is common practice for the T&C booklet to include the conditions of the mandate. The mandate obtains clear authority as to who can make withdrawals (either or all to sign). A bank may be liable to the injured party if it debits the account outside the scope of mandate.

In practice, some of the clauses in the Mandate for Joint Accounts contain alternative provisions, so that the joint account holder may select the appropriate provisions. The following are the common provisions in this mandate:

- "We, the undersigned, hereby request and authorise the Bank to open and continue current and other account(s) with the Bank in our joint names subject to such terms and conditions as the Bank may think fit and, at any time subsequently, to open such further account(s) in our joint names as both/or either of us may direct."
- "In accordance with the signing instructions set out below (the "Signing Instructions"), to close any account(s) so opened, to honour and comply with all cheques, promissory notes, instruments, orders and bills expressed to be drawn, signed, accepted, indorsed or made on our behalf, drawn upon or addressed to or made payable at the Bank, whether such account(s) is or are in credit or overdrawn, to accept and act on the lodgement or revocation of stop payment order(s), to accept all receipt(s) as a valid discharge to the Bank for any monies deposited with or owning by the Bank on our joint account(s) with the Bank at any time, and to comply with all other directions given for or in connection with the joint account(s) on our behalf, provided that such cheques, promissory notes, instruments, orders, bills, directions or receipts are signed with the Signing Instructions."
- "We will be jointly and severally responsible for the repayment of advances of money made by the Bank to us and of all other monies and liabilities due from us to the Bank together with interest, costs and expenses for such advances, other monies and liabilities (including legal costs for recovery of these items on a full indemnity basis) but without prejudice to the Bank's right to refuse to allow any overdraft or increase of overdraft."
- The Signing Instructions of a joint account may set out that both [all] or either [some] of the joint account holders are authorised to operate the joint account. If the joint account holders do not expressly authorise the bank to act on one signature, all the holders to a joint account must sign cheques and other orders.
- "We hereby authorise the Bank to hold on the death of any of us any credit balance(s) on any account(s) in our joint names and any securities, deeds, boxes and their contents, parcels and their contents, and property of any description held in our joint names to the order of the survivor(s) of us without prejudice to any right the Bank may have in respect of such balance(s), securities, deeds, boxes, parcels and property arising out of any lien, charge, pledge, set-off, counterclaim or otherwise whatsoever or to any step which the Bank may deem desirable to take in view of any claim by any person other than the survivor(s) of us." This clause or provision is commonly known as the "survivorship clause."

In practice, the Mandate for Joint Accounts has set out clearly all the authorisation and/or instructions from the joint account holders in most and/or whatever situations. In rare cases where the mandate has not clearly stipulated the authorisation or instruction regarding a special situation, the bankers should then seek the express authorisation from all of the joint account holders.

If a mandate for joint account provides that the cheque or order for payment etc. must be signed by two or more joint account holders of a joint account, and if any signature of any such account holder on a cheque or order is forged, the bank will not be entitled to debit the amount of such cheque or order to the joint account: *Jackson v. White and Midland Bank Ltd.*

In the case of a cheque deposit:

- Cheque in a sole name can be deposited to a joint account if the account mandate so stipulates it;
- If the mandate does not mention such stipulation, it may do so by asking the cheque payee to endorse and to make it more secure to add a statement—*credit to joint account no. xxxxxx*;
- A cheque payable in joint name cannot be deposited to a sole name account;
- Any party can stop payment of a cheque, even if it is drawn by another one (common practice); if disagreement arises or there is a wish to cancel the "stop," all parties should confirm before paying a cheque.

As mentioned earlier, a joint account is debt owed to the account holders jointly. This raises the question as to the rights of one of the joint creditors if the bank wrongly pays the other. *Catlin v. Cyprus Finance Corporation (London) Ltd.*, where a landmark decision in banking law was made, relates to joint accounts. In this case, the plaintiff and her husband had deposited funds in a joint account with the defendant bank. The deposit was made according to the terms of an express mandate, requiring that the bank would make payments out of the account only on the joint signatures of both account holders. In breach of the express term of that mandate, and without knowledge or authority of the plaintiff, the bank negligently transferred all the funds out on the instructions of her husband. The plaintiff brought an action against the bank claiming damages for breach of its mandate. The bank contended that in the absence of the husband as a party, the plaintiff's claim must fail because the bank owed a single obligation to the joint account holders jointly and the obligation could only be enforced in an action to which both account holders were parties. The court held that the bank's agreement to honour only those instructions signed by both account holders carried with it a duty not to honour instructions which were not signed in that manner. That duty was owed to the account holders severally and accordingly, where a breach of the mandate occurred, it could be enforced at the suit of the innocent account holder alone. It followed that the plaintiff was entitled to the relief that she sought.

In both the Jackson and the Catlin cases it was established that the funds paid into the joint account were the plaintiff's property. The respective plaintiffs were accordingly allowed to recover the full amount paid out on cheques that ought to have been dishonoured by the banks. Where such facts cannot be proved, all the innocent joint owner of the account is entitled to recover is a moiety of amounts paid out wrongfully against cheques not signed by him: *Arden v. Bank of New South Wales.*

In general, unless otherwise expressly agreed by the bank and its customers, the obligations and liabilities owed by a bank to joint account holders are joint and several.

Regarding the instructions relating to countermanding payment of cheques, it is generally assumed that any one joint account holder has power or authority to countermand payment of a cheque drawn on the joint account. However, that all depends on the instruction of the mandate. The Mandate for Joint Accounts provided by the banks should clearly set out the proper authorization for such instructions.

Joint Account Operations

The courts have held that where husband and wife are joint account holders, the bank has no concern over how they choose to operate the account so long as instructions are given in accordance with the mandate, unless the bank is aware of any restraints agreed between husband and wife. In the case of *Royal Bank of Scotland plc v. Fielding,* the mandate of a current account opened jointly by husband and wife provided for 'either to sign' instructions. The husband ran up a sizeable overdraft without the wife's knowledge. The court held that since the bank accepted instructions in accordance with the mandate, it had no duty or liability to the wife in respect of the overdraft.

When a dispute between the parties in an "either to sign" case is noted, the mandate can be considered revoked and the bank allows the withdrawal from signatures of all parties until the dispute is resolved.

Right of Survivorship

Joint account mandates typically include a survivorship clause, whereby the account holders authorise the bank to hold, on the death of any one of them, any credit balance on the account, and other assets held in their joint names, to the order of the survivor(s). So in the case where one of the account holders dies, the bank does not have to 'freeze' the account but can allow its continual operation on instructions from the surviving account holder(s). Upon notice of death, the bank will delete the name of the deceased from the account title and arrange for new cheque books etc. in the name(s) of survivor(s).

An adult and a minor may hold a joint account. Where all the monies in the account have been paid in by an adult, the principle of survivorship still applies, that is, upon the death of the adult, the minor gets the balance accrued: *McEvoy v. Belfast Banking Co. Ltd.*

What if two or more joint account holders died in circumstances making it uncertain which of them died first? Section 11 of the Conveyancing and Property Ordinance, Cap. 219 provides that the deaths are presumed to have occurred in order of seniority and accordingly the younger shall be deemed to have survived the elder. This presumption should be applied unless it is possible to say for certain who died first. However, the rule expressly excludes the case of husband and wife, where the intestate and his or her spouse die in circumstances rendering it uncertain who died first; the rule of intestacy applies as if the husband or wife had not survived the intestate: section 4(11) of the Intestates' Estates Ordinance, Cap. 73.

Where there is a dispute between survivor(s) and personal representatives, the claims of the representatives can usually be ignored if the intention is clear (i.e., if the survivorship clause was deleted).

If the intention is unclear, then the bank will only release monies:

- Against joint instructions of the survivor(s) and personal representatives;
- To the court – interpleading, that is, allowing both group to express their rights to the balance;

When applying the Rule of Survivorship consider:

- *Marshall v. Crutwell*: the balance automatically passed to his estate, rather than the survivor, because the prior intention of the husband was that the change was merely for convenience.

Bankruptcy or Mental Incapacity of Joint Account Holder

Unlike death, the bankruptcy or mental incapacity does not invoke the right of survivorship. Once a bank is aware of the presentation of a bankruptcy petition against the holder of a joint account or his/her mental incapacity, the account should be stopped immediately and the balance can only be released on the joint authority of the solvent party(s) and the trustee or Official Receiver. The further operation of the account should be subject to the joint instructions of the remaining account holders and the trustee or committee appointed to take over the estate of the bankrupt or mentally-incapacitated account holder. The appointment of the agent should be jointly authorised by all parties.

Service of a Garnishee Order

The effect of service of a garnishee order on a joint account is as follows:

- A garnishee order that names all the holders of a joint account as judgment debtors will attach the credit balance in the joint account.
- A garnishee order that names two judgment debtors will attach a credit balance in the name of one of them.
- A garnishee order that names only one of several joint account holders as judgment debtor will not attach the balance in the joint account.

Items held in Safe Custody

Banks often hold items in safe custody and there are various considerations when dealing with these items:

- Withdrawal of items will be covered by bank mandate, that is, either or both sign, etc.
- If not covered, all must sign
- If a party becomes insane—only release items against both sane party & receiver
- If a party becomes bankrupt—only release items against both solvent party & trustee/receiver
- If a party dies—survivorship does not generally apply, unless there is clear indication of joint ownership. Otherwise, obtain both survivor(s)' and personal representatives' instructions to release items

Minors

The Age of Majority (Related Provisions) Ordinance, Cap. 410 provides that a person shall attain full age at the age of 18 years. It also provides that the time at which a person attains a particular age expressed in years shall be the commencement of the anniversary corresponding to the date of his birth. Where a person has been born on 29 February in a leap year, the relevant anniversary in any year other than a leap year shall be taken to be 1 March.

In England, a person under 18 may be termed a 'minor' rather than an 'infant.' In Hong Kong, 'minor' and 'infant' are interchangeable. Bankers usually refer to them as 'minors.'

In summary:

- A minor is defined by the Age of Majority (Related Provision) Ordinance 1990 as being under 18 years of age;
- A minor can operate a credit account in the usual manner. This is of little practical importance as there should be no occasion for the bank to sue the minor;
- Minors are not allowed to hold debit accounts or loan accounts as the contract is void;
- It is acceptable for a minor to be named as a joint account holder, however, it is possible for the minor to avoid legal liability if the account becomes overdraft;
- A minor can become a member of a partnership and bind the firm in ordinary course of business;
- Under the S.3 Juvenile Offender Ordinance a minor below the age of 10 cannot commit any criminal offence;
- In practice, a bank may open a deposit account for a minor only when he/she reaches 11 years of age since that is the age when a child ID card is issued and the minor has the capacity to understand and appreciate the nature of the transaction.

Contractual Capacity

Briefly, minor's contracts are chiefly divided into two classes: valid or voidable.

- Valid contract
    i. Contract for necessaries:

    Section 4 of the Sale of Goods Ordinance, Cap. 26 provides: "Where necessaries are sold and delivered to an infant or minor, or to a person who, by reason of mental incapacity or drunkenness, is incompetent to contract, he may pay a reasonable price therefore."

    Necessaries are defined as "goods suitable to the condition in life of such minor and to his actual requirements at the time of sale and delivery." At common law, "necessaries" include services and goods, and if a minor is married (if over 16 years old), necessaries for his family are also included. The burden of proof is upon the seller, that is, it is for him to prove that any goods or services supplied were necessary.

    A minor is bound to pay a reasonable price for necessaries ordered by and supplied to him, although he is not liable on a cheque given by him in respect of those necessaries: *Re Soltykoff ex parte Margrett*.

    ii. Beneficial contracts:

    A minor is liable upon contracts which, though not for necessaries, are nevertheless for the minor's benefit, such as a service contract. Such a contract must be beneficial to the minor and must not be on the whole harsh or oppressive. A contract of service should be proper and not a pure trading contract notwithstanding that on the whole it may be for the minor's benefit.
- Voidable contracts:

    There are certain contracts of continuing liability, such as membership of a body corporate or contracts of partnership or tenancy, which bind a minor unless he expressly repudiates them during minority or within a reasonable time after coming of majority. A minor may escape or avoid any future liability under such contracts but not those that have already accrued. However, the minor cannot recover money paid unless there has been a "total failure of consideration": *Steinberg v. Scala (Leeds) Ltd.*

    Further, there are certain contracts that are not binding on a minor unless and until he ratifies them after attaining his majority, for example, a trading contract. This type of contract includes all contracts other than those for necessities, beneficial contracts of employment, and contracts for the acquisition of a permanent interest in property, which are valid unless expressly void. Thus, a minor may sue but not may not be sued upon an account stated or upon a contract for the sale of goods (other than necessaries) or any other simple contract (including banking transactions).
- Banking relations:

    In those cases where a minor's account is maintained in credit, the courts have not had to decide into which of the above-mentioned class of contracts the ordinary contract of banker and customer should be placed. It may be a special class of contract: a minor may sue, but may not be sued upon the contract. Accordingly, if a banker acts in breach of his duty of secrecy or wrongfully dishonours a cheque drawn by a minor, the banker will be liable for damages to the same extent as if his customer was an adult. Of course it is arguable whether the provision of banking services is one of contract for necessaries; if yes, then the contract is a valid contract at common law.

The fact that a banker is unable to sue a minor customer is of little practical importance. This is because if the minor's account is maintained in credit, there should be no occasion for a banker to sue the minor. The payment of cheques drawn by a minor does not place a banker in jeopardy. This is because section 22(2) of the Bills of Exchange Ordinance, Cap. 19 provides that where a bill [including a cheque] is drawn or endorsed by an infant, minor, or corporation having no capacity or power to incur liability on a bill, the drawing or endorsement entitles the holder to receive payment of the bill, and to enforce it against any other party thereto.

Most banks in Hong Kong would not open a current account for a minor because minors are not their target customers. If the bank allows a minor to open a current account he/she should be at least 16 years old. Even prior to 16 years of age, there can be no real risk in conducting a time deposit account and/or a savings account for a minor, provided that he has the capacity to understand and appreciate the nature of the transactions. Such an account could be opened for a child of about 7 years of age and upward. For children below 7 years of age, it is more prudent for the banker not to open any bank account, partly because it is an irrefutable presumption of law they cannot commit any criminal offence; and also partly because a child of that age would not be able to understand or appreciate the nature of banking transactions. In practice, banks open a savings or time deposit account for minors only when they reach 11 years of age since they should hold a child identity card. If the bank opens an account for a minor, the account name will be in the style of "Master Chan Siu Man (Minor)."

Prior to the age of 7, accounts for the benefit of a child may be opened in the name of a person of full age, usually the father or mother or guardian of the child, in the style of "Re X.Y., a minor." In fact, it should be a trust account for the child; some banks recently opened such accounts in the style of "Mr. A.B. in trust for X.Y., a minor." The person of full age is the customer and is the only person who may operate the account. Bankers may usually require that there is a close relationship between the adult and minor, for example, father/mother or guardian of the minor. Bankers should also check the identity of the minors, that is, check their birth certificates. In order to avoid any conversion, the bankers would not allow the minor accounts to be deposited with any cheque.

Lending to Minors

The position in regard to an overdrawn account in name of a minor is clear, that is, it is not enforceable. Repayment cannot be enforced even if the minor obtained an advance by a false representation that he was of full age: *R. Leslie Ltd. v. Sheill*. In practice, bankers would input a message code into the computer system so that there would be no overdraft facilities for a minor's account.

If the money is lent to a minor to enable him to purchase the necessaries, the lender (including a bank) is entitled to the right of subrogation, that is, the lender is allowed in equity the same right of recovery as the seller would have possessed if he had not been paid. However, no banker would knowingly lend money to a minor in reliance upon this rule.

Section 46 of the District Court Ordinance, Cap. 336 provides that no person under the age of 21 will be exempted from liability for any debt, damages, or demand arising under an agreement made before the date of commencement of the Age of Majority (Related Provisions) Ordinance where the debt, damages, or demand: (a) does not exceed $60,000 or (b) has been reduced to a sum not exceeding $60,000 by reason of the plaintiff having abandoned the amount in excess of $60,000 in his cause of action. This provision was no longer effective when the Age of Majority (Related Provisions) Ordinance took effect on 1 October 1990.

Other Banking Transactions

Despite not being of age, a minor is still able to perform several banking transactions:

- Joint account:

  A minor may be one of the account holders of a joint account. In such cases, if the current account is overdrawn or there is any advance through such a joint account, it is still possible for the minor to avoid the legal liability. In practice, the Mandate for Joint Accounts will invariably provide that the account holders of a joint account will be jointly and severally responsible for operation of the account and for the repayment of advances of money made by the bank to them.
- A minor as a witness:

  A minor may witness a document (including a banking document) provided that he is old enough to know or understand what is required of him, that is, the minor must know that the person whose signature he is witnessing is the person named in the document. However, in practice, bankers would not allow a minor to be a witness for any banking documents. If there was no independent adult witness, the bank would ask a staff member to be a witness for the banking documents.
- A minor as an agent:

  A minor may act as an agent and may bind his principal. Such agency relations may happen in banking transactions. A minor may be authorised by a customer to operate his banking account by letter of authorization or power of attorney, although such authorization may cause the account to become overdrawn or may increase the overdraft. However, it is very unusual for a customer to authorise a minor to operate his account. Bankers should make proper enquiries and ensure that the authorization is properly made.
- A minor as a partner:

  A minor may become a partner, and his act will bind the firm of which he is a partner. Accordingly, this minor may be authorised to operate the firm's bank account. A minor partner does not incur any personal liability for the debt of the firm during his minority. However, the other audit partners are entitled to insist that the partnership assets must be applied in payment of the liabilities of the partnership and that, until these are provided for, no part of them shall be received by the minor partner: *Lovell and Christmas v. Beauchamp.*

Bankers should give careful consideration as to whether it should accept a minor's personal assets as security to cover a partnership debt. The bankers should also note that if a minor does not repudiate his position as a partner of the firm, either before his majority or within a reasonable time of attaining it, he will be personally liable for the debts of the partnership incurred after his majority.

Executors and Administrators

An executor is a person appointed by a will or codicil to administer the property of the testator. He derives his title from the will of the deceased, but he is unable to deal with the estate and any balance in the deceased's bank account until such time as he has obtained probate. The probate will not be granted until the Estate Duty Office has issued some form of estate duty clearance.

An administrator is a person appointed by the court by a letter of administration to administer the property of a deceased. He derives his title entirely from the grant of administration. There are two main types of appointment, namely: (a) cases of intestacy where there is an entitlement to simple letter of administration; and (b) cases where there is a will but no proving executors, in which case the entitlement is to letters of administration with the will annexed.

The expression "personal representative" is used to describe either an executor or an administrator. A grant of probate to the executors, or a grant of letters of administration to administrators, is necessary in order that they may make title to the property of the deceased and thereafter administer, collect, and protect it for the benefit of the persons interested in the estate, whether as creditors, legatees, or next of kin.

Bankers may occasionally pay small balances of the deceased customer's accounts to the person who appears to be entitled to them under the customer's will or on his intestacy, without insisting that a grant of probate of letters of administration be produced. Such payments usually are paid out for the purpose of funeral expenses of the deceased customers. However, in such cases, the bankers would ask recipients to execute a letter of indemnity.

Opening an Executor's Account and an Administrator's Account

An account opened by executors or by administrators constitutes an account of the estate. The executors are the personal representatives of the estate and, unlike partners, have no personal interest in the account or in the estate's property. As each executor or administrator has the status of an agent, he is entitled to open an account with the bank in the name of the estate. He is also entitled to stop payment for any cheques drawn on it, either by himself or by another personal representative(s). In order to avoid any conflicts, the bankers should ask for clear instructions concerning the drawing of cheques on an account of an estate. The bank's mandate should be spelt out in indisputable terms. In order to minimize the possibility of misappropriation of funds, the arrangement should provide that each cheque be signed by at least two personal representatives.

An account can be opened for an executor or administrator in the usual way with references being taken up if the person is unknown. They may be introduced to the banks by their solicitors. The procedure for opening an administrator's account is similar to that for an executor's account. In practice, the account is styled as "Mr. X, executor/administrator of Mr. A, deceased."

Where two or more personal representatives are to act, a mandate similar to that of a joint account will be signed and the executors or administrators will undertake joint and several liability for any borrowing. They will instruct the bank whether the account is being operated on one or more signatures. The personal representatives are entitled to delegate.

Where a personal representative himself dies, the remaining personal representative may continue to act under the original will and, on production of his death certificate, the name of the deceased representative can simply be deleted from the bank records. Where the last surviving or sole executor dies, then his executors, on obtaining probate on his will, can take over the executorship, if they wish. Otherwise, parties interested in the estate of the original deceased will need to apply to the court for a letter of administration.

It is quite common that the account for the personal representatives is opened at the same bank as that where the account of the deceased was maintained. However, there is no right of set-off between the credit balance in the name of a personal representative and a debit balance in the name of the deceased or vice versa.

When probate or letters of administration are produced to the bank, the bank should obtain a suitable authority from the personal representative for any credit balance in the deceased's account to be transferred to the executor's or administrator's account. Items in safe custody may then be released against a valid receipt.

Advances to Personal Representatives

As stated previously, a personal representative needs to meet the estate duty payable on the deceased's estate before he can obtain probate or letter of administration. The personal representative may therefore approach the banks to bridge that period of time during which the personal representative is unable to deal with and realize the assets of the deceased, but needs the proceeds of these assets to pay the estate duty.

If it appears that there are sufficient, readily saleable assets of the estate to enable the advance to be repaid, the bank may usually be able to accede to the request on the advance. The bank should specially inform the personal representative that they are undertaking personal responsibility for the repayment of an advance. At this stage, they cannot mortgage or charge the assets of the estate until the probate or letter of administration has been granted. It is therefore important for the bankers to be fully satisfied with their integrity before the banks make any advance.

The advance should be granted on a loan account and the bank will charge an arrangement fee or upfront fee for handling such matters, as the income obtained merely by interest cannot be adequate.

Continuing the Business of the Deceased

A problem that often arises in cases involving personal representatives' accounts is whether or not the deceased's business can be carried on. The general rule is that, in the absence of a direction in the testator's will, executors have no power to carry on the business of the deceased, except for the purpose of winding-up or pending a sale in the very short term. The same situation applies to administrators. In other words, the personal representatives in general are not entitled to maintain the business as a going concern.

If the personal representatives wish to continue to run a business of the deceased, they have to establish their authority to do so in one of the following ways:

- Where there is express authority in the will;
- Where the business is continued in order to sell it as a going concern;
- Where the beneficiaries are all of full age and consent and agree to provide an indemnity;
- For intestacy, the power to postpone in the statutory trust for sale will enable the business to be carried on;
- The personal representatives may apply to the court and obtain an order authorizing them to carry on business.

The personal representatives are personally liable for any contractual obligations that they enter into whilst running the business of the deceased. They therefore must ensure that they are protected by the indemnity from such liability. That protection will arise from the authority in the will, or such carrying on the business of the deceased with a view to selling it soon as a going concern, or from the express consent of the pre-death creditors.

If the bank is asked to provide banking advances to enable the personal representatives to continue the deceased's business, there are three important matters for consideration.

- It is necessary to check whether the personal representatives have power to carry on the business of the deceased. A bank does not wish to get involved in details concerning the win-in of the estate of the deceased customer. It is necessary for the bank to obtain the personal representatives' personal assurance regarding the purposes of the banking advances. The bank is therefore in a position to recover from the personal representatives any losses incurred due to any invalidity of the transaction.
- Bankers must consider whether the deceased's creditors have been paid or, in the alternative, have consented to the carrying on of the business. It is essential for the bank to ensure that the deceased's creditors have been paid or that they have given their approval to the transaction. Otherwise, the creditors may take priority over the bank in regards to the assets of the estate.

- The bankers must consider whether the security for the proposed advance is valid or not. In general, the personal representatives have no power to charge the deceased's assets outside the business of the deceased as security for the repayment of the loan: *M'Neillie v. Acton*. However, they may give a valid charge upon the assets already engaged in the business: *Devitt v. Kearney*.

If the personal representatives have not given a personal undertaking to the bank or are financially unable to make reimbursement to the bank, the bank may still succeed against the creditors provided it has a possessory security. In *Berry v. Gibbons*, an executrix pledged with the bank a valuable picture belonging to the estate in order to secure an advance. The bank granted the overdraft because it was not aware that administration proceedings had been successfully instituted against the executrix shortly before granting the advance. As no receiver had been appointed at the time when the bank obtained the pledge, the court held that the bank was entitled to enforce its security because the security was a possessory security. It is questionable whether the bank can enforce a non-possessory security, for example, bills of sale or floating charge, in cases of determination of the personal representative's appointment.

Executors Becoming Trustees

A personal representative may concurrently be appointed as a trustee of beneficial trusts that are created by the will. Executors have the power to delegate while the trustees are in general unable to delegate and all of them must act. In handling an executor's account, a banker should beware of the administration becoming a trusteeship, in particular where the mandate is for any one executor to sign alone for operating the account. After about one year, if an estate has not been wound up, the executors should be interviewed to see if they are now really trustees; in that event a new mandate should be obtained, whereby all trustees will sign in the future. The account should then be restyled "Trustee of Mr. X, deceased" in the bank's record.

Trustees

A trust is defined as "an equitable obligation, binding a person (who is called a trustee) to deal with property over which he has control (which is called the trust property) for the benefit of the persons (who are called the beneficiaries or *cestuis que* trust), of whom he may himself be one, and any one of whom may enforce the obligation." Any act or neglect on the part of a trustee which is not authorised or excused by the terms of trust instrument, or by law, is called a breach of trust." (Underhill and Hayton, *Law Relating to Trusts and Trustees*, 15th edition, 1995).

Trusts may be divided into private trusts and public or charitable trusts. A private trust is for the benefit of an individual, or a number or class of specified persons, all of whom must be definitely ascertained. A public or charitable trust is one whose object is to promote the public welfare or benefit, even though it confers some benefit on an individual or class.

Trustee accounts are opened mainly by executors appointed as trustees under a will, and by persons such as solicitors or trust companies who administer family or charitable trusts.

A trust does not constitute a legal entity separate from that of the trustees. The trustees' function is to administer the trust in accordance with the trust deed under which they hold their appointment. In addition, certain powers and duties are conferred on them by the Trustee Ordinance, Cap. 29.

In most cases, a trust deed requires the appointment of two or more trustees. This ensures that the trust property is under the control of more than one designated person. For this reason trustees are usually not authorised to delegate their authority. Unless expressly stated otherwise in the trust deed, a cheque drawn on the trust account requires the signatures of all trustees. If the trust instrument contains a provision for delegation of power by the trustees, the bankers should examine the same carefully. There are certain exceptions under sections 25 and 27 of the Trustee Ordinance. Section 25 empowers trustees to appoint agents to do particular acts. Section 27 provides, *inter alia*, that notwithstanding any rule of law or equity to the contrary, a trustee may, by power of attorney, delegate for a period not exceeding 12 months the execution or exercise of all or any of the trusts, powers, and discretion vested in him as trustee, either alone or jointly with any other person or persons.

As the trustees have only the legal title to the property, the principle of survivorship does not apply. When a trustee dies, another person is appointed either under the provisions of the will or by the court. Until such appointment is made, section 20 of the Trustee Ordinance authorises the surviving trustee(s) to carry on the business of trust for the time being. Under section 20, the personal representatives of the sole surviving trustee can perform or exercise the power of the trust. It appears that in the case of the death of a trustee, the surviving trustee(s) (or the personal representatives of the last surviving trustee) are entitled to draw cheques on the trustees' account.

Opening an Account for Trustees

If trustees approach the bank to open a bank account, references should be obtained and followed up in the usual way, except if they are well-known by the bank. In practice, this type of account will be opened at the head office or in the private banking department of the bank. The title of the account should clearly indicate that it is a trust account, for example, "Trustees of Mr. Chan Tai Man," "Chan Siu Man's Family Trust Account," or "Trustees of Mr. X, deceased." If the trust instrument is produced, a copy should be obtained and the bankers will be bound to follow the provisions therein, in particular those related to banking transactions even if the bankers do not peruse it. However, it is not a must to require its production at the time when the account is opened.

The trustees should sign a mandate governing transactions on the account. In the case of public or charitable trusts, normally not less than two trustees will usually be authorised to sign the cheques drawn on the trust account.

Subject to the exceptions stated previously, a trustee of a private trust cannot delegate his authority. He is personally responsible for the exercise of his judgement and for the performance of his duty and cannot escape responsibility by leaving to another person the exercise of that judgement or the performance of that duty, even if he is one of several trustees and the person to whom he leaves it is his co-trustee. Consequently, in practice, the mandate for the trust account of a private trust should provide that the cheques drawn on the account must be signed by all trustees together. In the event that the trustees insist that they wish to delegate their authority to sign the cheques, the bankers should check with their legal advisers whether their request could be accepted. Even if legally acceptable, bankers should examine the integrity of the trustees before opening the trust account, in particular when not all trustees are required to sign for operating the trust account.

Advances to Trustees

Although the trustees are entitled to deposit trust money in a bank account, their right to borrow for the trust's purposes is restricted. When trustees apply to a bank for an advance, the bankers should examine whether the trustees have the power to borrow money from the bank for the purposes that they have in mind and whether they have power to give security for the proposed advance. Those powers may be conferred upon trustees by trust instrument, by statut, by the beneficiaries, and by the court.

- By trust instrument:

  The bankers should examine the trust instrument carefully in order to ascertain whether it confers the relevant powers upon the trustees to borrow money from a bank. To avoid any doubt, the bankers should refer the case to legal advisers for comment on the validity of the advance. This is particularly because the trust instrument rarely confers such powers upon the trustees.
- By statute:

  Under section 18 of the Trustee Ordinance, where trustees are authorised by law or under the trust deed to 'pay or apply capital money subject to the trust for any purpose or in any manner,' they are deemed always to have had the power to raise the money required by 'sale, conversion, calling in, or mortgage of all or any part of the trust property for the time being in possession.' Where the trustees have the power to mortgage, they also have the complementary power of borrowing.

  Section 19 of the Trustee Ordinance provides that no purchaser or mortgagee, paying or advancing money on a sale or mortgage purporting to be made under any trust or power vested in trustees, shall be concerned to see that such money is wanted, or that more than is wanted is raised, or otherwise as to the application thereof. In other words, the bankers are protected to advance the money to the trustees for the purpose of running the business of the trust provided that they have power to do so.

- By beneficiaries:

  If all the beneficiaries are of full age and if they are all prepared to authorise and indemnify the trustees to borrow money against a specified security, there is nearly no risk in acting with their wishes. However, bankers should directly verify their wishes.
- By the court:

  The trustees may make any application to the court to sanction a mortgage of trust property as a last resort. Under section 59 of the Trustee Ordinance, the court has statutory power to make the necessary order in such terms and manner as the court thinks just. After all, the bankers should ensure that all the trustees undertake joint and several liabilities for the repayment of the advance. Accordingly, the trustees will execute a joint and several guarantee (preferably under seal). If the advance is finally repaid, upon the release of security, all of the trustees should acknowledge receipt.

Duty of the Bank

Recall that the relationship of bankers and customers may, in certain cases, be the subject of fiduciary duties owed by the bankers. The bank's liability to the beneficiaries of the trust rests on a different basis. The beneficiaries of a trust are protected by equity. Equity frequently does so at the expense of innocent third parties who deal in good faith with a fraudulent trustee or with one who acts beyond his powers. A bank may be held liable as a constructive trustee in cases involving "knowing receipt" and "knowing assistance."

The bank of the beneficiaries will incur no liability unless the bank knows that the account involved is a trust account. However, even if the account has not been styled as a trust account, the actual knowledge of the nature of the account may not be excluded. In *Re Gross, ex parte Kingston*, an official maintained two accounts in his bank, his personal account and an other one which was marked "Police Account." The official absconded later on. At that time, his personal account was in debit and the Police Account in credit. The court held that the bank could not combine the two accounts to set off the credit balance in the Police Account against the official's debit balance on his personal account. When there is some specific circumstance known by the bankers, for example, the banker is familiar with the will under which the trustees have opened the account, it may be treated as a trust account. The bank should be aware of the fact that any knowledge of an officer or responsible staff member of the bank, who has acquired the knowledge within the scope of his employment, is to be imputed to the bank.

However, a banker should not presume that whenever a customer maintains more than one account with the bank, one or some of them is a trust account(s). There is no restriction for a customer to open and maintain more than one account with any one bank both in law and in practice.

In cases of breach of trust by the trustee, the bank's concern is to ensure that the trustees act within the scope of their apparent powers, in particular in relation to banking transactions. Accordingly, the bank must ensure that a cheque drawn on a trust account carries all required signatures (in most cases the signatures of all trustees of a private trust). In the absence of actual or express knowledge by the bankers of any improper or fraudulent acts done or intended by the trustees, in general bankers are not liable for the trustees' misconduct. After all, bankers are not required to assume the role of a detective in whatever sense.

However, a prudent banker should be alert to the scenario that a trustee draws a cheque on a trust account to pay into his personal account with the same bank. In *Foxton v. Manchester and Liverpool District Banking Co.*, a trustee drew a cheque from the trust account in order to reduce his personal overdraft. It was held that the bank had to establish that the payment was legitimate and proper. If the bank failed to discharge this burden of proof, it had to compensate the beneficiaries of the trust. The banker should pay more attention to the situation if the proceeds of a cheque drawn on a trust account are used to reduce the trustees' personal indebtedness to the bank. In *Gray v. Johnston*, it was observed that where a bank stands to benefit from the trustees' breach of trust, "that circumstance, above all others, will most readily establish the fact that the bankers are in privity with the breach of trust."

Sole Proprietors

A sole proprietor is one who owns and carries on a business and is the only person who bears the business risk and gains from the profit generated by the business. There is no separate legal entity and the proprietor bears unlimited personal liability on his business.

Any proprietor who is carrying on any business in Hong Kong is required to register under the Business Registration Ordinance, Cap. 310. If the proprietor is not carrying on a special licensed business, for example, stockbroker, leveraged foreign exchange trader, or employment agent, the business registration certificate is the only official document held by a proprietor.

As there is no separate legal entity, a sole proprietor is free to choose any name for his business save for those that are restricted such as banking or government names. The name of this type of business may include the word 'Company'; bankers should bear in mind that they should not confuse this with the companies which are body corporate, for example, limited companies under the Companies Ordinance and statutory companies.

Lending to sole proprietors should be similar to that for individuals except that the banking facilities and services offered will cater for business purposes, for example, trade finances.

Account Opening

The consideration for opening an account to a sole proprietor should be the same as an individual, except that he is a businessman.

In addition to checking the personal identity of the proprietor, the bankers should examine the business registration certificate and obtain a copy. The proprietor will be asked to sign the mandate for sole proprietorship.

Bankers should not just rely only on the business registration certificate provided by the customers. They should verify the information of the business directly from the

Inland Revenue Department by obtaining a certified true copy. The relevant charges are usually reimbursed from the proprietor's account. Until the certified true copy of the business registration certificate from the Inland Revenue Department is obtained, no cheque book should be delivered to the proprietor except if recognised professions certify the copy.

Partnership

Partnership is defined in the Partnership Ordinance as "the relation which subsists between persons carrying on a business in common with a view of profit."

Opening and Operating a Partnership Account

A partnership account resembles a joint account in that it is opened in the name of more than one person but it will be opened in the name of a firm. As a partnership does not have a legal entity as a body corporate, its account constitutes in effect a joint account of the partners.

Under section 7 of the Partnership Ordinance, each partner is his firm's agent and is therefore entitled to open an account on its behalf. However, in practice, the bankers require all the partners to open a partnership account together. Under section 8 of the Partnership Ordinance, a partner can operate the partnership account in his own right and is entitled to close it. In practice, whether one of the partners can operate the partnership account (including closing it) is determined by the instructions stated in the mandate. The bankers should invite all partners to sign the mandate that embodies precise instructions to the banks concerning the conduct of the partnership account.

When partners approach the bank in order to open a partnership account, the bankers should check the customers' authority, identity, integrity, and nature of business.

The bankers should check the full names and particulars of all the partners. The bankers should directly check with the records kept by the Office of the Commissioner of Inland Revenue. Relevant charges will be reimbursed from the partnership account.

A partnership account must be opened in the name of the partnership, that is, in the name of the firm, otherwise the partnership will not be bound. In *Alliance Bank v. Kearsley*, the court held that a partner did not have the authority to maintain an account of the firm in his personal name. The other partners were not liable to reimburse the bank in respect of losses incurred by the partner on the account concerned, although it was used solely for the purposes of the partnership.

Although the partnership agreement or articles is a written document for stipulating all the terms and conditions for the relations between the partners, if not only by word of mouth, a bank is not legally required to see this document. However, if partners do provide such document to the bank, the bank is obliged to examine the contents carefully and be bound by any terms relating to bank transactions; in particular those limitations imposed on by the authority of the partners. In practice, even if the partnership tenders the partnership agreement or articles, a prudent banker will ask the partners to provide a written confirmation that the banking transactions relating to the partnership are governed only by the terms of the mandate provided by the bank. Further, the said written confirmation also provides that if there is any conflict between the mandate and the partnership agreement/articles, the terms of the mandate will prevail.

The mandate for the account will incorporate a clause whereby each partner accepts joint and several liability for any overdraft or borrowing created or increased by any partner in respect of the partnership account. This is the most important clause as otherwise partners are only jointly liable and, in the event of the bankruptcy of the partnership, only one right of proof would be possible. As the several liability establishes, there are several rights against each partner's estate and through the joint liability clause there is also a right of proof against the firm and any assets held jointly. Further, it may be possible to set off a credit balance in a partner's personal account against the debt in the partnership account under the rights in the several liability clauses.

In the event that a partner has a personal account, it is not incumbent upon the bank to question the validity of transfers from the partnership account to the personal account, save and unless the amount and circumstances are such as to make the bank suspicious of fraud. A bank must not allow any partner to pay into his personal account cheques drawn in favour of the firm even if some other partners endorsed them. The bank allows a partner to do so only if all of the partners of the firm expressly authorise it in writing.

When a dispute arises between or among the partners, the bank must obtain clear instructions from all the partners of the firm to prevent the bank from being drawn into claim and litigation. However, bankers should also note that the knowledge of a third party that partners are in dispute does not amount to knowledge that authority has been withdrawn. The bankers should note that they must comply with a notice from one partner stopping payment of a cheque drawn on the partnership account.

In *Watts v. Christie*, the account of a partnership of X and Y was overdrawn whilst X's personal account with the same bank was in credit. When the bank failed, X assigned his credit balance in his personal account to the partnership account so as to facilitate a set-off of this credit balance against the partnership's debt balance. If such a set-off were exercised, the firm would have proved for the net credit balance rather than for the full amount of the credit balance, and would not have been obliged to pay the amount due under the overdraft to the trustee in bankruptcy. It was held that the purported assignment was ineffective. The bank did not have a valid lien on the personal account of the partner in respect of debts incurred by the firm. Therefore, the two accounts had to be kept apart; the bank could not have combined the two. It followed that, when the bank became insolvent, it was too late for the individual partner in question to effect a set-off by means of an assignment. It is because two balances had crystallised at the same time of the commencement of the bankruptcy.

Unincorporated Associations, Clubs, and Societies

Associations, clubs, and societies may be divided into two main categories:

- Incorporated clubs, associations, and societies, which are owned or controlled by a corporate body;
- Unincorporated associations, clubs, and societies, which have not been incorporated.

When a banker is requested to open an account for a club, association, or society, he has to determine first which category the customer falls into.

The objects of the unincorporated associations, clubs, and societies are primarily non-commercial and are usually formed for the mutual benefits of the members. They decide not to incorporate in order to avoid the expenses involved. They may also be motivated by a wish not to be mistaken for a trading enterprise. The funds of unincorporated bodies are usually obtained from subscriptions and donations.

Banking Accounts

As the unincorporated bodies are not incorporated, they are not legal entities and therefore cannot enter into any contract including banking transactions.

However, it is clear than an unincorporated body needs a bank account to deal with the payment and collection of cheques. Further, in some cases it may need to borrow money from the bank to carry out its objectives. For example, a club may wish to arrange a bank advance in order to purchase premises for the club. If a banker accepts such a body as a customer and opens an account, he has to be aware of the relevant fundamental principles.

Since an unincorporated body does not have an independent legal personality, it cannot sue nor be sued in its own name. Actions have to be brought against the committee of the body that acts for and on behalf of the body. For this reason, some banks prefer to open the account in the name or names of private individuals coupled with the indication that the funds belong to the body beneficially, instead of opening a bank account in the name of the body, for example, "Pang Tai Yan and Lee Siu Sheung, Old Boy's Association Account." In this way, the bank can ask the individuals to sign the mandate for a joint account; then these individual customers will be jointly and severally liable for the banking transactions and any overdraft.

However, in practice, most banks are willing to open an account in the name of the unincorporated body. There should be no risk provided that the account is kept in credit. In such cases, if the body has rules or articles, the account should be opened and conducted in accordance with these. Bankers should make sure that the relevant rules and articles are certified to be true and updated by the committee.

Most banks have a standard printed form of mandate for use by unincorporated bodies. The mandate usually embodies a resolution to be passed by the committee of the body authorising the bank to pay cheques, provided that they are drawn, for example, 'by any two nominated members of the committee for the time being and countersigned by the Chairman,' or otherwise may be required. Bankers should note that the committee of the body is not entitled to go beyond the powers conferred on it in the constitution of the body. As long as it remains within the scope of its authority, the committee has the power to delegate. Committee members are bound by the acts of a duly appointed agent.

Banking Advances

As the unincorporated body is not a separate legal entity, the lending of money on the account of such a body demands special safeguards, partly because it is difficult to obtain redress against the body's funds and partly because it is not easy to establish the personal liability of particular members of the body.

In most cases, the liability of members of an unincorporated body is expressly restricted to the amount of the subscription or membership fee due from them. An action, which has to be brought against the committee of the body, is generally instituted in order to recover the amount claimed from the funds of the body. However, the members of committee may be personally liable as well. In *Coutts & Co. v. Irish Exhibition in London*, a bank did succeed in establishing the personal liability of six individuals who had formed themselves into the executive council of an unincorporated body. The bank granted an overdraft of the body's current account on the personal assurance of the committee members. It was established that the account had not been officially transferred into the corporation's name and that the bank had not released the committee from their liability. It was held that the committee members were the bank's customers and, accordingly, they were obliged to reimburse the amount involved. The six individuals who were held personally liable were the signatories upon the account of the body. However, bankers should note that it does not follow that any signatory upon the account of an unincorporated body is necessarily personally liable for any lending on the account.

On the whole, a bank has to be more cautious when an unincorporated body requires any banking advances, as ordinary members of the body are not liable for its debts unless they have expressed their individual consent to the transaction. And since committee members may be personally liable, whether the bank can recover the money from them depends on their financial standing. The prudent banker will only extend credit to an unincorporated body against adequate security.

Other Unincorporated Clubs and Societies

- Societies are governed by the Societies Ordinance. Any society, club, or association of persons of whatever nature or objects must be registered under this ordinance unless it has obtained a certificate of exemption from registration.
- A search on the society can be conducted with the Registrar of Societies at police headquarters.

- Owner's incorporation is governed by the Building Management Ordinance. When opening an account, the bank should obtain certified true copies of the certificate of incorporation/registration or deed of mutual covenant or other similar document, which set out powers of the management committee.
- Schools may be registered with the Director of Education pursuant to the Education Ordinance or registered pursuant to certain ordinances in HK, for example, St. Joseph College Incorporation Ordinance. Accordingly, a certified true copy of the relevant ordinance and regulations of the school should be obtained when opening an account.

When Opening the Account

- Use the full title of the club as the account name.
- Ask for a copy of the club's rules and regulations (must be certified as being up to date) or the relevant ordinance governing its registration.
- Where appropriate, obtain a copy of the certificate of registration or certificate of exemption from registration.
- Get the committee members to sign a bank mandate.
- Check the rules and regulations to avoid the mandate contravening them.
- Ask for a copy of the resolution authorizing the appointment of various officers and, where appropriate, check it to ensure that authorization to open a bank account and appointment of authorised signers have been passed in accordance with the requirements of the relevant ordinance or regulations.
- Obtain ID copies of all committee members and authorised signers.

Borrowing Power

- General assumption: members do not intend to incur any liability beyond those stipulated by the rules, such as paying subscriptions.
- The rules and regulations must be read and ensure that:
    i. The club is expressly authorised to borrow;
    ii. All formalities for the borrowing must be strictly complied with;
    iii. The person's purporting to execute a document on behalf of the members are persons authorised by the rules and regulations.
- If the borrowing is not authorised by the rules and regulations, only those who contracted the loan or consented to the loan are liable.
- Security: 3rd party security, for example, a personal guarantee is thought necessary.
- If the club's own property, which is vested in the trustee, is taken as security, it must be permitted by both the club's rules and the trust deed; both documents should be checked.

Solicitors

The term 'clients' account' or 'solicitors' account' is an account opened by a solicitor or solicitors' firm in order to deposit clients' money. Such accounts have been the subject of legislation, which lays down an accounting procedure that precludes the co-mingling of clients' money with the funds of the solicitors or solicitors' firm. It is therefore necessary to treat a client's account as a separate fund. This procedure seeks to combat both carelessness and fraud in handling such trust funds. The provision conferring power to make rules on this subject is section 73 of the Legal Practitioner Ordinance, Cap. 159. These rules are the Solicitors' Accounts Rules.

Under Rule 4 of the Solicitors' Accounts Rules, the following may be paid into a client account:

- Trust money;
- Such money belonging to the solicitor as may be necessary for the purpose of opening or maintaining the account;
- Money to replace any sum which may by mistake or accident have been drawn from the account in contravention of rule 8(2) [further restrictions on drawing from client account]; and
- A cheque or draft received by the solicitor, which under rule 5 he is entitled to split but which he does not split.

Of course, solicitors and solicitors' firms may also open a banking account for their offices' purposes. This account will be used to maintain the records of all income and expenditures. This is a partnership account and is treated as such. The following considerations are only concerned with the clients' accounts.

Opening Accounts

Every practising solicitor or solicitor's firm must have not less than one client account. Bankers should ask a new solicitor customer whether he or his firm wishes to open a clients' account. Solicitors may open and maintain an office account with one bank and maintain the clients' account with other bank(s).

Most banks do not have separate mandates for solicitors' accounts. They will use the mandate for partnership or sole proprietorship as the case may be.

Conduct of Solicitors' Account

- No overdraft—it is a general rule that a "clients' account" should not become overdrawn. This is because the account is solely for the receipt of money belonging to clients.
- No right of set-off—there is no right of set-off for a credit balance on a client's account with a debit balance on the personal account of the solicitors or their office account.

- Possible breach of trust by solicitors—Unless the cheque is drawn on the clients' account in circumstances which are clearly suspicious or extraordinary, the bank is not liable to the solicitors' client for a misappropriation of the funds.

However, bankers should exercise common sense and not close their eyes to what appears to be a breach of trust. Transfers from the clients' accounts to the solicitor's office account or their personal accounts require special attention and necessary enquiries should be made. Transfers from the clients' accounts to the office account are frequently made for the purpose of enabling the firm to receive legal costs to which the firm is entitled.

Death of Solicitor

- Partnership—where a solicitor's firm has a bank account and one of the partners dies, the usual rules appertaining to the death of a partner apply.
- Sole practitioner—on the solicitor's death, the bank should be notified of the arrangement about his estate and another practising solicitor should be nominated (by will or Law Society) to manage the practice and to operate new bank accounts, pending the grant of probate or administration, to enable clients' matters to proceed and staff salaries to be paid.

The bank should note that the balance on the clients' accounts can be discharged by the authority of the Hong Kong Law Society but not by the deceased solicitor's personal representatives. The society must pay the money of the clients' accounts into a special account in the name of the society or of a person nominated on behalf of the society. The money will then be held in trust for the persons beneficially entitled to it.

Bankruptcy of Solicitor

- Partnership—except when the solicitors' firm is adjudicated bankrupt as a whole, the solvent solicitors can continue to operate the account.
- Sole practitioner—if a sole practitioner is adjudicated bankrupt, the balance standing to the credit of his clients' accounts do not vest in this trustee in bankruptcy. This is because the money is held by the bankrupt solicitor on trust for other persons. Two trustees shall be appointed to replace the bankrupt solicitor to operate the account until the balance of the clients' accounts has been distributed to the appropriate beneficiaries. The two trustees are usually nominated by the Hong Kong Law Society and trustee in bankruptcy.

Garnishee Orders

On some occasions, a creditor of a solicitor seeks to have a garnishee order applied to both the balance standing credit of a solicitor's personal account and to that of the of the client's account (i.e., attaching all sums owing by the bank to a solicitor).

In *Plunkett v. Barclays Bank Ltd.*, when a garnishee order was served on the bank, a clients' account was frozen. A cheque drawn by the solicitor on the clients' account was then dishonoured by the bank and returned to the holder with the answer 'refer to drawer.' The court dismissed the solicitor's action, brought against the bank in defamation and in breach of contract, and the account in question could be garnished by the solicitor's creditor. However, according to Order 45 rule 5 of the Rules of the Supreme Court, the solicitor was entitled to notify the court that certain moneys attached by the garnishee order nisi were the property of a third party. The court would then make the order required to protect the client's interest.

The bank should note that the order would not be made absolute except to the extent that the solicitor has a lien over the funds. Further, once the order nisi has been served, the solicitor is bound to notify the court that the balance in the client's account does not comprise his own funds. Accordingly, the bank should inform the concerned solicitors of the position and terms of the order once the order is served on it. The concerned solicitor should express his willingness to the court that the order will be drafted in terms that will exclude the clients' account. The court will usually give effect to this.

Incorporated Companies

The most important and large bank accounts, whether in credit or overdrawn, are those of companies registered under the Companies Ordinance, Cap. 32 (CO). It is essential for bankers to possess a general knowledge of company law, in particular those aspects that are relevant to the banking transactions. Company law as a whole must be considered here. For Hong Kong company law, bankers may refer to *V. Scott, Hong Kong Company Law.*

General Principles of Legal Personality

Strictly speaking, the word 'company' has no legal meaning. The word 'company' is normally used for organisations associated with economic purposes, that is, to carry on a business with a view to profit. Hong Kong law provides two main types of business organisation for such associations: partnerships (discussed earlier in this chapter) and companies registered under CO. Although the word 'company' is colloquially applied to both business organisations, lawyers and bankers regard registered companies and company law as distinct from partnerships and partnership law. The companies registered under CO will be referred to as 'company' hereinafter.

A company is a separate legal entity distinct from its members and directors: *Salomon v. Salomon & Co. Ltd.* It has a legal personality and is commonly described as an 'artificial person' or a 'body corporate.' A company can sue or be sued in its company name. However, until the Certificate of Incorporation is issued, the company has no contractual powers.

Bankers should note that courts will not allow the separate legal entity principle to be used where it might be unjust, and they will in exceptional circumstances lift the 'corporate veil' and look at the membership of the company. These circumstances include the following:

- National Emergency or paramount public interest;
- Where the company is formed principally as a sham to evade existing liability or to defeat the law;
- When a director has acted dishonestly with the company's property;
- Where a holding and subsidiary relationship exists;
- Where an existing partnership is converted into a limited company under CO and an application is made to wind up the company on the grounds that it is 'just and equitable' under section 177(1)(f) of the CO;
- Liability of a sole member for a company's debts: section 31 of CO;
- Liability of a disqualified person for a company's debts: section 156 of CO;
- Fraudulent trading under section 275 of CO.

Types of Companies

Any one or more persons, associated for any lawful purpose may, by subscribing their names to a memorandum of association (which may be printed in Chinese or English) and otherwise complying with the requirements of CO in respect of registration, form an incorporated company, with or without limited liability.

There are three types of companies:

- **A company limited by shares** – a company having the liability of its members limited by the memorandum to the amount, if any, unpaid on the shares respectively held by them;
- **A company limited by guarantee** – a company having the liability of its members limited by the memorandum to such amount as the members may respectively undertake to contribute to the assets of the company in the event of its being wound up; and
- **An unlimited company** – a company not having any limit on the liability of its members.

The most common type of company in Hong Kong is the 'company limited by shares.' This type of company is the most valuable bank customer.

Apart from the different types of companies set out above, the CO also distinguishes between private companies and public companies.

Private companies are usually comparatively small companies (members are limited to 50) and the right of transferring shares are restricted and invitations to public to subscribe shares or debentures are prohibited.

Public companies are generally much larger because they have the capacity to raise capital or funds from the public. However, public companies limited by guarantee may be large. Some public companies that list on the stock exchange are also called "listed companies."

Other important aspects of a limited company:

- A limited company has to make a Memorandum of Association that includes an object clause outlining the goals of a company. The Memorandum outlines specific powers of the company and its members to, for example, provide guarantees. In trading companies, the right to borrow and provide security is implied.
- Hong Kong has long abolished the *ultra vires* doctrine. From 10 Feb 1997, a company has the rights, powers, and privileges of a natural person according to S.5A of the Companies Ordinance.
- The Memorandum of Association and the Articles of Association are always deposited with banks, so bankers may be taken to have constructive and/or actual notice of the documents deposited. Then it may be not held in good faith when they deal with a company knowing that the deal is outside the company's scope of business. A prudent banker should adopt the same policy as before in checking a company's object clauses.
- A limited company should also have Articles of Association that govern its internal management. Bankers are particularly concerned with borrowing powers directors might have and with any requirements in respect to security given by the directors on behalf of the company.
- When opening a company account, the bank should do the following:

    i. Examine and make a copy of the Certificate of Incorporation;
    ii. Obtain two certified true copies of the Memorandum of Association and the Articles of Association;
    iii. Ensure the company has passed a board resolution to open the account with a quorum of the required number of directors;
    iv. Make a copy of the Business Registration Certificate;
    v. Generate a mandate;
    vi. Get signature specimen cards for authorised signers;
    vii. Conduct a company search to identify the individuals who own the company;
    viii. Obtain a list of directors and secretaries for future reference;
    ix. Obtain a copy of the ID of the directors and authorised signers;
    x. Accept an initial deposit and arrange for a checkbook;
    xi. Typically, do not allow withdrawals until all searches have been satisfactorily completed.

Overseas Company (or Non-Hong Kong Company)

As in opening any company account, there are requirements for opening an overseas company account:

- Obtain documentation comparable to that of a local company;
- Obtain a Certificate of Incumbency from the agent who has registered the company in the overseas country certifying that the company is in good legal standing, its registered

address and the names of shareholders/directors are correct, and no formal notice in the overseas country exist about default in laws, statues, regulations, etc.;

- Obtain a letter of undertaking: the company undertakes to notify the bank regarding any change of shareholders, director, name, registration office, commencement of liquidation, change of the laws of the country of incorporation, etc. It also undertakes to indemnify the bank any loss, costs, etc. incurred by reason or in respect of the bank's allowing the company to open and operate the account and/or in respect of the company's failing to furnish the bank with the change of information aforesaid;
- Conduct a company search: usually through an agent overseas;
- A local company search is also required to ensure "NIL" registration in HK.

Nominee Holding Company

The requirements for opening a nominee holding company account are the same as that of overseas company.

Definition of Different Types of Authorities

Authority of Directors

Shareholders appoint directors at a general meeting. The directors manage the business and must act collectively as a board. The board of directors may elect a managing director among themselves.

There are different types of authority that directors may hold. These include:

- **Actual authority.** Actual authority includes both express and implied authority. Express authority includes the express authority conferred on a director by the terms of the Articles of Association or by the Board of Directors. Implied authority arises from the position that the director holds. The managing director, for example, has the implied authority to do all acts and enter into transactions necessary for the company's business such as signing cheques, borrowing money, giving security, etc. Non-managing directors or the secretary do not have such implied powers. The Doctrine of Constructive Notice holds that a third party should be aware of any limitations or restrictions on this implied authority; as a result, it may be necessary to make inquiries. One example of when such enquiries would be necessary would be if a director mortgages company property to secure a personal loan.
- **Apparent authority.** Also known as ostensible authority, this arises when a director does not have express or implied authority but shareholders or the Board of Directors make representations that he or she does have such authority. The careful banker would establish that a representation, either in writing, verbally, or by conduct, has

been done and done by a person(s) with "actual" authority; that the representation provides the inducement to enter into a contract; and that that company's Articles of Association are not deprived of the capacity to enter into that particular kind of contract. The banker should be satisfied that the director of the company does not have power that is unlikely to have been delegated by the members of the board and that the Articles of Association give power to the directors (Article 82, Table A).

Directors' Power to Borrow

Article 81, Table A states that the directors may exercise all the powers of the company to borrow money and to mortgage provided that the amount (apart from temporary loan) does not exceed the nominal amount of the share capital issued.

According to the case of *Rolled Steel Ltd. v Bristish Steel Corp* a company can offer security for a debt to a third party but the deal has to provide a benefit for the company, otherwise the directors may have acted *ultra vires* or beyond their powers.

The Companies (Amendment) Ordinance of 1997 states that a deal, even if it does not benefit a company, is binding on the company, because the company has the right and powers of a natural person. However, the *Rolled Steel* decision prevails and any *ultra vires* acts by the directors are invalid unless they are adopted by general meeting.

There are ways to remedy *ultra vires* acts including altering the articles though a special resolution, ratifying the irregular borrowing though an ordinary resolution, or producing a doctrine of ostensible authority. The case of *Royal British Bank v. Turquand* suggests that anyone dealing with a company can presume that all internal requirements have been complied with and is not bound to inquire further. Nevertheless, as a safeguard, a bank should insist to have a properly executed board minutes, certifying all requirements under the company's article have been followed, or that the transaction be sanctioned by all members in its general meeting.

Loans to a Company Director

It is not lawful for a company to directly or indirectly enter into any guarantee or provide security in connection with a loan made to its directors. Such a guarantee is unenforceable against the company. This prohibition is relaxed if it is a private company and the transaction is approved in general meeting.

There are multiple circumstances in which these circumstances might occur:

- **Fixed charge.** A fixed charge is a charge on fixed assets such as land or plants or specific assets of the company. It takes the form of the first legal or equitable charge.
- **Floating charge.** A floating charge goes against assets that are not fixed charged such as a work-in-progress. The company is free to use its floating assets for its day-to-day business until the floating charge is crystallized. There are several disadvantages to a floating charge, including that the unpaid seller would acquire a lien on the assets of the company in priority to the floating charge and that a fixed charge would have priority. Under the "Ramalpa Clause," the ownership of the goods remains with the seller until

the seller receives payment in full. A floating charge is crystallized when the company ceases its business or is wound up, if a receiver is appointed, or in the event of specified debentures such as a written notice of a debenture holder tender or if there is further charging of charged assets. When a floating charge crystallizes, it becomes a fixed charge and has priority over all unsecured creditors. A floating charge on the undertaking of a company shall only be valid if the charge is created more than 12 months before the commencement of the winding up; if new money has been lent or paid to the company at the time of or subsequent to the creation of the charge but is relying on it (and then is valid only for the amount of new money); or if the company is solvent immediately after the creation of the charge. Applying Clayton's rule, a bank offering a running current account to a "floating charge" customer has an added advantage over other creditors. The last money received will reduce the oldest debt, which might not be "secured" by the floating charge.

Registration of Charges

Charges created by a company must be registered with the Registrar of Companies within 5 weeks of creation, otherwise the change becomes void against the liquidator and any creditor of the company (S.80).

It is the duty of the company to register it. Alternatively, any person interested therein may register, and banks always do so.

Partnership Converted to a Limited Company

There are a number of requirements to open an account for a partnership that is converted to a limited company. These include:

- The usual documentation.
- If a partnership account is in credit, an appropriately written authority for the transfer of the balance to the new limited company account signed in accordance with the partnership mandate is necessary.
- If the partnership account is in debit and is to be repaid by the company—a debit entry to the company's account should be authorised in accordance with the company's mandate.
- Adequate written instructions should be obtained to deal with any cheques which might thereafter be presented and drawn on the partnership account.
- If the newly formed limited company wishes to borrow and offer security formerly in name of the partnership or sole trader, the bank has to satisfy itself of the validity of this security. It can do this by confirming and making careful enquiries to ensure all creditors are paid off and that all creditors accept the new company as their debtor.

Handling of Cheques of Limited Companies

Collecting cheques of a limited company requires the bank to ensure a number of conditions are met. To pay cheques from a limited company, the cheque must be draw up by a sufficient number of authorised signers and the cheque book has to be in the company's name.

In *A.L. Underwood v. Bank of Liverpool & Martin,* a cheque payable to the company was collected to a director's private account even though the cheque was payable to the company. The bank was then sued for conversion as it failed to make inquiries as to the validity of the transaction and because it is rare for limited companies to negotiate cheques.

In *British Airways Board v. Parish,* a director was made personally liable for a dishonoured cheque or if an incorrect company name is on a cheque.

Virtually anyone in the company can stop a cheque but removal of the stop must be authorised in accordance with the account mandate.

Cheques can be paid outside the mandate but for legitimate purposes of the company.

Another important precedent on this issue is *B Liggett (Liverpool) Ltd v. Barclays Bank.* A bank may be open to a claim of wrongful debiting of the account but damages may be avoided if a company does not suffer a loss or the money is also used for the legitimate purposes of the company.

Companies (Amendment) Ordinance of 2003

Some sections of the Companies (amendment) Ordinance 2003 are worth noting.

S4(1) removes the statutory minimum of two members in a limited company. A company can be formed with just one member.

S153A notes that a private company can have only one director and S154 notes that the sole director of a private company cannot also be the secretary of the company.

Anti-Money Laundering and Counter-Terrorist Financing

Anti-Money Laundering

The term "money laundering" is defined in the Anti-Money Laundering and Counter-Terrorist Financing (Financial Institutions) Ordinance (Cap. 615). It generally covers all procedures to change the identity of illegally obtained money so that it appears to have originated from a legitimate source.

Cash lends anonymity to many forms of criminal activity and is the normal medium of exchange in the world of drug trafficking. This gives rise to three common factors:

- Criminals need to conceal the true ownership and origin of the money;
- They need to control the money; and
- They need to change the form of the money.

One of the most common means of money laundering that financial institutions encounter on a day-to-day basis takes the form of accumulated cash transactions, which are deposited in the banking system or exchanged for value items. These simple transactions may be just one part of a sophisticated web of complex transactions. Nevertheless, the basic fact remains that the key stage for the detection of money laundering operations is where the cash first enters the financial system.

It is an offence to enter into or be concerned in an arrangement which allows for the retention of the proceeds of drug trafficking on behalf of a drug trafficker, or whereby they are secured and placed at that person's disposal, or used for the person's benefit to acquire property by way of investment, knowing or having reasonable grounds to believe that that person is a drug trafficker and has benefited from drug trafficking: section 25(1) of DTRPO. It is also a similar offence under section 25(1) of OSCO in cases regarding the proceeds of indictable offences.

The Money Laundering Process

The need to launder the illicit proceeds of criminal activity through the financial system, particularly banks, is a vital component to the success of criminal operations. All bankers should understand the money laundering process in order to combat such activities.

The key to understanding any money laundering scheme is to recognize that money laundering is not a single act but a highly complex process, utilizing an infinite range of techniques. From this perspective, every attempt and device designed to hide and conceal the source and ownership of money illegally derived is an act of money laundering.

Six distinct stages can be identified in the money laundering process. They are: transportation; consolidation; placement; layering; integration; and repatriation.

It is vital to recognize that these stages do not have a universal application and that there are no easy formulae that can be conveniently applied to identify a money launderer. Money laundering operations vary infinitely in their structure, depending upon the speed with which such funds are to be integrated, the source and type of the criminal proceeds and their ultimate destination. The Guideline on Anti-Money Laundering and Counter-Terrorist Financing issued by the HKMA specifies three common stages: placement, layering, and integration. The above six stages of money laundering are considered in turn as follows.

Transportation

The transportation stage is an independent phase in the money laundering process. As many countries have introduced legislation that has criminalized money laundering, there has been an increasing trend for launderers to smuggle currency derived from criminal activity to jurisdictions (usually offshore) with extensive banking secrecy laws and fiscal laws devoid of money laundering legislation.

The physical smuggling of currency out of the country of origin via international air express companies, passengers, private aircraft, cargo shipments, and other outbound vehicles has increased dramatically. Such outflows of cash leave no audit trail and, therefore, cash often moves to renowned money laundering havens where a greater assurance of total disguise is provided.

There are a number of practical advantages that money launderers have with the transportation of currency. Not only does transportation put the proceeds out of reach of the authorities of the original jurisdiction, but it also evades any possibilities of an audit trail, thereby placing significant obstacles in the path of investigators seeking to obtain and secure admissible evidence. The currency transported offshore can then be placed directly or indirectly into the conventional financial system and routinely wire-transferred to institutions in other financial markets.

Consolidation

Prior to, or immediately after the transportation stage, criminals may pursue the independent preliminary stage of consolidation.

Consolidation is a time-consuming process that is quite often underestimated by regulators. However, in a drug network or other criminal enterprise generating small denominations of notes and coins, it is imperative that such money is converted into more manageable higher denominations so that it can be transported or placed into the financial system more effectively without raising suspicion. This will involve illegitimate money being introduced into a legitimate company on a transitory basis prior to a more permanent placement.

Those involved in consolidating cash at this stage of the laundering cycle will be most concerned to avoid the creation of any external records, which could be used to initiate an audit or paper trail and can connect the launderers to the subsequent stages of the laundering operation or, more importantly, to the initial criminal enterprise. The risks of the launderer are profound in that the consolidation by currency exchanges, or even commercial banks, represents the first infusion of criminal cash into the financial system. It is for this reason that small currency exchange houses on international borders are preferred. By actually acquiring the currency houses, using false identification papers and adopting a range of other techniques, the consolidation of funds through such houses will provide a more effective screen, therefore retaining anonymity and minimizing exposure.

Placement

Even if a launderer does not opt to transport cash to another jurisdiction or does not feel it necessary to consolidate, it will eventually become necessary to do so and the funds will need to be 'placed' into the financial system. Placement is the physical disposal of bulk cash proceeds derived from criminal activity into the conventional financial system with the objective of removing it from the location of its acquisition.

Since placement involves the first formal infusion of cash into the financial system on a more permanent basis than that envisaged in the consolidation state, the risks to the launderer are more profound. It is the weak link in the money laundering chain, where the proceeds of crime are most easily detected.

It is important to note the point made in the introduction stage that money laundering schemes can vary infinitely in their structure and scope. In fact, a simplistic placement by means of a cash purchase of goods may be the first stage in the laundering cycle, with the cash first being placed in the legitimate economy rather than in the formal financial system. Since the regulatory authorities have imposed increasing reporting obligations on financial institutions at the placement stage, this is a technique that is being increasingly utilised. Such purchases have limited use for significant sums and by implication they are an inconvenient and inflexible mechanism for placing cash.

More permanent and sophisticated placement programmes will utilise the banking and financial systems to a more significant degree. In most cases, cash will be placed after a transportation and/or consolidation programme within jurisdictions devoid of money laundering counter measures, where the regulatory framework is inadequate, exchange controls are non-existent, and banking secrecy laws are extensive.

Layering

Upon being placed into the conventional financial system, the true source of the illicit money must be concealed at once. In this sense, the layering stage is analogous to a stone gradually dropping to the bottom of a deep lake.

The launderer's objective is to create successive layers of complex transactions, typically involving a multitude of entities with various legal capacities, operating in a diverse range of jurisdictions. The money will eventually be cleansed through a number of artificial, spurious, misleading, and even fictitious transactions. The purpose of the transactions is to appease and convince sceptical financial institutions with whom the money has been placed, with the long-term goal of confounding the most dedicated and well-resourced investigators. By obscuring the audit trail, the risks of detention and confiscation are minimised and the criminal enterprise can become self-perpetuating. The complexity and sophistication of the layering programme will be dictated to a significant extent by the resources and the size of the criminal enterprise, together with the time at the launderer's disposal.

In a sophisticated money laundering operation, even specialist investigations will be unlikely to collect sufficient evidence to establish, to the standards required by a court, the true source of the money. A successful laundering is where tracing by forensic accounting techniques is rendered impossible.

Integration

Once the true source of the illicit proceeds has been obscured and the layering process has succeeded, the money can be progressively integrated into the mainstream economy in such a way that it appears as normal business funds generated by a conventional commercial enterprise. Integration provides a final coat of legitimacy for criminally derived wealth. By incorporating the money back into the economy in this way, a legitimate appearance is generated so that it is impossible to distinguish between the launderer's legitimate and illegitimate wealth. Such a distinction can only really be achieved through undercover infiltration, informants, and, sometimes, a stroke of luck.

Repatriation

Once the money has truly been legitimised to the satisfaction of the launderer, it will be necessary to place such funds into an 'end deposit.' Typically, this will involve a repatriation of the money to the jurisdiction in which it was initially generated, or, equally, given the global nature of organised crime, a proportion of the funds may be directed to a separate jurisdiction where a new criminal enterprise can be funded. In order to enjoy the fruit of the money laundering, transactions will have to be devised which will enable the cleansed money to resurface in a manner that is both explicable and justifiable. Repatriation highlights the underlying objective of any money laundering operation: once washed, the clean money has to resurface in a form that is readily accessible.

Despite strong anti-money laundering legislation, regulation and practice, money laundering continues in major financial centres. Laundering operations in such centres will tend to be orientated towards the more sophisticated and complex techniques that are common in the layering and integration stages.

The current trends in money laundering appear to be as follows:

- Increasing moves towards more sophisticated money laundering techniques and practice;
- Further internationalisation of money laundering networks;
- Greater investment of drug and other illicitly obtained funds in established legitimate businesses, in order to capitalise on such illicit funds and to mask the movement of money;
- The deliberate commingling of illicit proceeds obtained through various criminal acts to disrupt the audit trail for investigative authorities; and
- The increasing development of money laundering brokers who handle third party illicit funds that are unrelated to their own criminal activities.

Legislation on Money Laundering

During the early nineties the prevention of money laundering, particularly drug related, evolved into an important foreign policy and financial management priority in nearly all financial centres. Many governments put controls in place or are currently in the process of strengthening controls to counter a potential threat to both the integrity and stability of their financial systems.

Hong Kong has developed legislation to address the problems associated with the laundering of proceeds from drug trafficking and serious crimes. The Drug Trafficking (Recovery of Proceeds) Ordinance (DTRPO) and the Organized and Serious Crime Ordinance (OSCO) came into force in 1989 and 1994 respectively. They provide for the tracing, freezing, and confiscation of the proceeds of drug trafficking (DTRPO) and indictable offences (OSCO) and created the criminal offence of money laundering in relation to such proceeds.

Both Ordinances have a significant bearing on the duty to report suspicious transactions. In particular, there is now a clear statutory obligation to disclose knowledge or suspicion of money laundering transactions. All bankers must be aware of this statutory obligation. If the obligation is not complied with, the banker may be held personally liable. Each authorised institution must appoint a senior staff, as the authorised officer (compliance officer) under the Ordinances.

Section 25(1) of DTRPO and OSCO created the offence of dealing with any property, knowing or having reasonable grounds to believe it, in whole or in part, directly or indirectly represents the proceeds of drug trafficking as an indictable offence. The offence carries a maximum sentence of 14 years imprisonment and a maximum fine of HK$5 million.

It is a statutory defence under section 25(2) of both ordinances for a person to prove that he intended to disclose as soon as is reasonable such knowledge, suspicion, or matter to an authorised officer or has a reasonable excuse for his failure to make a disclosure in accordance with section 25A(2) of the Ordinances.

Section 25A(1) imposes a statutory duty on a person who knows or suspects that any property in whole or in part, directly or indirectly, represents the proceeds of drug trafficking or of an indictable offence, or was or is intended to be used in that connection, to make a disclosure to an authorised officer. Section 25A(7) makes it an offence for a person to fail to make such a disclosure. The offence carries a maximum penalty of a fine at level 5 (at present $25,001 to $50,000) and imprisonment for three months.

Section 25(4) of OSCO provides that references to an indictable offence in section 25 and 25A, include a reference to conduct that would constitute an indictable offence if it had occurred in Hong Kong. In other words, it shall be an offence for a person to deal with the proceeds of crime or fail to make the necessary disclosure under section 25A(1) even if the principal crime is not committed in Hong Kong, provided that it would constitute an indictable offence if it had occurred in Hong Kong.

Section 25A(2) provides that if a person who has made the necessary disclosure does any act in contravention of section 25(1) and the disclosure relates to that act, he does not commit an offence if:

- The disclosure is made before he does that act and the act is done with the consent of an authorised officer; or
- The disclosure is made after the person does the act and the disclosure is made on the person's own initiative and as soon as it is reasonable for him to make it.

Section 25A(3) provides that disclosure made under section 25A(1) shall not be treated as breach of contract or of any enactment restricting disclosure of information and shall not render the person making the disclosure liable in damages for any loss arising out of disclosure. Therefore, the authorised institutions need not fear breaching their duty of confidentiality owed to customers when making a disclosure under both Ordinances.

Section 25A(4) extends the provisions of section 25A to disclosures made by an employee to an appropriate person in accordance with the procedures established by his employer for the making of such disclosure, in the same way as it applies to disclosures to an authorised officer. This provides protection to employees of authorised institutions against the risk of prosecution where they have reported knowledge or suspicion of money laundering transactions to the person designated by their employers.

A "tipping-off" offence is created under section 25A(5) of both DTRPO and OSCO, under which a person commits an offence if, knowing or suspecting that a disclosure has been made, he discloses to any other person any matter which is likely to prejudice an investigation into money laundering activities. The "tipping-off" offence carries a maximum penalty of three years' imprisonment and a fine of HK$500,000. In other words, the "tipping-off" offence is more serious than just non-disclosure.

In addition, the Anti-Money Laundering and Counter-Terrorist Financing (Financial Institutions) Ordinance (Cap. 615) codifies customer due diligence and record-keeping requirements for financial institutions and provides for supervisory and criminal sanctions for contravention of the statutory requirements.

Basic Policies and Principles to Combat Money Laundering

The Statement of Principles issued by the Basle Committee in December 1988 seeks to deny use of the banking system to those involved in money laundering by application of the following principles (adopted by the HKMA in the Guideline):

- **Know your customer:** banks should make reasonable efforts to determine the customer's true identity, and have effective procedures for verifying the bona fides of new customers.
- **Compliance with laws:** bank management should ensure that business is conducted in conformity with high ethical standards, that laws and regulations are adhered to, and that a service is not provided where there is good reason to suppose that transactions are associated with laundering activities.

- **Cooperation with law enforcement agencies**: within any constraints imposed by rules relating to customer confidentiality, banks should co-operate fully with national law enforcement agencies including taking appropriate measures which are consistent with the law.
- **Policies, procedures, and training**: all banks should formally adopt policies consistent with the principles set out in the statement, and should ensure that all members of their staff concerned, wherever located, are informed of the bank's policy. Attention should be given to staff training in matters covered by the statement. To promote adherence to these principles, banks should implement specific procedures for customer identification and for retaining internal records of transactions. Arrangements for internal audit may need to be extended in order to establish an effective means for general compliance with the Statement.

Examples of Suspicious Transactions

The guideline provides, inter alia, the following examples of suspicious transactions regarding money laundering.

- **Money laundering using cash transactions**
  i. Unusually large cash deposits made by an individual or company whose ostensible business activities would normally be generated by cheques and other instruments.
  ii. Substantial increases in cash deposits of any individual or business without apparent cause, especially if such deposits are subsequently transferred within a short period out of the account and/or to a destination not normally associated with the customer.
  iii. Customers who deposit cash by means of numerous credit slips so that the total of each deposit is unremarkable but the total of all the credits is significant.
  iv. Company accounts whose transactions, both deposits and withdrawals, are denominated in cash rather than the forms of debit and credit normally associated with commercial operations (e.g., cheques, letters of credit, bills of exchange, etc.)
  v. Customers transferring large sums of money to or from overseas locations with instructions for payment in cash.
  vi. Large cash deposits using night safe facilities, thereby avoiding direct contact with the institution.
  vii. Purchasing or selling of foreign currencies in substantial amounts by cash settlement despite the customer having an account with the institution.
  viii. Customers making large and frequent cash deposits but cheques drawn on the accounts are mostly to individuals and firms not normally associated with their retail business.
- **Money laundering using bank accounts**
  i. Customers who wish to maintain a number of trustee or clients' accounts which do not appear consistent with their type of business, including transactions which involve nominee names.
  ii. Customers who have numerous accounts and pay in amounts of cash to each of them in circumstances in which the total amount of credits would be a large amount.

iii. Any individual or company whose account shows virtually no normal personal banking or business related activities, but is used to receive or disburse large sums which have no obvious purpose or relationship to the account holder and/or his business (e.g., a substantial increase in turnover on an account).
iv. Reluctance to provide normal information when opening an account, providing minimal or fictitious information or, when applying to open an account, providing information that is difficult or expensive for the institution to verify.
v. Matching of payments out with credits paid in by cash on the same or previous day.
vi. Large cash withdrawals from a previously dormant/inactive account, or from an account which has just received an unexpected large credit from abroad.
vii. Customers who together and simultaneously, use separate tellers to conduct large cash transactions or foreign exchange transactions.
viii. Companies' representatives avoiding contact with the branch.
ix. Customers who decline to provide information that in normal circumstances, would make the customer eligible for credit or for other banking services that would be regarded as valuable.
x. Large number of individuals making payments into the same account without an adequate explanation.
xi. Customers who maintain an unusually large number of accounts for the type of business they are purportedly conducting and/or use inordinately large numbers of fund transfers among these accounts.
xii. An account operated in the name of an off-shore company with structured movement of funds.

- **Money laundering involving off-shore international activity**
  i. Customers introduced by an overseas branch, affiliate or other bank based in countries where production of drugs or drug trafficking may be prevalent.
  ii. Use of letters of credit and other methods of trade finance to move money between countries where such trade is not consistent with the customer's usual business.
  iii. Customers who make regular and large payments that cannot be clearly identified as bona fide transactions (including wire transactions) to, or receive regular and large payments from, countries which are commonly associated with the production, processing, or marketing of drugs.
  iv. Numerous wire transfers received in an account but each transfer is below the reporting requirement in the remitting country.
  v. Customers sending and receiving wire transfers to/from financial haven countries, particularly if there are no apparent business reasons for such transfers or such transfers are not consistent with the customers' business or history.
- **Money laundering involving authorised institution employees and agents**
  i. Changes in employee characteristics, for example, lavish lifestyles.
  ii. Any dealing with an agent where the identity of the ultimate beneficiary or counterparty is undisclosed, contrary to normal procedure for the type of business concerned.

- **Money laundering by secured and unsecured lending**
  i. Customers who repay problem loans unexpectedly.
  ii. Request to borrow against assets held by the institution or a third party, where the origin of the assets is not known or the assets are inconsistent with the customer's standing.
  iii. Request by a customer for an institution to provide or arrange finance where the source of the customer's financial contribution to a deal is unclear, particularly where property is involved.
  iv. A customer who is reluctant or refuses to state a purpose of a loan or the source of repayment, or provides a questionable purpose and/or source.

The above list is not exhaustive and will be extended by banks taking into account their business activities. Bankers should consider the past history and general background of the customers concerned. If a transaction is suspicious, bank staff handling the transaction should be advised to pass such information to the "Money Laundering Reporting Officer" of the bank, who should evaluate the case and determine whether to onward report to the enforcement authority (the Joint Financial Intelligence Unit operated by the Police and Custom and Excise Department). If they fail to do so they may have committed an offence in law as well as a breach of the internal rules of the bank.

Burden of Proof

Section 25(4) of DTRPO places the burden of proof on the defendant (D). The Privy Council in *Attorney-General v. Lee Kwong-kut,* allowed an appeal by the attorney general against a high court decision that section 25(1) and (4) of DTRPO conflicted with the Hong Kong Bill of Rights Ordinance, Cap. 383 (BORO) article 11(1) (a person shall be presumed innocent until proven guilty). It ruled that article 11(1) had an implicit degree of flexibility which allowed for a balance to be held between D's interests and those of the state. Whether it is reasonable to impose some burden on D may depend on whether the nature of proof of a fact justified a presumption such as that contained in section 25(1) of DTRPO, that D was liable until the contrary was proved. The primary burden under section 25(1) of DTRPO lay with the prosecution; but it was "manifestly" reasonable for D to bear the burden of section 25(4) of DTRPO. The Privy Council held that BORO article 11(1) had not been infringed. In other words, article 11(1) of BORO cannot be invoked by the defendant.

Power of Authorised Officers

Section 20 of DTRPO gives wide power to law enforcement officers investigating the proceeds of drug trafficking and money laundering. The court may make an order that records and documents be produced and made available for examination if it is satisfied that there are reasonable grounds for suspecting that the person to whom the documents apply, has carried on or benefited from drug trafficking. On failure to comply with an order, a warrant may be issued under section 21 of DTRPO authorizing search and seizure.

A production order can be made for investigation abroad if the foreign jurisdiction allows sections 28 and 19 of DTRPO and Drug Trafficking (Recovery of Proceeds) (Designated Countries and Territories) Order 1991 permit designated overseas jurisdictions to apply to a Hong Kong court for recovery of drug trafficking proceeds.

Bankers must also note that the guideline provides that "Access to the disclosed information is restricted to financial investigating officers within the Police and Custom and Excise Department." Both DTRPO and OSCO place strict restrictions on revealing the identity of the person making the disclosure. As the guideline points out, maintaining the integrity of the relationship, which has been established between law enforcement agencies and an institution, is considered to be of paramount importance.

Bribery and Corruption

Bankers are usually offered some gifts from their customers. Bankers should bear in mind the law relating to bribery and corruption and should take appropriate actions when they face an issue of bribery. But the Hong Kong Bill of Rights Ordinance may provide defences to some charges under the Prevention of Bribery Ordinance (POBO). POBO has not expressly abolished the common law offence of bribery though it has effectively rendered it obsolete. The purpose of POBO is to prohibit and punish the giving and accepting of secret commissions.

Corrupt Transactions with Agents

It is an offence under section 9(1) of the POBO for an agent, without lawful authority or reasonable excuse, to solicit or accept any advantage as an inducement to or reward for or otherwise on account of:

- Doing or forbearing to do, or having done or forborne to do, any act in relation to the agent's principal's affairs or business; or
- Showing or forbearing to show, or having shown or forborne to show, favour or disfavour to any person in relation to that principal's affairs or business.

"Favour" has its ordinary meaning, but it must be something of substance. What is substantial must be decided according to the facts of each case.

Offence in POBO Section 9(2)

It is an offence for any person, without lawful authority or reasonable excuse, to offer any advantage to any agent as an inducement to or reward for or otherwise on account of the agent's:

- Doing or forbearing to do, or having done or forbore to do, any act in relation to the agent's principal's affairs or business; or

- Showing or forbearing to show, or having shown or forborne to show, favour or disfavour to any person in relation to the principal's affairs or business.

If the gift offered by the customer is trivial then the bankers should refer the case to senior level for approval. If the offer is substantial then the bankers should report to their senior and/or ICAC.

Offence in POBO Section 9(3)

It is an offence for any agent, with intent to deceive the principal, to use any receipt, account, or other document:

- In respect of which the principal is interested; and
- Which contains any statement which is false or erroneous or defective in any material particular; and
- Which to the agent's knowledge is intended to mislead the principal.

In *Lee Wing-Kwan MA*, the magistrate found that the agent was not acting strictly within his authority. On appeal it was held that all that was needed was that there should be a casual relationship between the agent's act and the principal's affairs.

In *Lui Kwok-wai*, it was held that there is no requirement of corrupt intent under section 9(3).

Advantage

Section 2 of POBO defines 'advantage' widely. Unless the context otherwise requires, 'advantage' means:

- Any gift, loan, fee, reward, or commission consisting of money or of any valuable security or of other property or interest in property of any description;
- Any office, employment, or contract;
- Any payment, release, discharge, or liquidation of any loan, obligation, or other liability, whether in whole or in part;
- Any other service, or favour (other than entertainment), including protection from any penalty or disability incurred or apprehended or from any action or proceedings of a disciplinary, civil, or criminal nature, whether or not already instituted;
- The exercise or forbearance from the exercise of any right or any power or duty; and
- Any offer, undertaking or promise, whether conditional or unconditional, of any advantage within the meaning of any of the preceding paragraphs (1), (2), (3), (4) and (5).

Certain specified donations are excluded.

Counter-Terrorist Financing

The term "terrorist financing" is defined in the Anti-Money Laundering and Counter-Terrorist Financing (Financial Institutions) Ordinance (Cap. 615). It generally refers to the carrying out of transactions involving funds that are owned by terrorists, or that have been, or are intended to be, used to assist the commission of terrorist acts. This has not previously been explicitly covered under the money laundering regime where the focus is on the handling of criminal proceeds, that is, the source of funds is what matters. In terrorist financing, the focus is on the destination or use of funds, which may have derived from legitimate sources.

The United Nations Security Council (UNSC) has passed various resolutions to require sanctions against certain designated terrorists and terrorist organisations. In Hong Kong, regulations issued under the United Nations (Sanctions) Ordinance give effect to these UNSC resolutions. In particular, the United Nations Sanctions (Afghanistan) Regulation provides, among other things, for a prohibition on making funds available to designated terrorists. The list of designated terrorists is published in the Gazette from time to time.

In addition, the United Nations (Anti-Terrorism Measures) Ordinance was enacted on 12 July 2002. This implements the mandatory elements of the UNSC Resolution 1373. The latter is aimed at combating international terrorism on various fronts, including the introduction of measures against terrorism financing.

The ordinance, among other things, prohibits the supply of funds or making of funds available to terrorists or terrorist associates as defined. It also makes it a statutory requirement for a person to report his knowledge or suspicion that any property is terrorist property. As with the above mentioned regulations, a list of terrorist names will be published in the Gazette from time to time for this purpose.

The HKMA requires the banks to be able to identify and report transactions with terrorist suspects. To this end, the banks should make use of a database of names and particulars of terrorist suspects, which consolidates the various lists that have been made known to it, and check the names of its customers against the names in the database. Where a bank suspects that a transaction is terrorist-related, it should make a report to the Joint Financial Intelligence Unit, even if there is no evidence of a direct terrorist connection.

Overview

In summary, guidelines issued by the Hong Kong Monetary Authority requires banks to identify their customers (including natural persons, legal persons, trusts, etc.) and verify the customers' identities under the Customer Due Diligence (CDD) principle, give special attention to the identification of ownership and safe-custody items, ensure significant transactions with the customer, cooperate with law enforcement authorities, train staff and promote adherence to the guidelines, and extend the scope of their internal audits.

The HKAB has a set of recommended guidelines that include appointing designated officers as Compliance Officer(s) or Money Laundering Reporting Officer(s) (MLRO), keeping a register of all reports, ensuring all accurate and necessary reporting is done to authorities, and taking steps to ensure all employees are aware of the guidelines.

The types of transactions that may fall within S.25 include large cash deposits, a substantial increase in cash deposits from a particular customer, the opening of numerous accounts and payments in cash, a company account with abnormal cash transactions, a reluctance to provide normal information when opening an account, and efforts to exchange large quantities of low denomination notes.

The HKAB has introduced a four-step approach to dealing with these issues. These four steps start with recognizing suspicious financial activity, undertaking appropriate questioning of the customer once an indicator has been identified if practically possible, reviewing information already known to the bank to decide if the suspicious activity is consistent with the normal operation of the account, and deciding whether to make a suspicious transaction report.

There is a significant amount of legislation against money laundering including the Drug Trafficking (Recovery of Proceeds) (Amendment) Ordinance, the Organized and Serious Crimes (Amendment) which has similar provisions, the Gambling Ordinance (Amendment) (effective 31 May 2002), and the United Nations (Anti-Terrorism Measures) Ordinance (passed on 18 July 2002) and the Anti-Money Laundering and Counter-Terrorist Financing (Financial Institutions) Ordinance (effective 1 April 2012).

Another area that requires care is remittances. In order to assist law enforcement authorities in their investigations of suspected money laundering through electronic message systems, banks should include the names, addresses, and/or account numbers of their customers in the electronic payment message (e.g., SWIFT MT103). Banks should also establish relevant customer acceptance policies and procedures as required under the "Guideline on Anti-Money Laundering and Counter-Terrorist Financing" issued by the HKMA.

Finally, the bank should develop anti-terrorist financing practices. A list of designated individuals and entities suspected to be terrorists or drug traffickers is posted regularly in the Gazette. At the same time, the HKMA has issued guidelines requiring banks to search against the list when opening accounts to avoid opening accounts for individuals or entities listed.

Summary

- Banks used to rely on legally implied terms, which incorporate into the contract various rights and duties of the contracting parties. Increasingly however, banks are now placing more emphasis on the importance of explicit contractual terms and the banker is expected to provide customers with a passbook or statements of account.
- Most banks now prepare consolidated terms and conditions on each category of banking products or banking services.

- A banker who wishes to cease transacting business for a customer must give that customer reasonable notice, and the period of notice must be long enough to enable the customer to make alternative arrangements.
- At law, a bank owes a contractual duty to exercise reasonable care and skill in performing its duties arising out of its relationship with the customer.
- Customer's duties to the bank involve: drawing cheques carefully so as not to mislead the bank or facilitate fraud or forgery and informing the bank once a forgery is discovered.
- An individual customer may appoint a third party to help operate a bank account on the customer's behalf in two ways: i) authorisation given in the account mandate by naming the third party an authorised signatory to the account; ii) power of attorney.
- Power of attorney is a document, executed under seal, whereby the donor authorises another (donee or attorney) to act on behalf of the donor.
- A garnishee order attaches or freezes debts due or accruing due by the garnishee to the judgement debtor.
- A Mareva injunction is a court order restraining a party to legal proceedings from removing from the court's jurisdiction assets located within and outside of the jurisdiction.
- Joint account mandates typically include a survivorship clause.
- Termination of relationship between banker and customer can be effected in a number of ways: mutual agreement, termination by the bank or the customer, death of the customer, mental incapacity of the customer, bankruptcy of an individual customer, or winding-up of a corporate customer.
- Money laundering schemes can vary infinitely in their structure and scope. Bankers need to be always on the lookout for possible money laundering activities.

Key Terms

Beneficial contract
Companies Ordinance (CO)
Contract of necessaries
Customer Due Diligence (CDD) principle
Garnishee order
Garnishee to order absolute
Garnishee to show cause (Nisi)
Incorporated companies
Joint account
Mandate
Mavera injunction
Minors
Money "gone out"
Money accruing due
Money due
Partnership
Personal customers
Power of attorney
Prevention of Bribery Ordinance (POBO)
Right of survivorship
Sole proprietorship
Solicitors
Trust
Trustee
Unincorporated associations, clubs, and societies
Valid contract
Voidable contracts

Study Guide

1. Mr. A and his wife opened a joint account with a mandate specifying that all withdrawals require the signature of both signatories. A few months after, Mrs. A signs a withdrawal slip for a substantial amount. The bank allowed the withdrawal and was later sued by the husband. What do you think is the outcome? Was the bank in error?
2. Mr. X was appointed as personal representative to Mr. Y's estate after his death. Both Mr. X and Mr. Y bank with the same bank. Prior to his death, Mr. Y ran up a debit balance with the bank. Being as Mr. X is his personal representative, is the bank allowed to set-off Mr. Y's debits against Mr. X's personal account? Why or why not?
3. Three men formed a partnership business and decided to open a personal bank account, which the bank agreed to do. Explain what the bank should have done in such a case.
4. A bank customer deals in luxury bags and routinely gives presents of accessories to the bank tellers. Would this be classified as a bribe? What steps should the bank tellers take, if any?
5. Give examples of money laundering scams involving institutional employees and agents. What are the possible signs?

Further Reading

Chan Bo-ching Simon. *Hong Kong Banking Law and Practice Vol. 1*. Hong Kong Institute of Bankers, First Edition, September 2000. Print.

Companies Ordinance website: http://www.hklii.org/hk/legis/ord/32/

Code of Banking Practice website: http://www.bankers.asn.au/ABAs-Code-of-Banking-Practice/default.aspx

Hong Kong Monetary Authority, *HKMA Guideline on Anti-Money Laundering and Counter-Terrorist Financing*. HKMA website: http://www.info.gov.hk/hkma/eng/guide/guide_no/attach/g33.pdf

BANKING OPERATIONS

Bills of Exchange and Promissory Notes

Learning objectives

After studying this chapter, you should be able to:

1. Describe the definitions, parties, and characteristics relating to bills of exchange and promissory notes
2. Identify the law applicable to these two types of negotiable instruments, including the rules codified in the Bills of Exchange Ordinance
3. Discuss the legal issues that a banker must be aware of when dealing with bills of exchange and promissory notes

Introduction

Negotiable instruments have the following key characteristics: they can be transferred from person to person, the person to whom they are negotiated obtains good title to them even though the transferor may have a defective title or no title at all, and the person to whom they are negotiated can sue on them in his own name.

Because banks deal with negotiable instruments every day, bankers need to understand the legal issues surrounding them. There are many types of negotiable instruments (and quasi-negotiable instruments), but we focus on two main groups in this book. These are bills of exchange and promissory notes.

In this chapter, we provide a general discussion of these two types of negotiable instruments and their functions, the role of the parties to these instruments, and the rights of the holder. The rules have evolved as part of common law and have been consolidated and codified in the Bills of Exchange Ordinance and other legislation.

Negotiable Instruments

Before we discuss bills of exchange and promissory notes, it is helpful to first summarise the key characteristics common to all types of negotiable instruments.

- A negotiable instrument and the rights it carries are capable of transfer by delivery of possession, as in the case of bearer instruments. If an instrument is payable to a specified person or order, it may be negotiated by indorsement (that is, affixing a signature on the instrument) and delivery.
- A distinctive feature of negotiability is that a holder of the instrument may acquire a better title to the instrument than the person who transferred it to him, subject to certain exceptions. This is the key distinction between negotiation and a mere transfer. In case of a mere transfer, the transferee can in no circumstances obtain a better title than his transferor.
- In the case of negotiation of a negotiable instrument, so long as the instrument appears complete and regular on its face, the person to whom it is negotiated obtains a good title if he takes it in good faith, for value, and without notice of any defect in his predecessor's title, notwithstanding that the person who transferred it to him may have a defective title or even no title to it. The only exception is where an essential signature to the instrument is proved to be forged.
- The person to whom an instrument is negotiated can sue on it in his own name.
- The transaction represented by the negotiable instrument is independent of the underlying transaction in respect of which the instrument was issued. For example, where a cheque is issued in payment for goods supplied pursuant to a contract for sale of the goods, generally speaking, a holder of the cheque may sue on it without any inquiry

being made as to the validity of the underlying contract or the parties' rights and obligations under it. A contractual party's failure to provide consideration for a cheque drawn payable to him will therefore not affect the rights of a subsequent holder of the cheque who took it for value and in good faith.

The types of negotiable instruments include bills of exchange, promissory notes, cheques, bankers' drafts, travellers' cheques, bearer bonds, and debentures. There are some instruments that possess the first two characteristics of a negotiable instrument, but not the third; in other words, a transferee takes them subject to any defects in the title of prior parties. These are called quasi-negotiable instruments and include postal orders and bills of lading.

Role and Responsibilities of the Bank

A bank is a frequent and integral part of transacting a negotiable instrument. Most bills represent an instruction by a customer to the bank to pay a certain amount to the customer or a third party. In the most common example of a negotiable instrument, the cheque, a bank is also involved in collecting the negotiable instrument. Both the paying and collecting bank have a specific role to play in the transaction and have specific responsibilities.

In carrying out this role, banks must exercise the requisite due diligence as they could be held liable for any losses to the customer. The Bills of Exchange Ordinance outlines the requirements that the bank must fulfill if they are to avoid liability:

- The bank must act in good faith;
- The banker must credit the customer with the funds;
- Payment must be received for the customer;
- The negotiable instrument negotiated must be one of those listed in subsection 2 of the ordinance. Cheques and drafts are the most important.;
- A bank must act without negligence in collecting the negotiable instrument.

The paying and collecting bank have a set of responsibilities when dealing with a negotiable instrument.

Paying bank

Dealing with the negotiable instruments of its customers is one of the major duties of a bank. This includes cheques. Paying on a negotiable instrument is only part of the responsibility of the bank. It is also incumbent on banks to at times dishonour an instrument.

The most common negotiable instrument that banks pay is the cheque, which may be presented over the counter or through the clearing system. A cheque is, in effect, a mandate from the customer to the bank to debit an account. Although a bank may deal with tens of thousands of cheques and other instruments on any given day, it still has a responsibility to exercise care and due diligence. This means that each cheque or other negotiable instrument has to be examined carefully to ensure that it may be safely paid.

In cases where it does not honour a negotiable instrument such as a cheque, the paying bank has a responsibility to explain the reason. Generally, this is done in a separate notice. The examination of a cheque involves the following:

- Checking the signature;
- Verifying whether the signatory has authority to sign that cheque in the case of a corporate cheque;
- Checking the date on the cheque. An instrument with a date in the future may not be paid;
- Checking the name of the payee to ensure, to a reasonable certainty, that the instrument is paid to the right person;
- Checking the amount, which must be in writing to meet the requirements of the Bills of Exchange Ordinance. The amount written out should match the amount provided in figures;
- Checking the crossing of the cheque. If a cheque is not crossed, there are no restrictions on the bank paying cash but crossed cheques should not be cashed;
- Checking whether the customer has countermanded payment;
- Checking whether notice has been received of the death of the drawer of the cheque;
- Verifying whether there are any circumstances, such as a bankruptcy or liquidation, that legally prevents the bank from paying the cheque;
- Considering any knowledge of a breach of trust, such as when a banker receives money from a customer that he knows is being held in trust;
- Determining whether there are enough funds in the customer's account to honour the cheque or unused overdraft facilities;
- Checking whether the cheque requires indorsement.

Collecting bank

Except in certain specific cases, banks generally collect negotiable instruments not on their own behalf but on behalf of their clients. In so doing, they must exercise the usual care and rely on their expertise. In several cases, the courts have made it clear that they expect a high standard of care on the part of a bank, regardless of the high volume of instruments (mostly cheques) that may be negotiated on any given day.

The bank should ensure that the negotiable instrument is paid to the right person. There are instances in which a third party may fraudulently cause an instrument to be paid, in turn depriving the true owner of the funds. The bank has a responsibility to ensure the owner of a negotiable instrument is the true owner or face significant liability. The action of paying a negotiable instrument to a party who is not the true owner without authorization is called "conversion," and conversion leaves the bank open to liability.

Should a negotiable instrument be returned unpaid, the bank must notify the customer immediately. This is generally done with a letter and a return of the instrument (most commonly a cheque) to the customer. A delay in advising the customer could result in the customer losing the right to take action to remedy the non-payment.

The bank should also consider the past history of an account when collecting a negotiable instrument. In cases where the past activity of an account raises questions, the bank should make further inquiries.

Particularly important are negotiable instruments payable to a third party. In these cases, the bank should ensure it is paying the instrument to the right person. In the case of a cheque, the bank should look to see whether the cheque is crossed with the words "account payee only."

Bills of Exchange[1]

The relevant legislation in Hong Kong is the Bills of Exchange Ordinance, which is modelled on the 1882 Bills of Exchange Act of the United Kingdom. It codifies laws relating to bills of exchange, cheques, and promissory notes. The ordinance and case law are technical and complex, but it is essential for bank officers to be familiar with their main principles.

Section 3(1) of the Ordinance defines a bill of exchange as:

- An unconditional order in writing;
- Addressed by one person to another;
- Signed by the person giving it;
- Requiring the person to whom it is addressed to pay on demand or at a fixed or determinable future time a sum certain in money to, or to the order of, a specified person, or to the bearer.

The Ordinance further provides that a bill of exchange is not made invalid by reason of:

- That it not being dated;
- That it not specifying the value given or any value that has been given therefor;
- That it not specifying the place where it is drawn or the place where it is payable.

Parties to a Bill of Exchange

There are at least two parties to every bill: the drawer and the drawee. The payee may either be a third party or is the drawer as well. When a bill is negotiated, it means that the bill is transferred by the payee, or by yet another party that the payee had negotiated the bill to, called a holder. The transferor—that is, the payee or holder—frequently adds currency to the bill by signing on the back (indorsement). This payee or holder then becomes an indorser, whose position is similar to that of a drawer.

In a straightforward transaction, the bill is addressed by one party (drawer) to another party, usually the drawer's bank (drawee), requiring this drawee to pay money to a third party (payee) in the case of a bill payable to a specified party, or to the bearer, in the case of a bearer bill.

---

[1]Chan, Bo-ching Simon; *Hong Kong Banking Law and Practice;* First edition; Hong Kong Institute of Bankers; Hong Kong, 2000

Drawer

The drawer is the party that makes the order. By writing and signing the order, the drawer assumes the dual functions of instructing the drawee to pay the bill, and making it understood that the bill will be accepted and paid when presented.

Section 55(1) of the Bills of Exchange Ordinance provides that the drawer of a bill, by drawing it:

- Engages that, on due presentment, the bill shall be accepted and paid according to its tenor, and that if it is dishonoured, the drawer will compensate the holder or any indorser who is compelled to pay it, provided that the requisite proceedings on dishonour are duly taken;
- Is precluded from denying to a holder in due course the existence of the payee and his capacity to indorse.

Drawee

The drawee is the party to whom the bill of exchange order is addressed. The drawee instructs the drawer to honour the bill, undertakes that on due presentation of the bill to the drawer it will be duly accepted (when acceptance is required) and paid, and acts as a surety that guarantees the payment of the bill.

Acceptor

The drawee becomes the acceptor when the drawee accepts the bill of exchange and warrants payment according to the tenor of the acceptance. The drawee then becomes liable as primary obligor or debtor. If the drawee refuses to accept the bill, this may be taken as a breach of contract with the drawer. For example, if a bank acting as drawee dishonours by non-acceptance a bill drawn in conformity with the provisions of an acceptance credit, that bank commits a breach of contract with the drawer.

Payee

The payee is the party to whom the bill is payable. The payee may be the drawer or may be a third party.

Holder

There are two types of holders: the holder for value and the holder in due course. The *holder for value* is the holder of a bill for which value has been given. Once value (consideration) is given for a bill, the holder giving value and all subsequent holders are holders for value. A holder for value has the rights of transferability conferred upon him by common law. The holder enjoys the same rights but is subject to the same defects in title, if any, of the transferor (the payee or another holder negotiating the bill). The value given may be any consideration sufficient to support a simple contract or an antecedent debt or liability.

A *holder in due course* is a holder who had taken a bill that is complete and regular on the face of it, even though that bill may have been previously dishonoured or the transferor had defective title to it. To qualify as a holder in due course, a holder must have become the holder of the bill before it was overdue, had no knowledge that it had been previously dishonoured (if this is the case), took the bill in good faith and for value, and had no notice of any defect in the title of the party that negotiated it.

A holder (whether for value or not) that derives title to a bill through a holder in due course and which is not party to any fraud or illegality affecting that bill has all the rights of that holder in due course with regard to the acceptor and all parties to that bill prior to that holder in due course.

Bearer

The bearer is a party that is in possession of a bill which is payable to the bearer and not to any specified party. The right to payment passes with physical possession and vests in the current holder without the need for indorsement.

Indorser

When the payee negotiates a bill, that payee is generally asked to indorse it by signing on the back of the bill. The payee therefore warrants that the bill will be duly accepted and paid, and that if the bill is dishonoured, the payee will compensate the holder or a subsequent indorser that is compelled to pay the bill. The indorser incurs liability towards every party that acquires the bill after that indorser and is compelled to pay it.

A bill may be indorsed where, for example, a bill payable at a future date has been accepted by a bank and the payee sells (or negotiates) it to another person at a discount before maturity in exchange for ready cash.

Accommodation Party

An accommodation party became a drawer, acceptor, or indorser without receiving value for it. This party's involvement is for the purpose of lending its name to some other party to enable that other party to raise money or obtain credit, for example. An accommodation party is liable on the bill to a holder for value, regardless of whether or not the holder knew such party to be an accommodation party when that holder took the bill.

Dating of a Bill of Exchange

A bill payable on demand is due on presentation at any time on or after the date of the instrument. Apart from bills drawn before that date, all bills are due and payable on the last day of the time of payment as fixed by the bill or, if that is a general holiday, on the succeeding business day. A general holiday is a day that must be kept as a holiday by all banks, education establishments, public offices, and governmental departments.

Where a bill is payable at a fixed period after date, after sight, or after the happening of a specified event, the time of payment is determined by excluding the day from which the time is to begin to run and by including the day of payment. Where a bill is payable at a fixed period after sight, the time begins to run from the date of the acceptance if the bill is accepted, and from the date of noting or protest if the bill is noted or protested for non-acceptance, or for non-delivery.

Signature on a Bill of Exchange

Section 23 of the Bill of Exchange Ordinance provides that "no person is liable as drawer, indorser, or acceptor of a bill who has not signed it as such."

The liability on a bill of exchange is by signature only: no person is liable upon a bill if he has not signed it. By the same principle, anyone who signs a bill becomes liable even if that person is not required to sign the bill. It is not necessary that it should be signed with his hand. The signature signed by some other person by or under his authority is sufficient. For example, a bank officer may sign on behalf of the bank for which he works provided he is an authorised signatory.

Section 26 of the Bill of Exchange Ordinance states that, "where a person signs a bill as drawer, indorser, or acceptor and adds words to his signature, indicating that he signs for or on behalf of a principal or in a representative character, he is not personally liable thereon."

The drawer must sign the bill in order to take legal effect. In other words, a document cannot be a bill of exchange unless it carries the signature of the drawer. No action lies on the bill against a person who has not signed it. Further, no title can be derived from a forged signature although the person in possession can acquire a status as holder through a subsequent indorsement and, if a holder in due course, he will then be entitled to claim against those who became parties subsequent to the forged signature.

Section 24 of the Bill of Exchange Ordinance provides that, "where a signature on a bill is forged or placed thereon without the authority of the person whose signature it purports to be, the forged or unauthorised signature is wholly inoperative, and no right to retain the bill, or to give a discharge therefor, or to enforce payment thereof against any party thereto can be acquired through or under that signature, unless the party against whom it is sought to retain or enforce payment of the bill is precluded from setting up the forgery or want of authority."

In general, a person cannot be liable for a bill if he or she has not signed it even though a forged signature is put on the bill. However, if that person is aware that his or her signature has been forged on a bill and by actions or silence may wittingly lead others to believe the signature is genuine, the courts will not allow that person to escape liability by claiming that the signature was forged.

Presentment for Acceptance

Presentment for acceptance is not always a requirement for payment. A bill can be discharged without presentment. Legally, it is necessary only in three cases:

- Where a bill is payable after sight, presentment for acceptance is necessary in order to fix the maturity of the instrument;
- Where a bill expressly stipulates that it must be presented for acceptance;
- Where a bill is drawn payable elsewhere than at the residence or place of business of the drawee.

The holder may wait until the maturity of the bill before presenting it for payment. As a rule, however, a bill is presented for acceptance before maturity, the objective being to secure the liability of the drawee. If the drawee refuses to accept the bill, the holder will then have an immediate right of recourse against prior parties.

"After sight" means after presentment for acceptance. So a bill payable after sight must necessarily be presented for acceptance before the holder can sue upon it.

Requisites of Acceptance

The acceptance of a bill is the signification by the drawee of his assent to the order of the drawer. An acceptance is invalid unless it complies with the following conditions:

- It must be written on the bill and be signed by the drawee. The mere signature of the drawee without additional words is sufficient;
- It must not express that the drawee will perform his promise by any other means than the payment of money.

A bill is usually complete when it is placed before the drawee for acceptance. However, the Bills of Exchange Ordinance provides that a bill may be accepted before it has been signed by the drawer, or while otherwise incomplete, or when it is overdue, or after it has been dishonoured by a previous refusal to accept, or by non-payment. When a bill payable after sight is dishonoured by non-acceptance and the drawee subsequently accepts it, the holder, in the absence of any different agreement, is entitled to have the bill accepted as of the date of first presentment to the drawee for acceptance.

Liability of Acceptor

Unless the drawee of a bill accepts it, the drawee is not liable for the bill at all. Once the drawee accepts the bill, however, that drawee becomes the primary liable party. In this regard, Section 54 of the Bills of Exchange Ordinance provides that the acceptor of a bill, by accepting it, engages that he will pay according to the terms of his acceptance. The acceptor is also precluded from denying to a holder in due course:

- The existence of the drawer, the genuineness of his signature, and his capacity and authority to draw the bill.
- In the case of a bill payable to a drawer's order, the then capacity of the drawer to indorse, but not the genuineness or validity of his indorsement.
- In the case of a bill payable to the order of a third person, the existence of the payee and his then capacity to indorse, but not the genuineness or validity of his indorsement.

Bankers should note that, although the acceptor of a bill is stopped from denying to a holder in due course the drawer's existence, capacity, and authority to draw the bill and the genuineness of his signature 'as drawer,' the acceptor may deny the genuineness or validity of the drawer's indorsement. If the bill is payable to his order or if it is payable to the order of a third person, the acceptor may deny the genuineness or validity of the latter's indorsement.

General and Qualified Acceptances

An acceptance is either general or qualified. A general acceptance assents without qualification to the order of the drawer. A qualified acceptance, on the other hand, varies the effect of the bill as drawn. In particular, an acceptance is qualified when it is:

- *Conditional*, meaning that payment by the acceptor is dependent on the fulfilment of a condition, such as acceptance of a bill of lading upon evidence of shipment of 100,000 metric tons of goods.
- *Partial*, or an acceptance to pay part of the amount for which the bill is drawn. For example, on a bill drawn for $200,000, "accepted payable for $150,000 only."
- *Local*, or an acceptance to pay only at a particular specified place and not elsewhere: "accepted payable only at XYZ Bank Ltd., Bank Street, Hong Kong."
- *Qualified as to time*, for example, on a bill drawn payable six months after date, "accepted payable twelve months after date."
- The acceptance of one or more of the drawees, but not of all. For example, on a bill drawn on A, B, and C, the acceptance of A only.

Section 44 of the Bills of Exchange Ordinance provides that the holder of a bill may refuse to take a qualified acceptance. If he does not then obtain a general acceptance, he may treat the bill as dishonoured by non-acceptance. Where a qualified acceptance is taken, and the holder does not have an express or implied authorisation from the drawer or an indorser to take a qualified acceptance, or the drawer does not subsequently assent to it, such a drawer or indorser is discharged from his liability on the bill.

However, this does not apply to a partial acceptance of which due notice has been given. When the drawer or indorser of a bill receives notice of a qualified acceptance and does not within a reasonable time express dissent to the holder, that party is deemed to have assented.

Accordingly, a banker should not take a qualified acceptance (except a partial acceptance) without the consent of his customer or correspondent. If the banker is offered a partial acceptance, he will usually take it. This is because the drawer and indorsers will be discharged. However, due notice must be given to them.

Bills Payable After Sight

As the maturity of a bill payable after sight cannot be fixed until it is presented for acceptance, unreasonable delay in making presentment may sometimes prejudice the position of the drawer or of an indorser, especially in cases where the financial position of the drawee is deteriorating.

The Bills of Exchange Ordinance provides that, subject to certain provisions, when a bill payable after sight is negotiated, the holder must either present it for acceptance or negotiate it within a reasonable time. If he does not do so, the drawer and all indorsers prior to that holder are discharged. In determining what is a reasonable time within the meaning of this provision, regard must be made to the nature of the bill, the usage of trade with respect to similar bills, and the facts of the particular case.

Rules for Presentment for Acceptance

Section 41(1) of the Bills of Exchange Ordinance provides that a bill is regarded as duly presented for acceptance when it is presented in accordance with the following rules:

- The presentment must be made by or on behalf of the holder to the drawee, or to some person authorised to accept or refuse acceptance on his behalf, at a reasonable hour on a business day and before the bill is overdue;
- Where a bill is addressed to two or more drawees, who are not partners, presentment must be made to them all, unless one has authority to accept for all, then presentment may be made to him only;
- Where the drawee is dead, presentment may be made to his personal representative;
- Where the drawee or assignee is bankrupt, presentment may be made to him or to his trustee;
- Where authorised by agreement or usage, a presentment through the post office is sufficient.

The Bills of Exchange Ordinance makes no provision concerning the place where a bill should be presented for acceptance. Usually, the bill will be presented for acceptance at the address of the drawee as stated on the bill but, if no address is given, presentment will be excused if the holder after exercising reasonable diligence cannot find the drawee.

Presentment for Acceptance Excused

Section 41(2) of the Bills of Exchange Ordinance provides that presentment for acceptance is excused, and a bill may be treated as dishonoured by non-acceptance, where:

- The drawee is dead or bankrupt, or is a fictitious person or a person not having capacity to contract by bill;
- After the exercise of reasonable diligence, such presentment cannot be effected;
- Although the presentment has been irregular, acceptance has been refused on some other ground.

The Ordinance specifically provides that even if the holder has reason to believe that the bill, on presentment, will be dishonoured, this does not excuse presentment.

Negotiation of a Bill

A bill is negotiated when it is transferred from one person to another in such a manner that the transferee is construed as the holder of the bill. Not every delivery of a bill has the option of negotiating it. For example, an indorsement followed by delivery may be effected only to facilitate the collection of the instrument. Hence, the indorser usually adds words expressing his intention, such as "pay Bank X for collection."

Transfer or negotiation is easiest where the bill is payable to bearer. It can be effected by the mere delivery of the bill by the transferor to the transferee. On the other hand, an order bill is negotiated by the indorsement of the payee, or the indorsee to whom it has been specially indorsed, and by the delivery of the instrument. If the holder of a bill payable to his order transfers it without executing an indorsement, the transferee acquires such title as the transferor has in the bill. Furthermore, the transferee acquires the right to have the transferor's indorsement. However, unless such an indorsement is obtained, the transferee remains a mere assignee and cannot acquire rights superior to the transferor's.

In practice, the transferor of a bill is asked to indorse it even where the instrument is payable to the bearer. This is because the transferee wishes to ensure that the transferor is liable on the bill as indorser. If a bearer bill is transferred without being indorsed, the transferor is known as a 'transferor by delivery.' Such a party is not liable on the bill. But by negotiating the bill, the transferor by delivery warrants to his immediate transferee that the bill is what it purports to be, that he has the right to transfer it, and that he is not aware of any fact that renders it valueless.

This warranty, which is given only to an immediate transferee that is a holder for value, enables the transferee to bring an action on the bill against the transferor. If the bill is worthless, the transferee may seek reimbursement of the amount paid by suing the transferor. The transferee's position must not be confused with the drawee's. A holder who presents a bill for acceptance or for payment does not seek to transfer it, and does not warrant the authenticity or validity of the instrument to the drawee.

Restrictions on Negotiability

Not every bill can be negotiated. In the first place, the drawer may insert in the bill words prohibiting transfer or evincing an intention that the bill be non-transferable. Thus, where a bill is made payable to 'Mr. A only,' a purported transferee cannot become its holder, let alone a holder in due course, or be entitled to sue on it. The intention to prohibit negotiation must, however, appear clearly on the face of the bill. If the drawer makes a bill payable to a particular person without adding the words "or order," but fails to add words prohibiting transfer, the bill is treated as payable to that person's order. Similarly, the mere cancellation of the printed words "or bearer" or "or order" in a bill does not in itself restrict its negotiability.

The second method that can be used to restrict the negotiability of a bill is the execution of a restrictive indorsement. An indorsement is restrictive if it either prohibits further transfer or states that it is not executed to effect transfer but constitutes a mere authority to the indorsee to deal with the bill as directed. Examples are indorsements accompanied by the words "pay D only," or "pay D for the Account of D" or "Pay D for collection."

A statement to the effect that consideration has been furnished by a third party does not render restrictive the indorsement which it accompanies. An indorsement of a bill to a specified person without the addition of the words "or order" is not restrictive. The bill remains negotiable and is to be treated as if the words in question are included.

A restrictive indorsement denies the indorsee the power to transfer the bill unless it expressly authorises him to do so. But the indorsee who takes the bill under the restrictive indorsement retains the right to receive payment of the instrument and is entitled to sue any party that is liable to his transferor. Where a restrictive indorsement authorises further transfer, all subsequent indorsees take the bill with the same rights and are subject to the same liabilities as the 'restricted indorsee.'

It follows that an indorsee who takes a bill under a restrictive indorsement and who is accordingly aware of the limitation of the title of the transferor, cannot be a holder in due course. At the same time, the restrictive indorsement does not put the drawee or acceptor on enquiry. Furthermore, the drawee is not liable to the indorser who restricted transfer if the indorsee misappropriates the amount paid to him against the bill.

In practice, a bill of exchange is negotiated a number of times following its discount. In some cases, a bill may be transferred back to the party already liable for it, such as the drawer or an indorser. Under section 37 of the Bills of Exchange Ordinance, such a party may reissue the bill and negotiate it over again. But he is not entitled to enforce the bill against a party to whom he has previously been liable, such as an indorser who became a party to the bill in the meantime.

Dishonour of a Bill

Most bills of exchange are duly accepted when presented for acceptance, and duly paid when presented for payment. However, in some cases, acceptance or payment of a bill is refused and the bill is then said to be dishonoured by non-acceptance or by non-payment. In general, the person who presented the bill (usually a banker) must give notice of dishonour to prior parties and take the appropriate steps to have the bill noted or protested. Failure to take proper steps promptly may have serious consequences.

Dishonour by Non-Acceptance

Section 42 of the Bills of Exchange Ordinance provides that when a bill is duly presented for acceptance and is not accepted within the customary time, the person presenting it must treat it as dishonoured by non-acceptance. If he does not, the holder shall lose his right of recourse against the drawer and indorsers.

The person who presents a bill for acceptance should deliver it up to the drawee if asked to do so. The drawee is entitled to retain it for 24 hours. At the end of that time, he must redeliver the bill as either accepted or unaccepted. In *Jeune v. Ward (1818) B & Ald 653*, where the drawee to a bill refused to accept it and the bill remained in his hands for a considerable time and was ultimately destroyed by him, it was held that the drawee was not liable as an acceptor.

Sector 43(1) of the Ordinance further provides that a bill is dishonoured by non-acceptance:

- When it is duly presented for acceptance, and such an acceptance as is prescribed by this Ordinance is refused or cannot be obtained;
- When presentment for acceptance is excused and the bill is not accepted.

Although "such an acceptance as is prescribed by this Ordinance" may be either general or qualified, it is specifically provided that the holder of a bill may refuse to take a qualified acceptance, and if he does not obtain an unqualified acceptance, he may treat the bill as dishonoured by non-acceptance.

The Bills of Exchange Ordinance provides that when a bill is dishonoured by non-acceptance, an immediate right of recourse against the drawer and indorsers accrues to the holder, and no presentment for payment is necessary.

The banker should note that the holder's 'right of recourse' is not to be confused with a 'right of action.' The holder will only acquire a right of action if he complies with the requirements of the Ordinance, such as giving notice of dishonour, and protesting the bill when necessary. If the holder complies with these requirements, he will then have an immediate right of action against the drawer and indorsers. The holder need not present the bill for payment before starting his action.

Section 18(2) of the Bills of Exchange Ordinance provides that a bill may be accepted after it has been previously dishonoured. It leaves it to the holder's discretion whether to permit the drawee to accept the bill or not in these circumstances.

Dishonour by Non-Payment

Section 47(1) of the Bills of Exchange Ordinance provides that a bill is dishonoured by non-payment:

- When it is duly presented for payment and payment is refused or cannot be obtained;
- When presentment is excused and the bill is overdue and unpaid.

When a bill is dishonoured by non-payment, an immediate right of recourse against the drawer and indorsers accrues to the holder. The consequences are similar to those which flow from dishonour by non-acceptance. The holder will have a right of action against the drawer and indorsers, provided that he complies with the requirements of the Ordinance, such as giving notice of dishonour, and protesting the bill when necessary.

When a bill is dishonoured by non-acceptance, there is no right of action on the bill or right of recourse against the drawee because he is not a party to the bill. But when an accepted bill is dishonoured by non-payment, there is an immediate right of action against the drawee in his capacity of acceptor. In this regard, Section 52(3) of the Bills of Exchange Ordinance provides that in order to render the acceptor of a bill liable, it is not necessary to protest it, or that notice of dishonour should be given to him.

Notice of Dishonour

If a holder wishes to preserve his rights against the drawer and indorsers of a dishonoured bill, the most important step he is usually required to take is to give due notice of dishonour to these parties. Section 48 of the Bills of Exchange Ordinance provides that when a bill has been dishonoured by non-acceptance or by non-payment, notice of dishonour must be given to the drawer and each indorser.

Any drawer or indorser to whom such notice is not given is discharged, although the discharge is not necessarily absolute. This is because a bill dishonoured by non-acceptance may subsequently come into the hands of a holder in due course. The ordinance expressly provides that, in this event, the rights of the holder in due course are not prejudiced by the omission to give notice of dishonour.

There are several exceptional cases where notice of dishonour is unnecessary. It has been considered unnecessary to give notice of dishonour to the acceptor of a bill. Where a bill is dishonoured by non-acceptance and due notice of dishonour is given, the Bills of Exchange Ordinance provides that it is unnecessary to give notice of a subsequent dishonour by non-payment unless the bill in the meantime has been accepted.

Section 50(2) specifies the following cases as cases where notice of dishonour is dispensed with:

- Where, after the exercise of reasonable diligence, notice, as required by the ordinance, cannot be given to or does not reach the drawer or indorser sought to be charged;
- By waiver, express or implied. Notice of dishonour may be waived before the time of giving notice has arrived or after the omission to give due notice;
- As regards the drawer of a bill, in the following cases, namely:
  i. Where the drawer and drawee are the same person;
  ii. Where the drawee is a fictitious person or a person not having capacity to contract;
  iii. Where the drawer is the person to whom the bill is presented for payment;
  iv. Where the drawee or acceptor is, as between himself and the drawer, under no obligation to accept or pay the bill;
  v. Where the drawer has countermanded payment;
- As regards the indorser of a bill, in the following case, namely:
  i. Where the drawee is a fictitious person or a person not having capacity to contract, and the indorser was aware of the fact at the time he indorsed the bill;
  ii. Where the indorser is the person to whom the bill is presented for payment;
  iii. Where the bill was accepted or made for his accommodation.

Validity of Notice

To be valid, a notice of dishonour must comply with the rules laid down in the Bills of Exchange Ordinance. The provisions may be considered under the following headings: who gives the notice; who benefits from the notice; the form of the notice; to whom the notice must be given; and when the notice must be given.

- **Who gives the notice.** Notice of dishonour must be given by or on behalf of the holder, or by or on behalf of an indorser who, at the time of giving it, is himself liable on the bill. Hence, notice cannot be given by an indorser "without recourse," or by an indorser who has himself been freed from liability by the holder's delay in giving notice to him. Notice of dishonour may be given by an agent either in his own name, or in the name of any party entitled to give notice whether that party is his principal or not.
- **Who benefits from the notice.** Notice of dishonour given by or for the holder is effective not only for the benefit of the holder but also for all subsequent holders and for all prior indorsers who have a right of recourse against the party to whom it is given. For example, A, B, C, and D are successive indorsers of a bill that is dishonoured. D gives notice to A, B, and C. Neither B nor C gives notice to A, but B and C each receive the benefit of D's notice because B and C are prior indorsers with a right of recourse against A.

  If there had been a subsequent holder (that is subsequent to D), that holder would not have received the benefit of D's notice. Accordingly, if a holder wishes to retain his rights against prior parties, it is in his own interest to give notice to all such parties rather than leave it to a previous indorser to give notice to parties prior to him.
- **The form of the notice.** The notice may be given in writing or by personal communication and may be given in any terms that sufficiently identify the bill and state that the bill had been dishonoured by non-acceptance or non-payment. The return of a dishonoured bill to the drawer or an indorser is, in point of form, deemed a sufficient notice of dishonour.

  A written notice need not be signed. It appears that there is no decided case as yet to determine whether an electronic communication, such as e-mail, is a valid form of notice.
- **To whom the notice must be given.** Where notice of dishonour is required to be given to any person, it may be given either to the party himself or to his agent. It may be the case that if a person is authorised to indorse a bill, he is also authorised to receive the notice of dishonour. However, the notice given to the referee is not sufficient.

  Where the drawer or indorser is dead and the party giving notice knows it, the notice must be given to a personal representative. If the death is known, there should be no difficulty in ascertaining whether there is a duly constituted personal representative or not by searching the Probate Registry. If the death is not known or no grant of probate or administration appears to have been made, sending the notice to the last known place of business or residence of the deceased would be sufficient.

  Where the drawer or indorser is bankrupt, notice may be given either to the party himself or to the trustee in bankruptcy (Official Receiver). Where a partnership has been dissolved and there are continuing partners carrying on the firm business, notice given to the continuing partners will be sufficient to charge a retiring partner. Where there are two or more drawers or indorsers who are not partners, notice must be given to each of them unless one of them has authority to receive such notice for the others.

- **When the notice must be given.** Notice may be given as soon as the bill is dishonoured or within a reasonable time thereafter. In the absence of special circumstances, notice is not deemed to have been given within a reasonable time, unless:
  i. Where the person giving and the person receiving notice reside in the same place, the notice is given or sent off in time to reach the latter on the day after the dishonour of the bill
  ii. Where the person giving and the person receiving notice reside in different places, the notice is sent off on the day after the dishonour of the bill, if there be a post at a convenient hour on that day, and if there be no such post on that day then by the next post thereafter

The Bills of Exchange Ordinance further provides that where a bill, when dishonoured, is in the hands of an agent, he may either himself give notice to the parties liable on the bill or he may give notice to his principal. If he gives notice to his principal, he must do so within the same time as if he were the holder and the principal, upon receipt of such notice, has himself the same time for giving notice as if the agent had been an independent holder.

In practice, a bank that collects a bill on behalf of a customer gives notice only to its principal, that is, to its customer, leaving that principal to give notice only to prior parties. However, if the bank is a holder for value and it wants to claim against prior parties, it will try to give notice to those parties.

Any party who receives notice of dishonour (and this includes a principal who receives notice from his agent) has the same time for giving notice to antecedent parties that the holder has after the dishonour.

Where a notice of dishonour is duly addressed and posed, the sender is deemed to have given due notice of dishonour, notwithstanding any miscarriage by the post office.

Finally, Section 50(1) of the Ordinance provides that delay in giving notice of dishonour is excused where the delay is caused by circumstances beyond the control of the party giving notice and not imputable to his default, misconduct, or negligence. When the cause of delay ceases to operate, the notice must be given with reasonable diligence.

Noting and Protesting

When a bill is dishonoured by non-acceptance or by non-payment, it may be necessary to obtain formal proof that it has been duly presented and dishonoured. The first step to this end is known as 'noting' the bill and the second step is known as 'protesting' it.

To have a bill noted, the bill should be handed to a notary public, who will present the bill again to the drawee for acceptance, or to the acceptor for payment, or to the bank where it was accepted payable. If acceptance or payment, as the case may be, is still refused, the bill is then noted. The notary, or his clerk, makes a note on the bill itself consisting of the notary's register where full particulars of the noting are kept. He also attaches to the bill a slip or ticket on which is written the answer, if any, given by the drawee or acceptor.

A "protest" is a declaration by a notary in a formal document under seal. A printed form is usually employed. A protest must contain a copy of the bill, and must be signed by the notary making it, and must specify the person at whose request the bill is protested and the place and date of protest, the cause or reason for protesting the bill, the demand made, and the answer given, if any, or the fact that the drawee or acceptor could not be found.

Inland Bills

An inland bill is a bill which is, or on the fact of it purports to be, both drawn and payable within Hong Kong, or drawn within Hong Kong upon some person resident therein. Any other bill is a foreign bill.

Where an inland bill has been dishonoured it may, if the holder thinks fit, be noted for non-acceptance or non-payment as the case may be; but it is unnecessary to note or protest an inland bill in order to preserve the recourse against the drawer or indorser.

In practice, it is quite usual to note and protest an inland bill if it bears foreign indorsements so that the foreign indorsers may be provided with formal proof of dishonour. Further, if it is not clear whether a bill is an inland or a foreign bill, prudent bankers should treat it as a foreign bill and have it noted and protested.

Foreign Bills

The legal requirements concerning foreign bills are very different from those relating to inland bills. Section 51(2) of the Bills of Exchange Ordinance provides that where a foreign bill, appearing on the face of it to be such, has been dishonoured by non-acceptance, it must be duly protested for non-acceptance. Where such a bill, which has not been previously dishonoured by non-acceptance, is dishonoured by non-payment, it must be duly protested for non-payment. If these rules are not observed, the drawer and the indorsers are discharged from all liability on the bill.

Hong Kong law thus makes it compulsory to protest a foreign bill only once. But the Ordinance does permit the holder, if he wishes, to protest a bill for non-payment even though it has previously been protested for non-acceptance. This is quite often done because the law of many other countries provides that protest for non-acceptance does not excuse protest on subsequent non-payment, and the holder of a bill in Hong Kong may wish to protect his position as against a foreign drawer or indorser.

Although the drawer and indorsers are discharged by failure to protest a foreign bill, the liability of the acceptor is unaffected.

Time Allowed for Protest

There are strict rules governing the time allowed for protest. The Bills of Exchange Ordinance provides that when a bill is noted or protested, it may be noted on the day of its dishonour and must be noted not later than the next succeeding business day. When a bill has been duly noted, the protest may be later extended as of the date of noting.

Noting a bill is thus an action that must be attended to very promptly. The formal protest of the bill may be completed at a later date. In theory, a bill may be protested within the prescribed time without first having been noted, but in practice it is more convenient to have it noted first.

The Ordinance also provides that delay in noting or protesting is excused when the delay is caused by circumstances beyond the control of the holder, and not imputable to his default, misconduct, or negligence. When the cause of delay ceases to operate, the bill must be noted or protested with reasonable diligence.

Place of Protest

In general, a bill must be protested at the place where it is dishonoured; this will usually be the place of presentment for acceptance or payment. However, when a bill is presented through the post office and returned by post dishonoured, it may be protested at the place to which it is returned, in which case it must be noted or protested on the day of its return if received during business hours, and if not received during business hours, then not later than the next business day.

When a bill drawn payable at the place of business or residence of some person other than the drawee has been dishonoured by non-acceptance, it must be protested for non-payment at the place where it is expressed to be payable, and no further presentment for payment to, or demand on, the drawee is necessary.

Discharge of a Bill

When a bill is discharged, it ceases to be a negotiable instrument and all rights based on it are extinguished. What is the position of a person who, in good faith and for value, takes a bill that does not show on its face that it has been discharged?

It is suggested that where such a party is able to establish that they are a holder in due course, they will be entitled to enforce the bill. However, someone can be a holder in due course only if he takes the bill before it is overdue. It follows, then, that the problem of negotiating a discharged bill could arise only in the case of bills payable on demand or where a bill payable is discharged before maturity.

A bill is discharged in any of the following five ways:

- By payment in due course;
- When the acceptor becomes its holder after its maturity;

- By express waiver or renunciation;
- By cancellation;
- In certain cases, by a material alteration executed without the assent of the parties liable on the instrument.

Payment in Due Course

Under the Bills of Exchange Ordinance, a bill is discharged by payment in due course when the drawee pays it at or after maturity to a holder, provided the drawee makes payment in good faith and without notice of any defect in the holder's title. The word 'holder' retains its technical meaning in this context—it encompasses the payee, the indorsee, and the bearer of a bill.

A transferee of an order bill who holds the instrument under a forged indorsement is, of course, not a holder. Payment to such a transferee is, therefore, not payment in due course and does not discharge the bill. But payment of a stolen bearer bill to a thief constitutes payment in due course as the thief or his transferee does not hold the bill under an indorsement. Payment in good faith by the drawee to an indorsee who has obtained the bill by fraud also constitutes a discharge.

The payment of a bill by the drawee does not constitute a discharge. If the bill is payable not to the drawer's own order but to that of a third party, the drawer who pays it is entitled to enforce it against the acceptor, but may not re-issue it. If the bill is payable to the drawer's own order and is paid by him after he has negotiated it to a third party, the drawer is restored to his former rights against the acceptor and any antecedent parties. Hence, he is entitled to strike out his own indorsement and to negotiate the bill over again. This is also the position of an indorser who pays the bill.

When a drawer pays a bill to the holder, he becomes entitled to the benefit of securities given to the holder by the acceptor. This is because the holder and the indorsers are sureties of the acceptor's debt to the holder. Accordingly, they are subrogated to the rights which the holder, as creditor, has against the acceptor (the debtor).

Acceptor Becomes Holder

A bill is discharged if its acceptor becomes its holder at or after maturity. The principle applies only if the acceptor acquires the bill in his own right. Thus, if the acceptor becomes the executor of the holder's estate, the bill is discharged. However, this would probably not be the case if the acceptor became an administrator as he would then not hold the bill "in his own right." If a bill, accepted jointly by a number of drawees, is indorsed at its maturity to one of them, it is discharged. The remaining acceptors cannot be sued on the bill although they may be liable to contribute as joint debtors.

Express Waiver

A bill is discharged if, at or after its maturity, the holder expressly and absolutely renounces his rights against the acceptor either in writing or by delivering the bill to him. A bill is also discharged if it is delivered to the acceptor's executors or administrators with the intention that it be discharged. An acceptance by the holder of the acceptor's offer to pay a composition is not a renunciation of the holder's rights. Other parties to the bill may also be released from their liability by the holder's renunciation of his rights. However, the holder's waiver does not affect the rights of a subsequent holder in due course.

Cancellation

A bill is discharged by an apparent cancellation, intentionally executed by the holder or his agent. The holder or agent may also discharge any party liable on the bill by cancelling his signature. In such a case, any indorser who had initially enjoyed a right of recourse against the party concerned would also be discharged. A cancellation is effective only if it is obvious. A holder is entitled to prove that a cancellation was effected unintentionally under a mistake of fact or without his authority. The cancellation is then inoperative.

Alteration

A bill is voided if the instrument itself, or an acceptance executed on it, is materially altered without the assent of all the parties to it. The only party who remains bound by it is the one who made the alteration and, presumably, all those who took the bill subsequently. It is provided that where a bill has been materially altered but the alteration is not apparent, it may be enforced by a holder in due course "according to its original tenor."

For example, if the amount of a bill has been fraudulently altered from $100,000 to $1,000,000, the holder in due course would be able to enforce payment of $100,000. An alteration on a bill is considered apparent if it would be noticed by a person who intends to acquire it and scrutinises it with reasonable care.

The Bills of Exchange Ordinance treats certain alterations as material. These include:

- Alteration of the date;
- Alteration of the sum payable;
- Alteration of the time of payment;
- Alteration of the place of payment;
- Where the bill has been accepted generally, the addition of a place of payment without the acceptor's assent.

Whether any other alteration is material or not is a question of fact. An alteration that is not deliberately executed by any person but is caused by an accident, does not invalidate the bill. An alteration made before a bill is completely issued, such as the alteration by the drawer of a purported place of issue inserted by an acceptor who has accepted the bill in blank, is not a material alteration. Of course, the very same alteration would be material if made after the bill had been issued.

Promissory Notes

As with bills of exchange, the law relating to promissory notes is principally the Bills of Exchange Ordinance. Section 89(1) defines a promissory note as "an unconditional promise in writing made by one person to another signed by the maker, engaging to pay, on demand or at a fixed or determinable future time, a sum certain in money to, or to the order of, a specified person [the payee] or to bearer." An instrument which promises the performance of some other act in addition to the payment of money is not a promissory note.

A document in which the person signing it agrees unconditionally to pay a sum certain in money to another 'on or before' a specified date is a promissory note, there being a specified date at which, if payment is not made, the holder can sue the person making the promise. In *Tsoi Kan v. Chung Tsim Kwai*, it was held that a Chinese borrowing note which contained a statement that the lender could demand repayment at any time was a promissory note, on the basis that there was a definite promise by the borrower to repay on demand. In *Li Fung Man v. Tam Chuk U* it was held that a document was a promissory note because the words 'no fault shall be made' contained an implied promise to pay on demand.

A note is inchoate and incomplete until its delivery to the payee or bearer. Like bills of exchange, promissory notes may be payable with interest or by stated instalments. In practice, the maker of a note promises to make payments monthly, quarterly, or half-yearly and to pay interest at a specified rate on the amount outstanding. It is also quite usual to insert a provision that, upon default in payment of any instalment, the whole outstanding balance shall become due.

An instrument in the form of a note payable to a maker's order is not a note within the definition unless and until it is indorsed by the maker. A note is not invalid by reason only that it contains a pledge of collateral security with authority to sell or dispose thereof. A note which is, or on the face of it purports to be, both made and payable within the Hong Kong SAR is an inland note. Any other note is a foreign note.

The common forms of promissory notes include ordinary promissory notes, colloquially known as IOUs ('I owe you'), cashier orders, bank drafts, and bank notes. Bank notes differ in some important respects from ordinary promissory notes in that they may be reissued after payment. In Hong Kong, bank notes issued by the three commercial banks—Hong Kong and Shanghai Banking Corporation Limited, Standard Chartered Bank (Hong Kong) Limited, and Bank of China (Hong Kong) Limited—are part of the currency of the realm and put on statutory basis.

Promissory Notes and Bills of Exchange

Section 95(1) of the Bills of Exchange Ordinance states that the provisions relating to bills of exchange apply, with the necessary modifications, to promissory notes, except where otherwise provided. However, there are differences between a promissory note and a bill of exchange:

- A promissory note is a promise to pay while a bill of exchange is an order to pay;
- A note has a maker and a payee as the two main parties while a bill has the drawer and the drawee, and the payee, who may be the drawer or a third party;
- Presentment for acceptance and acceptance are not required for promissory notes;
- A promissory note does not require protest to establish liability when it is dishonoured.

Parties to a Promissory Note

The two main parties to a note are the maker and the payee. The others are the indorser and the holder or bearer.

- The maker is the person who is primarily liable on the note and corresponds to the acceptor of a bill of exchange. The maker promises to pay the note according to its tenor, and is precluded from denying to a holder in due course the existence of the payee and his then capacity to indorse.
- The payee is the person being promised payment under the note.
- The indorser bears the same meaning as for bills of exchange. The first indorser of a note corresponds with the drawer of an accepted bill payable to a drawer's order.
- The holder or bearer is defined in the same way as in bills of exchange.

A promissory note may be made by two or more makers, who may be liable on it jointly, or jointly and severally, according to its tenor. Usually the words 'We promise to pay' are used where joint liability is intended, and 'We jointly and severally promise to pay' are used to indicate joint and several liability. Where a note says 'I promise to pay' and is signed by two or more persons, it is deemed to be their joint and several note (section 91(2), BOEO).

Where the makers are jointly liable on the note, if the holder sues one or more, but not all, of the makers on the note, the defendant(s) may apply to court for a stay of proceedings until all the makers are joined in the proceedings: Order 15, Rules of the High Court. Where the liability of the makers is joint and several, the holder may elect to choose one or some or the makers without the need to join in all of them.

Negotiation of Promissory Notes

Promissory notes may be negotiated in the same way as bills of exchange. Thus a note payable to bearer is negotiable by delivery alone, whereas a note payable to order is negotiated by the indorsement of the holder and then completed by delivery.

There is a special rule which applies to promissory notes, namely that where a note payable on demand is negotiated, it is not deemed to be overdue for the purpose of affecting the holder with defects of title of which he had no notice, by reason that it appears that a reasonable time for presenting it for payment has elapsed since its issue. This may be contrasted with the rule relating to bills, namely that where an overdue bill is negotiated, it can only be negotiated subject to any defect of title affecting it at its maturity. Hence, no person who takes it can acquire or give a better title than that which the person from whom he took it had.

Liability of the Maker

The maker of a promissory note is the principal debtor. He is also the party primarily liable on the instrument, which differentiates the maker from the drawer of a bill of exchange. The maker's obligations correspond with those of the acceptor of a bill of exchange, rather than those of the drawer.

The liability of the maker of a note is defined in Section 94 of the Bills of Exchange Ordinance. By making a note, the maker:

- Engages that he will pay the note according to its tenor;
- Is precluded from denying to a holder in due course the existence of the payee and his then capacity to indorse.

Where, in the body of it, a promissory note is made payable at a particular place, it must be presented for payment at that place in order to render the maker liable. In any other case, presentment for payment is not necessary in order to render the maker liable.

These points are important when considering the position of the maker under the Limitation Ordinance, Cap. 347. In the usual case, the maker of a promissory note payable on demand remains liable for six years from the date of the note, or of its issue, if later. After six years, the right of action against the maker becomes statute-barred by virtue of the Limitation Ordinance. However, if a note is, in the body of it, made payable at a particular place, the statutory period runs from the date of its presentment because that is the date when the liability of the maker arises.

Liability of the Indorser

The indorser of a note engages that, on due presentment, it will be paid according to its tenor and that, if it is dishonoured, the indorser will compensate the holder or any subsequent indorser who is compelled to pay it, provided that the requisite proceedings on dishonour are duly taken. Note that this is not expressly provided in the Bills of Exchange Ordinance, but it clearly seems to be the effect of a number of its provisions.

The Ordinance does expressly provide that presentment for payment is necessary in order to render the indorser liable. Section 93(3) provides that where a note is, in the body of it, made payable at a particular place, presentment at that place is necessary in order to render an indorser liable. When a place of payment is indicated by way of memorandum only, presentment at that place is sufficient to render the indorser liable, but a presentment to the maker elsewhere, if sufficient in other respects, suffices to make the indorser liable.

The Bills of Exchange Ordinance also provides that where a note payable on demand has been indorsed, it must be presented for payment within a reasonable time of indorsement. If this is not done, the indorser is discharged. The determination of what is a 'reasonable time' should take into account the nature of the instrument, the usage of trade, and the facts of the particular case.

There is a similar provision in the Ordinance with reference to bills payable on demand but, in practice, there is an important difference between bills and notes. A bill payable on demand is usually intended to be presented and paid immediately, whereas a promissory note payable on demand is often intended as a security. Therefore, 'reasonable time' with regard to notes usually connotes a much longer time than with regard to bills.

Summary

- A negotiable instrument and the rights it carries are capable of transfer by delivery of possession. A holder of the instrument may acquire a better title to the instrument than the person who transferred it to him. The person to whom an instrument is negotiated can sue on it in his own name. The transaction represented by the negotiable instrument is independent of the underlying transaction in respect of which the instrument was issued.
- A bill of exchange is a negotiable instrument that is an unconditional order in writing, addressed by one person to another, signed by the person giving it, and requires the person to whom it is addressed to pay on demand or at a fixed or determinable future time a sum certain in money to, or to the order of, a specified person, or to bearer.
- There are at least two parties to every bill: the drawer and the drawee. The drawer is the party that makes the order. The drawee is the party to whom the bill is addressed. The payee, the party to whom the bill is payable, may either be a third party or is the drawer as well. The drawee becomes the acceptor when the drawee accepts the bill of exchange and warrants payment according to the tenor of the acceptance.
- A holder for value is the holder of a bill for which value has been given. A holder in due course is a holder who had taken a bill that is complete and regular on the face of it, even though that bill may have been previously dishonoured or the transferor had defective title to it.
- When the payee negotiates a bill, that payee is generally asked to indorse it by signing on the back of the bill. The payee therefore warrants that the bill will be duly accepted and paid, and that if the bill is dishonoured, the payee will compensate the holder or a subsequent indorser that is compelled to pay the bill. The indorser incurs liability towards every party that acquires the bill after that indorser and is compelled to pay it.
- The banker must know the legal issues around bills of exchange, including dating and signing, requisites for presentment of acceptance, general and qualified acceptances, negotiation of a bill, and dishonour of a bill.

- The dishonour of a bill is of particular interest because the person presenting the bill is usually a banker. If acceptance or payment of a bill is refused, the person who presented it must give notice of dishonour to prior parties and take the appropriate steps to have the bill noted or protested. Failure to take proper steps promptly may have serious consequences.
- As with bills of exchange, the law relating to promissory notes is principally the Bills of Exchange Ordinance. Section 89(1) defines a promissory note as "an unconditional promise in writing made by one person to another signed by the maker, engaging to pay, on demand or at a fixed or determinable future time, a sum certain in money to, or to the order of, a specified person [the payee] or to bearer."
- The two main parties to a note are the maker and the payee. The others are the indorser and the holder or bearer. The maker of a promissory note is the principal debtor. He is also the party primarily liable on the instrument, which differentiates the maker from the drawer of a bill of exchange. The maker's obligations correspond with those of the acceptor of a bill of exchange, rather than those of the drawer.

Key Terms

acceptor
accommodation party
after sight
bearer
bill of exchange
Bills of Exchange Ordinance
dishonour by non-acceptance
dishonour by non-payment
dishonour of a bill
drawee
drawer
foreign bill
general acceptance
holder
holder in due course
holder of value
indorsement
indorser
inland bill
IOU
maker
negotiable instruments
notice of dishonour
payee
presentment for acceptance
promissory note
qualified acceptance
right of action
right of recourse
transferee
transferor by delivery

Study Guide

1. Define what a bill of exchange is. How does it differ from a promissory note?
2. What might be the roles that a bank could take as a party to a bill of exchange? Can a bank be a drawer? A drawee?

3. Suppose a holder of a bill of exchange comes to your bank to have the bill accepted. Detail the steps that you, as the bank's duly authorised representative, should take before binding your bank to be an acceptor of the bill.
4. Assume that your bank is offered a qualified acceptance on a bill of exchange it presented on behalf of a customer. What do you need to do before agreeing to the offer?
5. What might be the roles a bank can assume in terms of promissory notes?

Further Reading

Bills of Exchange Ordinance website, http://www.hklii.org/hk/legis/en/ord/19/.

Chan Bo-ching Simon. 2000, *Hong Kong Banking Law and Practice Vol. 1*. First Edition. Hong Kong: Hong Kong Institute of Bankers.

Limitation Ordinance website, http://www.hklii.org/hk/legis/en/ord/347/.

CHAPTER 4

Other Banking Operations

Learning objectives

After studying this chapter, you should be able to:

1. Understand the legal issues around other bank services such as credit cards, investment advice, safe custody, and automated teller machines
2. Appreciate the evolving legal environment for electronic banking
3. Gain awareness about strategies and remedies that bankers can use to protect themselves and their banks from liability

Introduction

In addition to bank accounts and negotiable instruments, banks offer many other services, including credit cards, investment advice, safe custody, direct debiting, and automated teller machines. The way these traditional and new services are delivered is also constantly evolving, resulting in platforms such as Internet and mobile phone banking to complement brick-and-mortar banking. All these give rise to legal issues that bankers must know.

This chapter focuses on the legal and regulatory issues around these other bank services and how bankers should approach them, as well as those around new delivery platforms including Internet banking.

Credit Cards

The term "credit card" generally refers to a plastic card assigned to a cardholder with a credit limit that can be used to purchase goods and services on credit or obtain cash advances. Credit cards permit cardholders to pay for purchases made over a period of time, and to carry a balance from one billing cycle to the next.

The most important feature of a credit card is revolving credit. A credit limit is set for each card; the cardholder is advised of the limit and then agrees that he will not exceed this ceiling. Credit card purchases normally become payable after a free credit period, during which no interest or finance charge is imposed.

The credit card should be distinguished from a charge card. Unlike a credit card, a charge card normally does not have a pre-set spending limit and the cardholder has to repay the outstanding balance billed on the monthly statements in full on the due date. The most popular international charge cards are American Express and Diners Club.

Each credit card bears a specimen signature of its holder and is embossed and encoded by the issuing bank with the holder's name and number. The cardholder can use the credit card to purchase goods or to acquire services from merchants who display the issuer's insignia or logo. The merchant supplies the relevant items against the sales slip imprinted by the imprinter machine, and the cardholder authorises the issuer to debit his account with the amount due. The merchant receives payment from the issuer, who obtains reimbursement from the cardholder.

Settlement by the cardholder may be made either when the account is submitted, in which case he does not incur a finance charge, or by instalments, each of which must not be less than a given percentage (usually 5%) of the outstanding balance at the time of payment. Where the payment is made by instalments, interest is charged on the balance due at the end of each billing cycle (in most cases a calendar month).

Parties to a Credit Card

In terms of the legal environment and contracts, the parties to a credit card operation are the cardholder, merchant, and card issuer (the bank or other issuing organisation), which may also be the merchant acquirer. For an international credit card, the card organisation, for example, Visa International, is also a party.

- **Cardholder.** In Hong Kong, any adult 18 years old or older judged to be creditworthy may become a credit card holder. The definition of creditworthiness typically includes monthly salary (for example, wages of more than HK$4,000 per month) and a clean credit history. Cardholders can use the card as a convenient and flexible medium of exchange. The cardholder is allowed 25 to 30 days (depending on the card issuing bank) from the date of his monthly statement in which to settle the outstanding amount. If a cardholder's statement is normally sent on the first of the month, any purchase he makes on the second of the month could carry the benefit of 55 to 60 days' free credit. However, if the cardholder obtains cash advances over the counter of the member banks or through the ATM network, that transaction will incur interest from the transaction or posting date.
- **Card Issuer.** This is a credit card company that is typically owned by banks or their subsidiaries, which have the capital to finance credit card operations and the ability and means to issue credit facilities. It is the issuer that enters into a contract with the cardholder, in which the issuer undertakes to pay for the purchases and services made by the cardholder within the credit limit granted.
- **Merchant.** There are tens of thousands merchant outlets in Hong Kong that accept credit cards as a means of payment for their goods or services. The card company assigns to each merchant an agreed 'floor limit' up to which the merchant may accept customers' cards at its own discretion, subject to the Restricted Card List. Beyond that limit, the merchant must call the card company's authorisation centre.
- **Merchant Acquirer.** This may be the issuer itself or a separate organisation that enters into agreements with merchants to process their credit card transactions. The acquirer agrees to pay the merchant the amount due from the cardholders (less the merchant's discount), provided that the goods and/or services have been supplied on the agreed terms.
- **Credit Card Association.** The two leading organisations are Visa International and MasterCard International, which were set up by groups of banks and other card issuers in order to sponsor and control card programmes. The credit card association is neither an issuer nor an acquirer. Its role is confined to the participating banks and financial institutions, and basically consists of providing a common interface for them, handling all their international authorisation and settlement systems and operations, and holding the service mark for the card programme.

Legal Environment

In Hong Kong, there is no statutory framework that caters specially for credit cards and no comprehensive rules which must be complied with. However, bankers should be aware of the contents of the Code of Practice on Consumer Credit Data, issued by the Office of the Privacy Commissioner for Personal Data in pursuance of Part III of the Personal Data (Privacy) Ordinance, Cap. 486. The Supervisory Policy Manual on "Credit Card Business" issued by the HKMA provides guidance to banks on managing their credit card business. The Code of Banking Practice sets out the minimum standards pertinent to card services that banks are expected to observe when dealing with their personal customers.

A bona fide credit card scheme operated by a company to any holder of a credit card issued under that scheme is exempted from the coverage of the Money Lenders Ordinance, Cap. 163. In other words, there is no need to have a special licence to operate a credit card programme, provided that the operator has sufficient funds to run the operation.

Cardholder Agreement

The detailed terms of the agreement between the issuer and the cardholder are stipulated in the Cardholder Agreement. In practice, the applicant for credit card services does not know the detailed terms of the Cardholder Agreement when he completes the application form. In fact, he has already agreed to accept the terms and conditions of the Cardholder Agreement upon signing the application. When the application is approved and the card is issued, the cardholder is then required to sign the card to acknowledge receipt of the card and to confirm and accept the terms and conditions of the Cardholder Agreement annexed or attached thereto.

The most important terms in the Cardholder Agreement include the following:

- The cardholder must exercise due diligence to prevent the loss or theft of the card or use of his card/Personal Identification Number (PIN) by any third party.
- The card remains the property of the issuer and the Cardholder Agreement may be cancelled by the issuer at any time without giving any reason/prior written notice to the cardholder.
- The principal cardholder and each supplementary cardholder shall remain jointly and severally liable for the transactions, fees, and interest in the card account(s).
- The issuer will under no circumstances be liable in the event of the card not being honoured by the merchant(s) or for defective goods and services obtained by use of the card. Any complaints against the merchant shall be resolved between the cardholder and merchant. No claim by the cardholder against the merchant(s) may be set-off or counter-claimed against the issuer.
- The issuer will debit the card account with the amount of all card transactions effected by the cardholder and a statement of account will normally be sent to the cardholder monthly.

- The whole outstanding balance of the card account will be payable (a) if there is any breach of the conditions and terms of use by the cardholder, or (b) in the event of the death or bankruptcy of the cardholder.
- The cardholder authorises the issuer to contact the cardholder's employer, banks, credit reference agencies and other information sources and to obtain, exchange, and disclose any information the issuer may require to operate the card account.
- The issuer shall be entitled to employ any debt collection agency to collect the balance from time to time outstanding in the card account. The cardholder shall be liable to indemnify the issuer in full for all costs and expenses incurred by the issuer in respect of such action.
- The cardholder must use the card within the credit limit assigned by the issuer.

What is the bank's liability if a credit card it issued is stolen and charges were subsequently made on it? In *OTB International Credit Card Ltd. v. Michael Au (1980)*, the credit card company sued a cardholder who refused to pay charges that were made after his credit card was stolen. Upon discovering the theft, the cardholder had immediately telephoned the company. Details of the loss were recorded and the cardholder was told to confirm the loss in writing as soon as possible. He did so the following morning. However, the stolen card was honoured by two department stores although the signature on the purchase slips did not resemble the cardholder's signature on the back of the card.

The court ruled that when the cardholder applied to the company for his credit card, he completed and signed an application form. By this action, he expressly agreed to be bound by the rules of membership that were printed on the back of that form, under the title "Terms and Conditions Governing the Use of OTB Card." One provision contains these words:

> "In the event of loss or theft of the card, the Holder must immediately notify the Company by registered mail or telegram and until such notification is received by the Company the Holder will remain responsible for all purchases charged through the use of such Card."

On appeal, the Court of Appeal held that 1) the credit card company could not be held vicariously liable for any negligence on the part of the department stores, since there was no evidence to show they were servants or agents of the appellant, and 2) the clause in the contract relied upon by the credit card company was a reasonable one and was also reasonably necessary for the protection of the legitimate interests of the company and commensurate with the benefits secured to the cardholder under the contract. The cardholder was found to be bound by the terms of his contract.

Bankers should note that the terms and conditions stipulated in the Cardholder Agreements may be held by the court as unenforceable. In *Hang Seng Credit Card Ltd. and Others v. Tsang Nga Lee and Others (2000)* (10 cases in total), it was held that the cost provisions of these credit card agreements were unconscionable and were therefore unenforceable. In these cases, the plaintiffs in the ten actions before the court were seeking to appeal on the decision that the costs of each of the actions should be the fixed costs as set out in the Second Schedule to Order 62, as opposed to costs on an indemnity basis, as claimed by the various plaintiffs in the actions on the basis of the agreement as specified in the Card Members Agreement of various credit cards.

Merchant Agreement

The Merchant Agreement is between the merchant and the acquirer (which may also be the card issuer, i.e., the bank). Under this contract, the acquirer promises to pay the merchant the amount due from the cardholder. (In the case of international cards, for example, Visa or MasterCard, the terms of the merchant agreement are based on the by-laws of the international schemes administered by the international card organisations.) In return, the merchant agrees to pay the acquirer a certain percentage of every purchase of the cardholder, as consideration for the services rendered to the merchant, that is, merchant discount.

In the past, one of the most important terms in the Merchant Agreement was the floor limit set by the acquirer, that is, the merchant cannot supply goods or services to the cardholder without making a credit enquiry if the price exceeds a given figure. Nowadays, due to advanced technology, most merchants in Hong Kong have been provided with a Credit Authorisation Terminal (CAT) and all authorisations of purchases will be directly authorised by the host computer of the issuer via international or local networks. Therefore, the floor limit set for those merchants with CAT will be zero.

Under the contract, the merchant is obliged to check whether the card produced by the cardholder is covered by the card scheme stipulated in the merchant agreement. Then the merchant should compare the signature appearing on the sales slip with the cardholder's signature on the card. If a CAT is provided, the merchant is expected to compare the credit verification code or value from the CAT with those on the card. The merchant is also expected to compare the card number embossed and the indent of the card. The acquirer provides training to staff members of merchants to prevent counterfeiting.

Sales or Services Agreement

This agreement is between the merchant and the cardholder. It is a contract of sale or a contract for the provision of a service, save and except that the payment is guaranteed and reimbursed by the acquirer in accordance with the merchant agreement, and ultimately paid by the cardholder.

In *Re Charge Card Services Ltd. (1989)*, the Court of Appeal held that the contract between a cardholder and a merchant was distinguishable from the contract of sale stipulating the furnishing of a banker's documentary credit covering the price of the goods. The buyer, who furnishes the documentary credit, has the right to select the issuing bank. He can then be expected to bear the loss if his chosen bank becomes insolvent and consequently, defaults.

In cases involving credit cards, the merchant and cardholder agree that a specified procedure, namely payment by the specified issuer, is a valid means for the discharge of debt incurred by the cardholder. When a credit card is used to effect payment, the merchant agrees to accept the sales slip in lieu of the cardholder's personal payment obligation. The parties further agree that the sales slip signed by the cardholder is furnished to the merchant in full discharge of the amount for which it is made out.

International Card Systems

Nearly all credit cards bear a logo or insignia such as "Visa" or "MasterCard." Such a logo is held by a body corporate, set up by a group of banks and other card issuers for the purpose of sponsoring and controlling the card programmes concerned. Each international system has a team of staff members that oversees the activities of member banks, but the system is actually a reflection of its members, rather than an independent servicing organisation. In most jurisdictions, including Hong Kong, it is legal for banks to be members of more than one international card corporation.

Each international system has a set of by-laws and additional operating regulations that members must comply with. The following list gives a general idea of the subjects covered by the detailed regulations:

- Use of logs and service marks;
- Plastic card specifications (including credit verification code/value and indent specifications);
- Authorisation rules;
- Floor limits;
- Restricted card lists;
- Relationships with merchants;
- Cash advances;
- Settlement/interchange;
- Charge backs;
- Compliance;
- Security/fraud;
- Counterfeiting.

Code of Banking Practice

Chapter 1, 3, and 5 of the Code of Banking Practice apply to credit card business. The more important sections are as follows:

- **Section 25.** This section mainly deals with the issuance of cards. It provides that banks should satisfy themselves of the identity of the person applying for the card (Sec.25.3); in addition to the detailed terms and conditions, banks should make readily available to customers general descriptive information on the use of cards, for example, security of the cards and personal identification numbers, credit facilities granted to the customers and fees, charges and interest that apply (Sec. 25.4); and the requirements for the issuance of subsidiary cards (Sec. 25.5 and 25.6).

- **Section 29.** This section deals with transaction records that banks should provide to customers. Such records include printed transaction records when transactions are made through electronic terminals, and monthly statements of account (with certain exceptions).
- **Section 30.** Focusing on bank's practices in handling unauthorised transactions, this section points out that banks should advise customers to examine their statements with 60 days from the statement date and customers should be warned that the banks may reserve the right to regard the statement as conclusive if the customers fail to report any unauthorised transactions within the specified period. Banks should not avail themselves of this right if the unauthorised transactions arise from forgery or fraud under certain circumstances.
- **Section 32.** This section describes the liabilities of banks and customers with respect to losses incurred from the use of the cards.

Direct Debiting

Direct debiting facilitates the prompt payment of amounts due under commercial and consumer contracts. It enables a supplier, dealer/merchant, or other creditor to obtain payment of the amount due him by issuing a direct demand for payment to the debtor's bank. The creditor asks the debtor (who is a bank customer) to sign a mandate executed on a standard form, which is sent by the creditor to the debtor's bank.

The creditor usually arranges for direct debit facilities with its bank and signs a letter of indemnity, agreeing to keep the bank indemnified against all actions, claims, damages, costs, and expenses arising directly or indirectly from such debiting. The creditor also authorises the bank or banks involved to admit, compromise, or reject any claims without reference to the creditor.

The standard form authorises the bank to pay the amount demanded by the creditor. There is no need to require, on each occasion, confirmation of the indebtedness of the debtor. When the amount or dates of payment are subject to change, the creditor must give written notice of the change to the debtor at the agreed period (say 14 days) before the next payment is due.

The legal nature of direct debiting transactions was considered by the English Court of Appeal in *Esso Petroleum Co. Ltd. v. Milton (1997)*. The court held that, in modern practice, such a giro payment (direct debiting in Hong Kong) is comparable to payment by cheque and as such, is equivalent to payment by cash. In general, payment by direct debiting for goods or services received is not subject to a defence of set-off.

Standing Order

The standing order is a direct debiting service offered by banks in Hong Kong. This involves an authorisation to a bank to debit the customer's account for making regular payments in a fixed currency and amount at a fixed date of the month. A standing order may be paid by issuing a cashier's order or draft or telegraphic transfer. Handling fees are collected on the establishment of the order or upon each payment, and when making a change to the payment details.

Items commonly seen as the subject matter of standing orders are annual subscriptions to clubs and societies, the payment of rates, instalments due to hire purchase companies, and premiums to insurance companies.

The risk to the bank in a standing order is that it will make an error and pay the wrong amount or omit making a payment, which can have damaging effects for the customer. For example, a new standing order authority may be issued to replace a previous standing order that was cancelled. If the bank fails to notice the change, the customer's account will be over-debited and problems can arise in recovering the monies wrongly paid.

Where the bank is unable to make a payment on the due date because of lack of funds, it is usual to advise the customer by an advice note, which instructs him to make his own arrangements for payment of that instalment. On some occasions, banks are prepared to hold over a standing order for a day and then to check whether covering funds have been provided; the extra work occasioned by this is not justified in the provision of the service. Accordingly, banks usually do not perform such extra work except for valuable customers.

In *Whitehead v. National Westminster Bank Ltd. (1982)*, the customer's account occasionally had sufficient funds to enable a monthly mortgage payment to be made by banker's order but often there were insufficient funds and the bank made no payment. However, if the account then subsequently reverted to credit, from time to time the bank agreed to make the first payment but this was not always the position. Eventually, the arrears under the mortgage payments reached such a level that the building society took possession of Mrs. Whitehead's property and sold it.

She then brought an action against the bank, claiming that the bank had a duty to ensure that each banker's order payment had been made on the due date, or the next date on which her account had been in sufficient credit to enable payment to be made. The court ruled that the bank's duty related simply to complying with the payment of the standing order on its due date each month. The court further ruled that if there were insufficient monies in the account on that date, then the bank had no further obligations to its customer in respect of that instalment.

Bankers must bear in mind that a beneficiary has no authority to amend the customer's written instructions. If a payment is not made, the bank must not disclose the reason to the beneficiary (or his bankers). This is because the bank's normal duty of secrecy applies to the customer, not the beneficiary. Similarly, a beneficiary cannot give instructions to the remitting bank for the payment to be cancelled; again the bank must take instructions from the customer.

Direct Debit

In direct debit, the bank of the receiver (for example, a gas utility) sends a direct debit authorisation form, filled and signed by the debtor (for example, a customer of the gas utility) to the debtor's bank to debit the debtor's account for payment to the receiver's account via the electronic clearing system. Direct debits are flexible in timing and payment amounts, which make them popular for paying utility bills.

There are two ways to process a direct debit authorisation (DDA): the standard method and the simplified method. A bank adopts the one that is most appropriate for its systems and procedures. Regardless of the method, it is important to be aware of the legal issues around DDA, including the need to have the creditor sign a Creditor's Indemnity or Letter of Indemnity and to have the debtor completely fill in and sign the DDA.

Each of the two approaches has its pros and cons and the features of each are outlined below. The standard method is well established while the simplified method is faster bur requires the creditor's bank to issue an indemnity to the debtor's bank.

Standard Method

- The creditor (for example, a club membership) applies to its bank to use autodebit facilities and completes a Creditor's Indemnity.
- The creditor obtains supplies of standard direct debit authorisation (DDA) forms from its bank.
- After filling in the DDA form with information regarding the creditor's bank, account number, name of account to be credited and the pre-assigned debtor's reference, the creditor submits the DDA to the debtor. The bank name and account number are usually pre-printed on the DDA form.
- The debtor completes the form, signs it, and sends it to his or her bank.
- The debtor's bank checks the DDA for validity (e.g., signature and limit for each payment). If the payment limit is not specified by the debtor, the debtor's bank may at its discretion determine its own maximum amount of each payment.
- If everything is in order, the debtor bank forwards an authenticated copy of the DDA or a Confirmation of DDA Form, a listing with the relevant details, to the creditor's bank.
- Upon receipt of confirmation from the debtor's bank, the creditor's bank will inform the relative creditor that debits may be initiated.
- The creditor may then generate autodebit transactions in settlement of the debtor's outstanding balance.

Simplified Method

- The creditor signs a Letter of Indemnity that binds it to indemnify its bank against any losses.
- The debtor completes the debtor's application/agreement form (with a clause added to authorise the debtor's bank to debit his or her account for payment to the creditor) and sends it to the creditor.
- The creditor then submits an authorisation instruction list of new debtors who have signed their application/agreement to the creditor's bank.

- The creditor's bank sends the Authorisation Instruction List to the respective debtor's bank for setting up autodebit instructions.
- The debtor's bank checks the validity of the account number, account name, and Hong Kong Identification Card number in the Authorisation Instruction List. Discrepancies found will be reported to the creditor's bank.
- If all details are in order, a confirmation will be sent by the debtor's bank to the debtor to confirm that the autodebit instruction has been set up.

Payment and Return

Once the DDAs have been validated and approved, the creditor initiates autodebits by providing details of debits to its bank. The creditor's bank prepares all autodebit transactions for the day on a tape or electronic file and sends it to the Hong Kong Interbank Clearing Limited (HKILC), which provides interbank clearing and settlement services to all banks in Hong Kong. The debtor's bank, on receipt of the listings from the HKILC, checks the transactions against the DDAs. If the transactions are in order, the debtor's bank passes the transactions.

The debtor bank should not process the transaction if it detects infirmities such as no authority, exceeds authority, insufficient funds, account closed, authority cancelled, and so on. All returns must be received by HKICL before 12:45 p.m. on day D+1.

Automated Teller Machines

An automated teller machine (ATM) provides many services, including cash withdrawal, cash deposit, balance transfer within the issuing bank, statement request, cheque book request, change of PIN, and change of language for ATM. ATM cardholders can also access electronic funds transfer at the point of sale (EFTPOS) services, known in Hong Kong as the Easy Pay System (EPS). ATMs are open 24-hours a day without interruption, except during maintenance or a system or mechanical breakdown.

In granting a customer an ATM card, the bank typically does not undertake a credit investigation, except for 'bad list' checking. The bank must make sure the customer signs the ATM cardholder agreement and acknowledges receipt of the card. The personal identification number (PIN) should be sent to the customer under separate cover. The PIN should be generated by the host computer of the issuing bank under prudent security measures and should be known only by the cardholder.

Legal Considerations

The provisions of the Code of Banking Practice discussed earlier for credit cards are also applicable to ATM cards. Bankers should also note the contents of section 37 and

Chapter 6 of the Code, which relate to other payment services and electronic banking services respectively. The use of ATM cards is governed by the ATM cardholder agreement provided by the issuing bank. The provisions in the ATM cardholder agreement relating to PIN will usually be the same as for the credit card cardholder agreement.

Most ATM cardholder agreements have clauses excluding contractual and tortious liability. Whilst such clauses would have to be 'reasonable' under the Control of Exemption Clauses Ordinance, Cap. 71, it is highly probably that the courts would not hold the ATMs to be a 'guaranteed' service. Hence, banks would not be liable for failures of ATM provided that they had followed their normal procedures and so long as a 'reasonable' exemption clause applies.

The bank permits customers to use an ATM to make cash withdrawals as a banking service. Therefore it is bound by Section 5 of the Supply of Services (Implied Terms) Ordinance, Cap. 457, to act with care and skill. This section provides that, in a contract for the supply of a service where the supplier is acting in the course of business, it is implied that the supplier will carry out the service with reasonable care and skill. In short, the bank should:

- Set up and design the ATM system to ensure its compliance with customers' instructions;
- Design a reasonable updated ATM system so that the bank has timely and accurate information that will guide it in debiting the customers' bank accounts;
- Maintain all ATM systems and equipment in good working order and condition. This duty does not extend to ensuring all systems and equipment are in working order all the time. However, they must be repaired within a reasonable time.

In Hong Kong, ATM cards can access the local network (except for cards issued by HSBC and Hang Seng Bank, which can access only the ATM network of those two banks) and/or international network(s). The legal position has become more complicated as banks have set up such networks so that the customers of one bank can use the ATMs of other banks to obtain cash and/or other services. In most cases, the originating bank acts as an express agent of the card issuing bank and the detailed terms and conditions of such provision of services has been stipulated in the ATM cardholder agreement.

When an ATM cardholder consents to the use of his ATM card by another person, or is negligent in protecting the card and/or PIN, he will be liable to the bank, which can debit his account.

The most frequent problem in ATM services is that the ATM dispenses an amount different to what the customer keyed in, but debits the customer's account with what he had requested. The general principle remains that a bank cannot debit its customer's account unless it has been authorised to do so. If an ATM dispenses less than requested, then the bank must adjust the customer's account to reflect what was dispensed. The bank must maintain a tally-roll printout of amounts dispensed, which is the admissible evidence. The burden of proof lies on the customer if he seeks to dispute this evidence.

If an ATM dispenses more than the requested amount, then the customer is regarded as holding the excess in trust for the bank. Under the law of restitution, the bank can sue for the return of a payment made under a mistake of fact.

Electronic Funds Transfer at the Point of Sale

ATM cards in Hong Kong can be used to access the electronic funds transfer at the point of sale (EFTPOS) payment system. EFTPOS links customers and merchants via the bank system, simplifying transactions by enabling direct fund transfers from the bank accounts of customers directly to the bank accounts of merchants without the need for any paper voucher.

The company that operates Hong Kong's EFTPOS system is operated by the Electronic Payment Services Co. (H.K.) Ltd. (EPSCO), a limited company owned by 36 Hong Kong licensed banks. The company has two core businesses: 1) Retail EFTPOS, which allows ATM cardholders to make debit card transactions at retail merchants, and 2) Self-service payment, which enables ATM cardholders to make payments (for example, to pay electricity, telephone, and credit card bills) through self-operating devices and systems.

EPSCO Services

EPSCO offers the following payment services:

- **Easy Pay System (EPS).** Virtually all ATM cards and credit cards that have bank accounts encoded issued by the 36 banks can access EPS. There is no restriction to the services except the available credit balances on the bank accounts. The customer uses the EPS terminal to complete the transaction.
- **Payment by Phone Service (PPS).** This service facilitates bill payment by means of a tone phone. Users can settle various types of bills such as bank payment (credit card bill, hire-purchase, loan instalment, etc.); government payments (income tax, rent and rates, housing authority rent and fee, etc.); utilities (gas, water, electricity, etc.); telecommunications (telephone bill, mobile phone bill, etc.) and many others.
- **Payment Express Terminal (PET).** This service is jointly provided by EPSCO and the four utility companies (China Light, Hong Kong Electric, Hong Kong Telecom, and Town Gas). The service facilitates bill payment through payment kiosks installed at the four utilities' outlets and other strategic locations.
- **Hong Kong Jockey Club Telebet Accounts.** These are deposit and withdrawal services and cash voucher sales provided by EPSCO for the Hong Kong Jockey Club (HKJC), which operates horse racing, lotteries, and other games of chance. The telebet

accounts enables customers to transfer funds from their bank accounts to the HKJC's bank accounts and vice versa. Using the telephone, HKJC customers can make deposits to and withdraw funds from their telebet account almost in real time.

Legal Considerations

There is no legislation as yet in Hong Kong on EFTPOS, so its legal status may depend on the ruling in the case *Re Charge Card Services Ltd. (1989)*. In general, there are five contractual relationships in EFTPOS:

- **Relationship 1:** Between cardholder and merchant (purchase of goods or services);
- **Relationship 2:** Between cardholder and card issuer (debiting of payment);
- **Relationship 3:** Between merchant and 'merchant-acquirer' which operates the debit card scheme, that is, EPSCO (supply of terminal and authorisation procedures);
- **Relationship 4:** Between merchant-acquirer and card issuer (agreement on operating scheme);
- **Relationship 5:** Between merchant-acquirer and merchant's bank (crediting of payment).

In the *Re Charge Card Services* case, the court ruled that once the person has handed over his payment card and the merchant has allowed him to take the goods, the customer's liability is extinguished; it is unconditional payment. This extends to debit cards (ATM cards) by virtue of the fact that, as part of debit card and EFTPOS systems, the card issuer makes an unequivocal agreement to transfer funds to the merchant's bank. Therefore, contractual relationship 1 above is discharged immediately.

Under contractual relationship 2 above, the ATM card issuer (that is, the cardholder's bank) agrees with the ATM cardholder that it will pay the merchant when the cardholder initiates the transaction using his ATM card, and that the bank will debit the cardholder's account accordingly.

Contractual relationship 3 is entered into when the merchant agrees with the merchant-acquirer that he will accept the EFTPOS equipment and that the merchant-acquirer will sponsor him to the system. This results in contractual relationship 4 between the merchant-acquirer and the card issuer. Finally, contractual relationship 5 is between the merchant-acquirer and the merchant's bank, which credits the merchant's account on receiving the EFTPOS instructions.

Investment Advice

One service that banks offer to their customers is that of assisting them in the investment of their money. Some banks offer their customers a fee-based investment management service, which is available for investment portfolios above a prescribed minimum size. The customer may elect whether the bank is to make purchases and sales of investments with his consent or whether such investments are to be made without reference to him.

In most cases, the customer's investments are transferred into the name of the bank's nominee company (usually a subsidiary of the bank) so that all communications from company registrars may be sent to the nominee company, which is thus able to deal with such matters as new issues of shares on the customer's behalf. A special fee is payable for this service, depending upon the size of the funds. Some merchant banks even specialise in this type of work.

In other cases, bank officers may be asked by customers or prospective customers for advice on investments or on the commercial merits of a proposed transaction or venture. In all of these, the banker owes a duty of care even if the advice given is gratuitous.

Legal Considerations

Investment-related activities of authorised institutions and bankers are generally required to comply with the Securities and Futures Ordinance and the relevant guidelines issued by the HKMA and the Securities and Futures Commission.

In *Banbury v. Bank of Montreal (1918)*, the existence of a duty of care was recognised where advice is given within a branch manager's authority. The plaintiff was not, though he had been previously, a customer; he was merely recommended to the bank's office by a customer. He was charged nothing for the advice he got as to the credit and standing of the company in which he invested and lost his money. The question narrowed down to whether it was part of a bank's business to advise on this investment and, if it was, whether a branch manager had the necessary authority to do so.

The case was treated as analogous to that of gratuitous services rendered by a person professing special knowledge and skill. The judge ruled that "the limits of a banker's business cannot be laid down as a matter of law . . . if he undertakes to advise, he must exercise reasonable care and skill in giving the advice. He is under no obligation to advise, but if he takes upon himself to do so, he will incur liability if he does so negligently."

The question in Banbury's case, whether advising on investments was within the scope of the bank's business, depended on whether the branch manager had authority to bind the bank, whether negligence on his part was negligence on the part of the bank authority.

Bankers should pay due care on such advising. In *Woods v. Martins Bank Ltd.* (1959), the bank had held itself as willing to advise through its managers, though it alleged that this was not part of the business of banking and that, therefore, the bank was under no duty and could not be responsible for any loss.

But it had advertised that it had 'six district head offices with boards of directors and general managers, so that the very best advice is available through our managers.' Since the bank manager could be consulted freely on all matters affecting one's financial welfare, the bank's argument did not find favour with the judge. However, these were special facts which may render the decision unsafe for general application. Each case will have to be considered on its own facts.

Whether a branch manager has authority to advise is a matter of fact. It is likely, however, that even where he is not authorised, advising is sufficiently within his ostensible authority to entitle a customer to assume that he is authorised and to find a claim for negligence if he falls short of the standard which the customer would be entitled to expect.

In Hong Kong, most prospectuses for initial public offerings (IPOs) state that, if there is any query on the prospectus, the intending subscribers may consult their bankers/bank managers. For most customers in Hong Kong, this would refer to the branch managers or relationship officers of the bank branch where they opened their accounts, who in fact may not have adequate expertise to advise on IPOs. It is prudent for such branch managers or officers not to advise customers for the particular prospectus directly, but rather direct them to consult the specialist department of the bank.

In summary, the legal position of the banks in relation to investment and/or financial advice is:

- Where it is within the ordinary scope of a bank's business to give investment advice, the bank owes a duty to its customers to advise with reasonable care and skill. In fact, it is an implied term as provided in section 5 of the Supply of Services (Implied Terms) Ordinance, Cap. 457.
- Where it is part of a bank's business to give investment advice to potential customers, the law imposes on the bank an obligation to advise potential customers with reasonable care and skill.

Safe Custody

One of the services a bank offers to customers is that of keeping in safe custody valuables of various kinds, including jewellery, share certificates, life policies, and title deeds. In general, property which is thus left with a banker for safe custody is deposited in a locked box, the key of which is retained by the customer, that is, safe deposit box services.

Alternatively, items such as deeds, share certificates, and life policies may be enclosed in an envelope, which is sealed with sealing wax. If the customer possesses a personal seal, he makes an impression from this in the molten wax. If not, he signs his name in ink across the wax when it has set; alternatively, he may be asked to sign his name across the flap of the envelope, the signature being then covered with a special form of sealing tape which, if removed, takes the signature with it. The banker thereby voluntarily becomes a bailee.

Safe Facilities

The banker's duty of care applies to the provision of bank deposit box services. We will consider two areas where liability may arise for the bank with regard to safe facilities: death of a customer and provision of overnight safekeeping of money.

Death of a Customer

The bank may release the items in a deceased customer's safety deposit box to the deceased's personal representative. However, the banker must require that the personal representative of the deceased produce an authorization from the Director of Home Affairs of Hong Kong allowing for the removal of specific items. The Home Affairs Department oversees the process of administration of the estate of a deceased person and provides the necessary certificates that allow executors or persons responsible for the estate of a deceased person to access a safety deposit box held by a bank. The Estate Beneficiaries Unit of the Home Affairs Department is in charge of the overall process.

The Revenue (Abolition of Estate Duty) Ordinance 2005 took effect on 11 February 2006. The ordinance eliminated the need to file estate duty affidavits or accounts, or seek estate duty clearance papers for an applicant to grant a representation in respect to a death since that date. Prior to July 2005, estate duties were charged on a sliding scale depending on the type and value of the deceased's assets.[1]

There are several requirements incumbent upon the bank that holds a safe deposit box for a customer who passes away. Sections 60C to 60I of Chapter 10 of the Probate and Administration Ordinance outline the responsibilities of the bank:

- **Inspection of a Bank Deposit Box.** An executor of a deceased person, a person entitled to administer the estate or a surviving renter (in the case of a jointly held box) may apply to inspect a safety deposit box. Importantly, the applicant should have a key to the safety deposit box. The Home Affairs Department has a set of requirements for applicants to acquire a certificate for inspection.[2] The banker should accept the certificate but also ask for proof of identity of the holder of the certificate and a staff member of the bank should be present during the inspection. In the case of a jointly held bank deposit box, the other party should be present. An officer of the Estate Beneficiaries Support Unit of the HAD should be present during the inspection, which will typically be prearranged.
- **Removal of Will.** In cases where a will is found inside a deposit box, the bank should allow its removal provided the holder of the Certificate of Inspection is named as an executor. In other cases, the bank should make a copy of the will or instrument, place the original back, and give the copy to the public officers present. No other document or article should be removed from the box at the inspection.
- **Preparation of Inventory.** The holder of the Certificate for Inspection should prepare an inventory of the contents of the box in cases where no will or similar document is found in the box, when the holder is named as an executor, or when the holder is the surviving renter of a jointly held box. Both the holder of the certificate and the public

---

[1]More detailed information on the *Revenue (Abolition of Estate Duty) Ordinance 2005* is available at the Hong Kong government website at: http://www.ird.gov.hk/eng/tax/edu.htm#11

[2]The detailed requirements for applicants are available in the *Probate and Administration Ordinance* and summarized in the Home Affairs Department website here: http://www.had.gov.hk/en/public_services/estates/deposit_box.htm

officers should verify the truthfulness and accuracy of the inventory by signing on the original copy of the inventory of the contents. The holder of the certificate will keep the original and copies will be provided to the other parties present, including a staff member of the bank. It is incumbent upon the bank to keep that copy for six years.

- **Removal from Bank Deposit Box.** An authorization for removal will be issued only after an inventory of the contents of the box has been prepared. Removal without authorisation may constitute intermeddling, which is a criminal offence. Authorization for removal of items from the box will be granted if an item is a document necessary for an application for summary administration, a grant representation or sealing of a foreign grant, or in cases where the document belongs to someone else, is urgently needed, and when its removal will not prejudice the legitimate interests of any person in the estate of the deceased. Applications for removal of items follow a similar process as the Application for a Certificate of Inspection and can be done by the executor of a deceased person, someone who is entitled in priority to administer the state, or a surviving renter in the case of a jointly held box.
- **Other circumstances.** In some cases, the lease of a safety deposit box includes a survivorship arrangement. In this case, the surviving renter may apply to remove items from the box with the HAD. The surviving renter may access the safe deposit box within 12 months of the death provided the items of the box have been inventoried according to the legal requirements.

Overnight Safe Custody

Although hardly common in Hong Kong, some banks offer a special form of safe custody to their business customers at selected branches for the safe keeping of money overnight. Such cash is deposited in the branch night safe, access to which is available from the street.

The provision of night safe services opens the bank to liability, so it is important to have proper procedures in place such as the following:

- The customer is provided with a key to the door which opens in the wall, and with a wallet in which the cash is to be secured and locked with another key by the customer.
- The customer agrees to be responsible for any loss, and the bank undertakes to hold the wallet simply under a contract of bailment, and not under that of debtor-creditor. The debtor-creditor relationship only arises when the monies are deposited in the bank account on the following business day.
- The wallet is extracted from the bank safe by two bank staff before the branch opens for business.
- Property should be kept in a locked box and the key kept by the customer, or in a sealed parcel/envelope.
- The customer should sign a receipt with general description (e.g., name and total number of shares) of what has been passed to the bank.

Contract of Bailment

In practice, banks try to avoid acting as bailee, but they may agree to act as such when they cannot refuse requests from the customer, for example, because the customer is a very important person. By acting as bailee, the bank opens itself to two types of liability under a contract of bailment: negligence and conversion.

Negligence

A bank that accepts articles for safe custody is a bailee for reward, and as such, is liable for want of ordinary care. Where bailed goods are lost from the custody of the bailee or are damaged, the onus is on the bailee (that is, the bank) to prove that the loss or damage "occurred without any neglect of default or misconduct of himself or any of the servants to whom he delegated his duty," Lord Deming ruled in *Morris v. CW Martin & Sons Ltd.*

Conversion

Conversion means that the wrongdoer has deprived the true owner of the use and possession of goods by treating the goods as if the wrongdoer had the right to deal with them. The act of conversion denies the true owner possession of the goods. The act complained of in conversion is that the wrongdoer has interfered with the goods and so prevented the owner from having possession of them, either permanently or temporarily.

As a bailee, a bank may be liable for conversion if it delivers the goods to a person other than the depositor. Such liability is strict as it does not matter whether the bank concerned acted in good faith or was not negligent.

Where anyone other than the original depositor applies for redelivery of the goods but cannot show his authority, the practical course for the bank as bailee would be to decline to deliver. However, if the application is genuine, the bank may be guilty of technical conversion of the goods. For a successful defence, the bank must prove that it had reasonable grounds for suspicion as to the title of the goods. It must also show that it had detained the goods only for a reasonable time and did so to clear up the doubt.

Practical Considerations

Where goods are deposited to a bank by two or more persons jointly, the authority of all is ordinarily required before they can be withdrawn. In practice, most banks have specific mandates that require the signature of all bailors as a prerequisite to withdrawal or that grant authority for delivery to some of the depositors. Whatever the mandate, the banker's duty is to comply with it.

If delivery is demanded by a transferee of the goods, the banker is entitled to first satisfy himself regarding a derivative title of those goods. Bankers should be aware that the transferee has no direct claim against the bailee until the bailee has attorned (that is, formally acknowledged the transfer of the goods) to him. The banker is not the debtor immediately affected by the assignment of a chose in action (the right to enforce payment of a debt by legal proceedings), nor the person to receive notice if the assignment is under the Law Amendment and Reform (Consolidation) Ordinance, Cap. 23. The banker is a mere depository.

The banker must not remove the goods from the premises where they were received for custody if part of the agreement is that they be stored at a particular place. If the banker stores them elsewhere, he may be liable for their loss or destruction, apart from any question of negligence, even though he would have had a defence if goods had been lost by a similar peril while in the place where, under the contract, they should have been.

However, the banker would be justified in removing the goods if danger threatened, as in a case of a dangerous structure of the building, but it would be wise to obtain the bailor's consent before the removal, if possible.

Other Banking Services

There are many other banking services that give rise to legal issues. We focus on three of these in this section: hire-purchase, factoring, and leasing.

Hire-Purchase

In Hong Kong, there is no legislation directly relating to hire-purchase agreements and so such transactions are governed by common law. In common law, a hire-purchase agreement may be defined as a contract for the hiring of goods under which there is conferred on the hirer an option to buy the goods. Hire-purchase is a common method used by consumers to obtain goods before payment in full. A bank may provide such consumer credit directly or through a subsidiary, for example, a deposit-taking company or registered money lender.

The banker must be aware that a hirer under a hire-purchase agreement is entitled to put an end to his future rental liability by exercising his contractual right to terminate. A clause designed to ensure that upon such termination the owner recovers the full price is likely to be struck down as a penalty, on the grounds that it seeks to impose on the defaulting hirer a liability greater than that which he would have incurred if he had not broken the agreement.

Factoring

Some bankers arrange for the financing of sales, particularly overseas sales, by providing factoring services. Under such an arrangement, the bank (or its subsidiary or "factor") takes over the book debts of the customer (manufacturer or exporter) on a non-recourse basis. In other words, this is receivables financing, which in practice is usually provided by a subsidiary of a bank.

A factor in the context of factoring is not a mercantile agent. Rather, he is one who, pursuant to a continuing relationship with a supplier of goods or services to trade customers, purchases debts from time to time arising in respect of supplies to those customers. The assignor is commonly called the client or supplier, and the account debtor is the customer. The factor offers three main types of service:

- Acceptance of risk of non-payment by customers;
- Provision of finance by prepayment of part of the purchase price of the debts;
- Administration of the sales ledgers.

The relations between the factor and the trader (client) are governed by a detailed master agreement, the factoring agreement, which regulates the terms upon which the factor will purchase receivables due to the client from those to whom he supplies goods or services (customers). The debts or receivables that the factor is prepared to purchase on a non-recourse basis are termed approved receivables. These are receivables arising from transactions specifically approved by the factor, or falling within an overall funding limit authorised by the factor, or falling within an overall funding limit authorised by the factor in respect of a particular customer.

The factoring agreement will require the client to stamp on his invoices to customers notice of the fact that the invoiced account has been assigned to the factor and that payment should be made directly to the factor at the factor's stated address. In the case of maturity factoring, the client is not paid the price of a receivable until it matures or the customer becomes insolvent, whichever occurs first. In the case of advance factoring, the client is given the facility of drawing on the account with the factor against the receivables prior to maturity, paying a discount charge for the privilege.

When a receivable has become vested in the factor in equity, pursuant to the factoring assignment being given to the customer, it is the customer's duty to pay the factor, not the client. However, mistakes occur in the best-regulated circles and it is common for the customer's accounts department to overlook the notice of assignment and send a cheque to the client.

Factoring agreements usually provide that cheques and money received from customers are to be made over to the factor and are meanwhile to be held on trust for the factor. Even when the factoring agreement does not have such provision, it is clear that the client is a trustee for the factor as to cheques and money so received. If the client wrongfully retains or deals with them in defiance of the factor's title, it commits a conversion and is liable for the face value of any cheque so converted. So too is a director of the client company who causes it to commit the act of conversion, for he is then guilty of conversion himself.

Where the client pays the cheque into its overdrawn bank account, the bank or its subsidiary can retain the proceeds of the cheque to the extent to which it gives value for them without notice of the factor's rights. Subject to this, the factor can trace the proceeds into the account and, through it, into the hands of volunteers and third parties taking with notice of the factor's rights, in accordance with the ordinary rules of tracing.

Leasing

A lease of goods is a hire contract whose essential characteristic is that goods are rented out by one party, X, to another party, Y, for Y's use or enjoyment in exchange for payment of rent. It is distinguished from hire-purchase in that Y has neither the option nor the obligation to purchase the goods, but is required to return them to X, or deal with them as X directs, at the end of the lease.

Leasing periods may range from 20 years at one end to one day at the other, and may encompass equipment ranging from 'big ticket' items such as power generators, oil tankers and aircraft, to relatively small items of business equipment such as fax machines and photocopiers. Many banks have subsidiaries that cater specially to the leasing business.

In most cases, the initiative for a leasing transaction comes from the lessee. It is the lessee who selects the equipment and the supplier. He then requests the bank to purchase the equipment from the supplier and let it to him on lease. The bank places the order with the supplier, who invoices the bank and later delivers the equipment directly to the lessee. Upon receipt of a certificate by the lessee that the equipment has been delivered in satisfactory condition, the bank pays the supplier and signs the leasing agreement with the lessee.

The relationship between the bank and the lessee is governed by the terms of the agreement between them. In general, the parties are free to agree to such terms as they choose. However, there are two types of contractual provisions that are subject to judicial scrutiny.

The first type is the clause usually found in leasing agreements by which the bank seeks to ensure that, if it has to terminate the agreement because of the lessee's default, the bank will not suffer a loss. It is necessary to ensure that a minimum payment clause, designed to give the bank the value of its defeated contractual expectation, is not struck down by the court as a penalty.

The other type of clause seeks to exempt the bank from liability for defects in the equipment. Such a clause is effective for excluding common law implied terms, but only as it satisfies the test of reasonableness under the Control of Exemption Clauses Ordinance, Cap. 71. In the context of a transaction in which the lessee relies essentially on his own skill and judgement and/or that of the supplier, such an exemption clause would seem to be reasonable.

However, if the effect of upholding the clause is to deprive the lessee of all remedy, this may induce the court to take a more jaundiced view of the clause. So the prudent bank will do what it can to also protect the lessee, for example by incorporating undertakings, imperfect though their effect may be, to assign the lessee's rights as a buyer or to enforce such rights for the lessee's benefit.

Internet and Phone Banking

Banking practice in new technology is not yet sufficiently established to provide the guidance that courts would look for. In fact, there is no judicial precedent in most areas of electronic banking and no legislation directly relating to its provision. Section 37 and

Chapter 6 of the Code of Banking Practice sets out the minimum standards pertinent to Internet and phone banking that banks are expected to observe when dealing with their personal customers. Section 37.3 of the Code of Banking Practice provides that in providing telephone or computer banking services for transfer of funds to the accounts of third parties other than utility companies, the authorised institutions should adopt adequate measures to maintain the security of such transactions, for example, if appropriate, by requiring customers to designate in writing a list of accounts to which funds can be transferred from the customer's account through such services. In practice, most banks in Hong Kong follow this provision in providing telephone and Internet banking services.

The various rights and liabilities involved in electronic banking can be covered in the ad hoc contracts used for particular banking services or products. The banker's 'due care' seems likely to be expanded as technology continues to develop and the bank's systems are regularly updated to respond to rapidly changing times. The Supervisory Policy Manual on "Supervision of E-Banking" issued by the HKMA provides guidance to banks on the general principles for risk management of Internet banking. Banks are required to adhere to the 'fit for purpose' principle when implementing the relevant risk management controls, that is, the controls should be commensurate with the risks associated with the types and amounts of transactions allowed, the electronic delivery channels adopted, and the risk management systems of individual banks. Whilst banks do not need to seek formal approval from the HKMA to offer new Internet banking services and major enhancements to existing services, they should "discuss their plans with the HKMA in advance before launching such new services."

Legal Considerations

As discussed in Chapter 1, the mandate is fundamental in the banker and customer relationship. Within the widening range of paperless transfers, the issue of the mandate is posing a number of questions. Can a signature be effectively verified in an electronic transmission and will such transmission make it more difficult to detect alterations? How effective can the PIN be as a replacement of the customer's signature? Bankers should stipulate detailed terms on such issues in the contract the bank uses for a particular electronic banking service.

Because an EFTPOS transaction is validated or rejected in real time, it is possible that a customer's right to confidentiality may be breached by giving a reason for non-authorisation. Further, information on customers, because it is electronically held, can be disseminated easily. Banks must be careful to breach neither confidentiality nor the Personal Data (Privacy) Ordinance, Cap. 486.

In electronic banking, there may be a lack of proof that the transaction either took place or was authorised because the PIN has replaced the signature. Bankers must keep records and maintain an audit trail.

Electronic Transactions Ordinance

The Electronic Transactions (Amended) Ordinance 2004 (ETO) also has implications on some aspects of electronic banking. It defines a digital signature in relation to an electronic record as "an electronic signature of the signer generated by the transformation of the electronic record using an asymmetric cryptosystem and a hash function." A person that has access to the initial untransformed electronic record and the signer's public key should be able to determine: a) whether the transformation was generated using the private key that corresponds to the signer's public key; and b) whether the initial electronic record has been altered since the transformation was generated.

Section 5 of the ETO provides that:

- If a rule of law requires information to be given in writing or provides for certain consequences if it is not, an electronic record satisfies the requirement if the information contained in the electronic record is accessible so as to be usable for subsequent reference.
- If a rule of law permits information to be given in writing, an electronic record satisfies that rule of law if the information contained in the electronic record is accessible so as to be usable for subsequent reference.

Section 9 of the ETO provides that, without prejudice to any rules of evidence, an electronic record shall not be denied admissibility in evidence in any legal proceeding on the sole ground that it is an electronic record.

Schedule 1 of the ETO specifies the areas of activities and other matters that are excluded from the application of the ETO. The opening of bank accounts and provision of most other banking services are not specifically excluded. The matters excluded are the following:

- Creation, execution, variation, revocation, revival, or rectification of a will, codicil, or any other testamentary document;
- Creation, execution, variation of a trust;
- Creation, execution, variation of revocation of a power of attorney;
- Any assignment, mortgage, or legal charge within the meaning of the Conveyancing and Property Ordinance or any other contract relating to or effecting the disposition of immovable property or an interest in immovable property;
- A document effecting a floating charge referred to in section 2A of the Land Registration Ordinance;
- Negotiable instruments.

Summary

- In addition to bank accounts and negotiable instruments discussed in previous chapters, banks offer other services that can give rise to legal issues and liability that bankers must be aware of. The way these traditional and new services are delivered is also evolving, resulting in platforms such as Internet and mobile phone banking that can expose banks to further liability.

- In Hong Kong, there is no statutory framework that specifically governs credit cards and no comprehensive rules which must be complied with. However, bankers should be aware of the Code of Practice on Consumer Credit Data issued by the Office of the Privacy Commissioner for Personal Data, in pursuance of Part III of the Personal Data (Privacy) Ordinance, Cap. 486, and the relevant sections in the Code of Banking Practice. The Supervisory Policy Manual on "Credit Card Business" issued by the HKMA provide guidance to banks on managing their credit card business. The Code of Banking Practice sets out the minimum standards pertinent to card business that banks are expected to observe when dealing with their personal customers. The legal nature of direct debiting transactions was considered by the English Court of Appeal in *Esso Petroleum Co. Ltd. v. Milton (1997)*. The court held that, in modern practice, such a giro payment (direct debiting in Hong Kong) is comparable to payment by cheque and as such, is equivalent to payment by cash. In general, payment by direct debiting for goods or services received is not subject to a defence of set-off.
- The provisions of the Code of Banking Practice for credit cards are also applicable to Automated Teller Machine (ATM) cards. Bankers should note the contents of Section 37 and Chapter 6 of the Code, which relate to other payment services and electronic banking services respectively. The use of ATM cards is governed by the ATM cardholder agreement provided by the issuing bank. The provisions in the ATM cardholder agreement relating to the personal identification number (PIN) will usually be the same as for the credit card cardholder agreement.
- There is no legislation as yet in Hong Kong on electronic funds transfer at the point of sale (EFTPOS), so its legal status may depend on the ruling in the case *Re Charge Card Services Ltd. (1989)*. The court ruled that once the person has handed over his payment card and the merchant has allowed him to take the goods, the customer's liability is extinguished; it is unconditional payment.
- Investment-related activities of authorised institutions (including banks) are generally governed by the Securities and Futures Ordinance and the relevant guidelines issued by the HKMA and the Securities and Futures Commission. The legal position of the banks in relation to investment and/or financial advice is that it owes existing and potential customers a duty to advise with reasonable care and skill. For an initial public offering, it is prudent for branch managers or officers not to advise customers on the particular prospectus directly, but rather direct them to consult the specialist department of the bank.
- The banker's duty of care applies to the provision of bank deposit box services. Two areas where liability may arise for the bank with regard to safe facilities are death of a customer and provision of overnight safekeeping of money. Alternatively, the provision of safe custody may take the form of a contract of bailment. When this happens, the bank opens itself to two types of liability: negligence and conversion.
- Other banking services that have legal implications for bankers include hire-purchase, factoring, and leasing. The rise of Internet banking and phone banking also pose

potential liabilities. There is no judicial precedent in most areas of electronic banking and no legislation directly relating to its provision. Section 37 and Chapter 6 of the Code of Banking Practice sets out the minimum standards pertinent to internet and phone banking that banks are expected to observe when dealing with their personal customers.

Key Terms

ATM card
automated teller machine (ATM)
card issuer
card organisation
cardholder
cardholder agreement
contract of bailment
conversion
credit card
direct debit
Easy Pay System (EPS)
electronic banking
electronic funds transfer at the point of sale (EFTPOS)
factoring
hire-purchase
investment advice
leasing
MasterCard
merchant
merchant acquirer
merchant agreement
negligence
night safe services
Payment by Phone Service (PPS)
Payment Express Terminal (PET)
sales or services agreement
standing order
Visa

Study Guide

1. What are the legal principles that have been set by common law with regard to a lost credit card and subsequent transactions made on it by people who are not the cardholder? Frame your answer with reference to the cardholder agreement, including potentially unenforceable provisions in that agreement.
2. What is a contract of bailment in the context of safe custody services? Explain why bankers are reluctant to become a voluntary bailee. Reference negligence and conversion in your answer.
3. The risk to the bank in a standing order is that it will make an error and pay the wrong amount or omit making a payment. Outline the procedures a bank should put in place to minimise the likelihood that this error will be made and to help protect it from liability should the bank face a lawsuit.
4. After an automated teller machine stayed offline for two days, a frustrated customer sued the bank for causing damage to his business. Under what circumstance may the courts rule for the bank? Reference the Supply of Services Ordinance in your answer.

5. Mr. A rented a safety deposit box in Bank B and stored important documents in it, including his will. Mrs. A later came to retrieve the documents, bringing with her the key to the safety deposit box. If you were the banker, will you allow her to open the box and retrieve the documents? What are the procedures you must follow to protect the bank from legal action?

Further Reading

Chan Bo-ching, Simon. 2000, *Hong Kong Banking Law and Practice Volume 1*. First Edition. Hong Kong: Hong Kong Institute of Bankers.

Code of Banking Practice website, http://www.info.gov.hk/hkma/eng/consumer/code_eng.pdf.

Code of Practice on Consumer Credit Data website, http://www.pcpd.org.hk/english/files/ordinance/CCDCode_eng.pdf.

Electronic Transactions Ordinance website, http://www.ogcio.gov.hk/eng/eto/ecap553.htm.

Hong Kong Monetary Authority. "Credit Card Business" in *Supervisory Policy Manual*, http://www.info.gov.hk/hkma/eng/bank/spma/attach/CR-S-5.pdf.

Hong Kong Monetary Authority. "Supervision of E-Banking" in *Supervisory Policy Manual*, http://www.info.gov.hk/hkma/eng/bank/spma/attach/TM-E-1.pdf.

Privacy Commissioner for Hong Kong website, http://www.pcpd.org.hk/.

LAW RELATING TO SECURITY

Guarantee

Learning objectives

After studying this chapter, you should be able to:

1. Describe the characteristics and legal implications of different types of guarantees

2. Describe the doctrine of undue influence, its application in the area of bank lending, and practical considerations for bankers in taking guarantees

3. Identify the rights, duties, and liabilities of the parties to a guarantee

4. Describe the circumstances in which a guarantee may be discharged or terminated

Introduction

Osborn's Concise Law Dictionary defines security as "a possession such that the grantee or holder of the security holds as against the grantor a right to resort to some property or some fund for the satisfaction of some demand, after which satisfaction the balance of the property or fund belongs to the grantor." When granting loan facilities, most banks in Hong Kong look first to the adequacy and validity of the security offered by the borrower, except in the case of personal loans, tax loans, and credit cards.

In pledging a security, a borrower enters into a legal agreement with the bank. As such, it is important for banking professionals to recognise the legal implications of taking a security so as to protect the bank from liability and avoid legal disputes.

In this chapter, we focus on guarantees, which are the most common forms of security taken by creditors, banks, and other businesses. We will discuss the tripartite relationship among the debtor (the borrower), the guarantor, and the creditor (the bank), their liabilities and rights, types of guarantee, and other legal issues around this form of security.

What is a Guarantee?

A guarantee is a promise by one person (guarantor) to another (creditor) to answer for the debt, default, or miscarriage of a third person (debtor or principal obligor) towards the creditor. A guarantee is by nature a contract and is therefore governed by the common law rules relating to contracts. In addition, statutory provisions are applicable, including the Law Amendment and Reform (Consolidation) Ordinance and the Unconscionable Contracts Ordinance.

The guarantor undertakes to execute his promise only when the debtor or primary obligor defaults or fails to perform his obligations to the creditor under the contract between the creditor and the debtor/principal obligor. The guarantor's liability is only secondary or collateral. It is dependent on the debtor's obligation, and only arises when the debtor defaults.

Written and Oral Guarantee

In Hong Kong, there is no requirement that guarantees be done in writing or have evidence in writing. In other words, there is no special formality for a contract of guarantee. A person may bring an action against another person based on that other party's oral promise to answer for the debt default.

This is made clear in Section 14 of the Law and Reform (Consolidation) Ordinance. The relevant provision reads thus: "No special promise made by any person to answer for the debt, default or miscarriage of another person, being in writing, and signed by the party charged therewith or some other person by him thereunto lawfully authorised, shall be deemed invalid to support an action, suit or other proceeding to charge the person by whom such promise has been made, by reason only that the consideration for such promise does not appear in writing or by necessary inference from a written document."

However, in practice, nearly all bankers will ask the guarantor to sign or execute the standard guarantee forms. The prudent banker will not rely only on the oral promise made by the guarantor.

Guarantee and Indemnity

Typically, the standard guarantee forms provide not only guarantees but also indemnities. They have a 'principal debtor' clause which allows the bank to make a claim against the guarantor as if he were the principal debtor, notwithstanding any legal limitation or incapacity on the part of the debtor whose obligations are being guaranteed.

Whether a contract is drafted purely as a guarantee or as an indemnity has implications on the bank. In a guarantee, if the principal contract is found to be unenforceable, the guarantor would be discharged from liability. On the other hand, a person who gives an indemnity undertakes a primary obligation that is not dependent on the debtor's liability or default. Therefore, that person remains liable even if the principal debtor is found to be ineligible to be a debtor.

For example, where a person wishes to become surety for someone who is under disability (e.g., a minor), it should be made clear in the contract that the surety is to be liable as a principal. The legal document may be worded as both a guarantee and as an indemnity. If the principal debtor is later found to be under disability with the result that sums advanced to him could not be made the subject of a guarantee, the indemnity provision will still bind the guarantor and the bank will be able to bring legal action against the guarantor.

Types of Guarantees

A guarantee may be a single/specific guarantee, continuing guarantee, or limited/unlimited continuing guarantee.

- **Single/specific guarantee.** This is a guarantee limited to a single transaction. It is discharged when the creditor makes a first advance up to the agreed limit of the guarantee, and the guarantor is liable for that amount only. This type of guarantee is risky for banks where an active account is used for the advance because the rule in Clayton's Case (see Chapter 1) could operate to discharge the guarantee.
- **Continuing guarantee.** This is a guarantee intended to cover a series of transactions over a period of time. It will not be discharged by a single transaction. An example is where a guarantee is given for an overdraft facility, or for all sums from time to time outstanding

under general banking facilities granted by the bank to the debtor. Thus, guarantees commonly contain a clause stating that the guarantee shall be a continuing security for the ultimate balance due from the debtor to the bank from time to time and at any time.

- **Limited/unlimited guarantee.** An unlimited guarantee is one where the guarantor undertakes liability for all of the borrower's debts to the creditor without limit as to amount (commonly known as an 'all monies' guarantee). A limited guarantee is one where the guarantor assumes liability up to a fixed amount. Bank guarantee forms typically contain an 'all monies' clause, with a proviso to cater for cases where a limit is to be imposed and which can be deleted if the guarantee is unlimited.

Code of Banking Practice

Section 23.2 of the Code of Banking Practice requires banks to advise an individual surety (that is, a guarantor or provider of third-party security to secure a debtor's liabilities) in writing that, by signing the guarantee or giving third-party security, the surety might become liable instead of, or as well as, the debtor. The bank should also inform the surety whether the guarantee or security provided by the surety is limited or unlimited as to amount.

If the guarantee is limited, the bank should advise the guarantor of the limits of that guarantor's liability.

If the guarantee is unlimited, the bank should inform the guarantor of the implications of signing such a guarantee. For example, the guarantor will be liable for all the actual and contingent liabilities of the debtor, currently and in the future, including more money that the bank may lend to the debtor without the guarantor's consent.

The Code of Banking Practice expects banks to advise the guarantor to seek independent legal advice before signing the guarantee forms. Banks are also expected to inform the guarantor in writing:

- Whether or not the liabilities under the guarantee are payable on demand;
- What the circumstances are under which the guarantor would be called upon to honour his or her obligations;
- What the circumstances are that will allow the guarantor to extinguish his or her liability and the timing within which this can be done.

The Code requires banks to include or attach to the guarantee forms a clear and prominent notice on the above provisions. Banks should provide the guarantor the option to choose whether the guarantee should be limited or unlimited in amount.

Before an individual signs the guarantee forms, subject to the consent of the debtor, the bank should provide him or her with a copy or summary of the contract evidencing the obligations to be guaranteed. Upon request by the guarantor, subject to the consent of the debtor, the bank should provide a copy of the latest statement of account it provided to the debtor, if any. The guarantor should also be provided with a copy of any formal demand for overdue payment that the bank sends to the debtor who has failed to settle the overdue amount after the customary reminder. However, a debtor's prescribed consent must be obtained before these documents can be provided to the guarantor. The bank should obtain such consent before accepting a guarantee. If the debtor declines to give consent to the provision of the above documents to the guarantor, the bank should inform the guarantor in advance so that the guarantor can decide whether to provide the guarantee or the security.

Where a guarantee is unlimited in amount, the bank should give notice to the guarantor as soon as reasonably practicable when further facility is extended to the debtor or when the nature of the facility extended to the debtor is changed.

Undue Influence

In Hong Kong, there is no statutory rule regarding the formal requirements for the execution of a guarantee. Common law rules therefore apply, specifically the common law principle that allows a contract to be voided if Party A obtains a benefit from Party B by exerting influence over Party B. That influence is so strong that Party B is prevented from exercising his or her independent judgment in deciding whether or not to confer the benefit on Party A.

Under common law, contracts that are voidable because of undue influence fall under two categories:

- Where there is a special relationship between the parties that enables one party to exert influence over the other, the court presumes that undue influence has been exerted unless there is evidence to the contrary. Such special relationships include solicitor-client, parent-child, husband-wife, and trustee-beneficiary relationships.
- Where evidence of the relationship between the parties and other facts are sufficient to justify the court in finding, on a balance of probabilities, that the transaction in question was procured by undue influence. A common type of situation is where one party reposes trust and confidence in the other.

Legal Implications

If a bank accepts a guarantee under circumstances where it is subsequently proved that the guarantee was obtained because of the debtor's undue influence over the guarantor, the court may rule that the guarantee should be set aside. The judge may conclude that the bank had actual or constructive notice that such undue influence had been exercised and it should have taken steps to ensure that the guarantor fully understands the nature of the transaction.

For example, where a wife acts as guarantor for the debts of her husband or a company in which the husband has an interest, the court will put the bank on constructive notice (that is, it will assume that the bank should have known) that there was undue influence if the transaction, on its face, is not to the wife's financial advantage. The second circumstance for putting the bank on constructive notice is if there is a substantial risk that, in having the wife act as guarantor, the husband has committed some wrong doing such as exercising undue influence or misrepresenting material facts such as the nature of the document or extent of the guarantor's liability.

If either (or both) of these circumstances are present, the bank must take "reasonable steps" to explain to the wife the risk she is undertaking in acting as guarantor and to advise her to take independent advice. The proposed "reasonable steps" would include arranging a private meeting with the wife and a representative of the bank, in the absence of the husband, where she is informed of the extent of her liability as guarantor, warned of the risk she is assuming, and urged to take independent legal advice.

Execution of a Guarantee

To avoid allegations of undue influence or misrepresentation and to discharge its duty of ensuring that a guarantor understands the nature and effect of the transaction, it is now the practice of banks in Hong Kong to require guarantors to execute the guarantee document in the presence of a bank employee at the bank's premises or, where the bank is legally represented, in the presence of the bank's lawyer at the lawyers' office.

For the same reasons, it is the practice of banks to provide the guarantor with a copy of the guarantee in advance, together with a copy of the loan agreement between the bank and the debtor (subject to the debtor's consent), in accordance with the recommendations of the Code of Banking Practice. Banks also prepare a written statement notifying the guarantor of matters specified in the Code, as previously discussed in this chapter. Most banks require the guarantor to acknowledge that they have received the statement and understood its contents.

While attestation of a guarantor's signature is not a legal requirement, a typical bank guarantee form requires attestation by a bank employee or a lawyer. It is no longer regarded as prudent or acceptable to entrust to the debtor the task of obtaining the guarantee document from the guarantor.

Guarantees by Minors

Persons below the age of 18 are incapable of entering into a contract of guarantee because they do not possess full contractual capacity in law. A bank runs the risk of having the contract declared void if it fails to check whether the guarantor is of age. A guarantee given by other persons that similarly lack contractual capacity at law, such as a mentally incapacitated person, is voidable as well at the option of that person who lacks capacity.

When a person reaches the age of 18, he or she is endowed with full contractual capacity. However, bankers should be aware that there is one type of guarantee given by such a person that requires special care—namely, where he or she becomes a guarantor for a parent or for someone standing in the place of a parent. Because of the special relationship of the parties, undue influence is presumed to exist.

Even if the child is married and is no longer living at the parents' home, undue influence may still be presumed. Whether the parental domination has ceased is a question of fact depending upon the particular circumstances of each case. These rules were laid down by the Court of Appeal in *Lancashire Loans Ltd. v. Black (1934)*, where a married daughter, aged 22, was relieved from liability as guarantor for her mother in respect of an advance to the mother by moneylenders.

Guarantees by Partnerships

In the ordinary business transactions of a partnership, each partner is an agent for the firm and his other partners. Section 7 of the Partnership Ordinance provides that "the acts of every partner who does any act for carrying on in the usual way business of the kind carried on by the firm of which he is a member bind the firm and his partners, unless the partner so acting has in fact no authority to act for the firm in the particular matter, and the person with whom he is dealing either knows he has no authority, or does not know or believe him to be a partner."

In other words, one partner has no implied authority to give guarantees such as to bind the partnership. The exception is if it can be shown that the giving of guarantees is necessary for carrying on the business of a particular partnership in the ordinary way. Unless the partnership deed or partnership agreement clearly states that the giving of guarantees is part of the ordinary business of the firm, the banker should either have the guarantee signed by all the partners or require that the one partner signing the guarantee has the express written authority of the others.

The second alternative is seldom adopted in practice, chiefly because the authority ought to refer specifically to the execution of the bank's own form of guarantee, a copy of which should be attached to the authority. So, instead of signing an authority of this nature, the partners might just as conveniently sign the guarantee itself. All partners who sign the guarantee forms in order to bind the partnership are personally liable on the guarantee.

The clauses employed in a guarantee given by partners are similar to those in a joint and several guarantee, which we discuss later in this chapter. In fact, some banks, instead of having a special form for guarantees by partners, make use of their ordinary 'joint and several' form. Partners must expressly undertake joint and several liability because, in absence of express provision, they incur only joint liability for the debts and obligations of the partnership.

Corporate Guarantees

As we discussed in Chapter 2, the doctrine of *ultra vires* has been virtually abolished in Hong Kong. It is therefore no longer necessary for a banker to examine the company's memorandum of association to see whether it contains an express power to execute a guarantee. However, the banker must check the articles of association in order to determine whether the execution of a corporate guarantee is within the powers of the directors.

The board of directors of the company should pass a resolution authorising certain officials to execute the guarantee instrument on the company's behalf, and the bank should be given a certified copy of the resolution. It is prudent for the bank to supply the company with a draft resolution worded as follows: "Resolved that the Chairman and Secretary be authorised to execute a guarantee for HK$________ in favour of __________ on account of _________ in the form and terms of the specimen guarantee attached hereto."

The specimen should be initialled for purposes of identification. This effectively precludes the company or its liquidator from arguing upon some subsequent occasion that the guarantee actually executed (containing all the special clauses found in bank guarantees) was not specifically authorised by the directors.

Some banks achieve the same object by having a certified copy of the resolution endorsed on the guarantee itself. The resolution is worded: "Resolved that the Chairman and Secretary be authorised to execute a guarantee for HK$________ in favour of __________ on account of _________ in the form and terms of the guarantee produced to the board on which guarantee a certified copy of this resolution shall be inscribed."

Finally, when a company is proposing to execute a guarantee, the bank must ensure that the directors who pass the resolution do not have a personal interest in the transaction. Section 157 of the Companies Ordinance makes it unlawful for a company, directly or indirectly, to enter into any guarantee (including an indemnity) to any director of the company itself, its holding company, or another company in which any of the directors holds a controlling interest.

Where the company is listed in Hong Kong or is a member of a listed group, the prohibition extends to loans made to a spouse, child, or partner of a director. The Ordinance provides for certain exceptions, including cases where the loan is made to a company that is a member of the same group of companies, or where the transaction is approved by shareholders in general meeting in the case of a private company that is not a member of a listed group.

For corporations that are incorporated by legislation, the bank should check the relevant legislation to make sure that the corporation is indeed empowered to make guarantees.

Joint and Several Guarantees

When a customer is asked for suitable security for a proposed advance, he may inform the bank that two or more of his relatives or friends are prepared to sign guarantees on his behalf. He may be making application for an overdraft of, say, HK$6 million, and he may state that three persons, G1, G2, and G3, are willing to sign guarantees to the amount of HK$2 million each.

It is sound policy for the banker, under these circumstances, to ask that all three guarantors join in signing one instrument for HK$6 million, that is, each guarantor accepts joint and several liability. If and when the bank has to enforce the security, it may happen that G1 will be in a strong financial position, whereas G2 and G3 will not. Under a joint and several guarantee, the bank would be able to demand the whole HK$6 million from G1, leaving it to him to claim contributions from his or her co-guarantors.

Bank guarantee forms in Hong Kong invariably provide for joint and several liabilities of co-guarantors.

Special Problems

Guarantees executed by two or more persons give rise to special problems. There is an important difference between joint liability on the one hand, and joint and several liability, on the other. Where a guarantor is only bound jointly with his co-guarantor and not severally as well, his liability both for existing and for future debts of the debtor comes to an end with his death. The survivor or survivors alone become liable both at law and in equity. This is known as the doctrine of survivorship.

It is not necessary for co-guarantors to sign the guarantee in the presence of each other. However, all co-guarantors must sign the document. Where a guarantee is given by more than one guarantor, and one of them fails to sign or the signature turns out to have been forged, those who did sign will be discharged from liability. However, they will still be liable if the bank can prove that those who signed consented to non-execution by the others. Bank guarantee forms now commonly provide that failure by any proposed co-guarantors to execute the document will not affect the liabilities of the other parties.

The release of one co-guarantor in respect of his or her liability under the guarantee will release the other co-guarantors. A release will also be effected if there is any variation in the liability of any co-guarantor, such as a reduction in the limit of his or her liability. However, this does not apply if those intended to remain under liability consented to the release or variation.

To avoid this result, bank guarantee forms typically provide that the bank shall be entitled to release or vary the liability of any co-guarantor in respect of his liability under the guarantee, without prejudice to the liability of the others. The guarantee forms also provide that the guarantee shall remain in force until notice of termination has been given by all of the co-guarantors (and, where any of them dies, the personal representative of the deceased guarantor). This precludes termination of the guarantee by notice given by one guarantor only.

Drafting a Joint and Several Guarantee

To make it clear that the liability of the guarantors is to be joint and several, the words "The liability and obligations of each Guarantor are joint and several…" should be used.

The other clauses will be similar to those inserted in guarantees executed by an individual. However, the joining together of two or more persons as guarantors in the same instrument makes it advisable to incorporate certain special provisions.

It is common to find a clause worded thusly: "Each Guarantor shall be bound even though any other Guarantor(s) or any other person(s) intended to be bound by this Guarantee is not. The Bank shall be entitled to deal separately with a Guarantor on any matter, including the discharge of the liability of that Guarantor to any extent, without affecting the liability of any other Guarantor(s)." The value of this clause is that it excludes the rule that the release of a joint and several guarantor releases the other or others from liability.

Another clause usually found in a joint and several guarantee reads: "This Guarantee is a continuing security and shall secure the whole of the Guaranteed Moneys until six calendar months after receipt by the Bank of notice in writing by each Guarantor to terminate it. Nevertheless and despite the giving of such notice, this Guarantee shall continue to apply to the Guaranteed Moneys in respect of which the Customer is or becomes actually or contingently liable up to such termination and the Guarantor guarantees to pay such Guaranteed Moneys to the Bank on demand whether that demand is made before, at the time of or after such termination."

Liability of Guarantors

The scope of liability of a guarantor is a matter of contract law. The extent of such liability depends on the terms contained in the guarantee forms. In practice, the guarantee forms are drafted by the bank, which in most cases will not allow customers to vary the terms, except in cases relating to project finance or syndicated loans.

Conditional Guarantee

A guarantee may be conditional, meaning that if the condition is not met, the guarantor has no liability. This is not a case of the guarantor being released or of a breach having been committed by the creditor. Rather, it is a case of the guarantee never coming into force because the condition that would make it valid has not been met. It is therefore important for a banker to recognise the various cases in which guarantees have been held to be conditional.

A common problem is the failure of one or more contemplated guarantors to sign the guarantee, which as discussed earlier will make none of the guarantors liable. Their 'release' is not dependent on any fault on the part of the creditor. Even if a guarantee bears all the signatures required, but it is discovered that one is forged, all the guarantors are also released.

Another common problem is the failure to execute the consideration. Thus if the consideration for the guarantor is the making of future advances and none is made, the guarantor will have no liability.

In most cases, the guarantee is only one of several forms of security taken by the banker. The question is whether the taking of the other security is a condition of the guarantee. In *Greer v. Kettle (1938)*, the House of Lords held in that case that the guarantor only undertook to guarantee a debt secured by a charge on shares, and such a debt never having existed, the guarantor never had any liability. But the English Court of Appeal in *Gray v. TCB Ltd. (1988)* puts the onus on the guarantor to establish that the existence of the other security is a condition of the guarantee.

In any event, it would be prudent for a banker to address the issue. If the bank is not willing to have the guarantee conditional on the other forms of security taken, precautions should be taken to ensure that this does not become the case.

To guard against a guarantee being held void for failure of a condition, a banker should include protective provisions that address the issue of conditions. For example, the guarantee clause should state that the guarantor guarantees unconditionally. It is also desirable to refrain from referring to the debt guaranteed as the 'mortgage' or 'mortgage debt.' As statements of consideration for the guarantee are not required by law, recitals and consideration clauses should be kept to the bare minimum. A consideration clause or recital clause that refers to the 'mortgage debt,' for instance, would support the argument that the guarantee is conditioned on the existence of a valid mortgage.

Guarantee Limits

As discussed earlier in this chapter, a guarantee may be unlimited (no limit as to the amount guaranteed) or limited up to a certain stipulated amount. A prudent banker will ask for an unlimited guarantee, but in most cases, the prospective guarantor will decline and only agree to execute a guarantee for a certain amount.

It is important to distinguish between a guarantee of the whole debt subject to a limitation of liability, and a guarantee of a part of a debt. If the guarantee is a guarantee of the whole debt subject only to a limitation of liability, the guarantor has no rights to subrogation (the substitution of one person in place of another person with reference to a lawful claim) or to indemnity until the entire debt is paid, even if he has paid up to the limit.

Thus, the banker may have to present proof of debt for the entire debt in case of the debtor's insolvency and retain all the dividends from the debtor's estate. The banker may also sue the debtor for the entire amount of debt, even after payment by the guarantor. Where the guarantor is insolvent in such a case, the banker may prove for the entire debt, though the amount of dividends cannot exceed the limit of liability.

If the guarantee is a guarantee of a part of the debt, once the guarantor has paid the amount guaranteed, the guarantor has all the rights of a guarantor who has discharged his liability. These include the right to share in the security held by the banker for the whole debt and to file a proof in the debtor's insolvency and share the dividends. It follows that, if the guarantor is insolvent, the banker may prove for the amount of the guarantee and not the entire debt.

Whether the guarantee is one of the whole or part of the debt is a matter of construction. There are two basic rules:

- Where the guarantor has given a continuing guarantee, limited in amount, to secure the floating balance which may from time to time be due from the debtor to the banker, the guarantee is applicable to a part only of the debt, co-extensive with the amount of his guarantee. The reason is that it is inequitable to allow the banker to increase the balance at the expense of the guarantor.
- Where the guarantee limited in amount is for a debt ascertained which exceeds that limit, it is prima facie construed as a guarantee of the whole debt.

In practice, the standard continuing guarantee form is usually drafted as a guarantee of the whole debt, subject to a limited amount. The problem may arise where a preprinted limitation clause is left blank. In such an event the guarantee will be construed as unlimited.

Guarantor's Rights as Against the Creditor

The guarantor enjoys rights under the contract of guarantee he or she has executed vis-à-vis the creditor, that is, the bank. Bankers must be aware of and respect the guarantor's rights to ensure the bank is protected in the event of a legal dispute. Unless there are contrary terms in the guarantee, a guarantor has the following rights as against the creditor bank:

- At any time during the life of the guarantee, a guarantor can ask the bank for information as to the amount for which he is liable under the terms of the guarantee. The bank should inform the guarantor of the exact amount of the debt, if it is an unlimited amount guarantee, or if the debt has not exceeded the amount guaranteed. The bank should inform the guarantor that he has maximum liability if the debt has already reached or exceeded the maximum amount of a limited amount guarantee.
- The bank must exercise care in supplying this information to protect the confidential relationship it has with the customer (i.e., the debtor) and the debtor's prescribed consent should be obtained before providing the information. Information given should be strictly limited to a statement of the guarantor's present liability.
- If the debt exceeds the amount of the guarantee, the guarantor should merely be told that he is liable for the full amount of his guarantee. If the debt is less than the amount of the guarantee, the guarantor should be told the actual amount of the debt, including bank charges. The guarantor should also be reminded that, as a period of notice is required if he wishes to determine his liability, the position may change before that period has expired.

- As soon as a definite sum of money has become payable by the guarantor, he has the right to have it paid by the debtor. It was held in *Thomas v. Nottingham Incorporate Football Club Ltd.* [1972] that after the guarantor has given notice to the creditor bank about the determination of the guarantee, he was entitled to call upon the debtor to pay, even though the guarantor was only liable on demand and no such demand had yet been made. The ruling observed that it would be strange if the guarantor could not seek to remove the cloud until it had started to rain.
- At any time after the debt has become due, the guarantor may apply to the creditor bank and pay off the debt. After giving an indemnity for costs, the guarantor may then proceed to sue the debtor in the creditor bank's name or even under the guarantor's name, provided that the guarantor obtains an assignment of the guaranteed debt.
- After paying the debt in full, the guarantor has the right to subrogate (i.e., take over by substitution) to all the rights to which the creditor bank is entitled. If the guarantor offers to pay the debt on condition that the remedies due the creditor bank are made over to him and the credit bank refuses, the guarantor is entitled to pay the money into court, and then bring an action for an assignment of the remedies.
- The right of a guarantor to the securities deposited with the creditor bank extends not only to those given by the debtor, but also those given by any other person (whether a guarantor or not) for the purpose of securing the debt. Accordingly, a guarantor who has paid more than his due proportion of the common liability is entitled to have such securities assigned to him.
- The guarantor has the right to be informed of any term in the loan agreement which renders the position of the guarantor different from what he would expect.
- The creditor bank owes a duty of care to the guarantor when selling the debtor's property deposited by the debtor in support of his indebtedness.
- Subject to any explicit term in the guarantee, a material variation of the principal agreement between the creditor and debtor without informing or obtaining consent from the guarantor may discharge the guarantor from liability.
- It is arguable whether the guarantor has a right to compel proceedings. Some standard guarantee forms have a provision whereby the guarantor waives any right to require the creditor to proceed first against the debtor or other security. In *Hongkong and Shanghai Banking Corp. v. Cheung Kung Hai*, it was held that in the absence of any agreement to the contrary, enforcement of other securities or proceedings against the debtor is not a condition precedent to the enforcement of a guarantee.

Guarantor's Rights as Against the Debtor

As part of the tripartite relationship among itself, the debtor, and the guarantor, the creditor bank is affected by the rights of the guarantor as against the debtor. The prudent banker should be aware of these rights to protect the interests of his bank in case of a legal dispute between the guarantor and the debtor that can have an impact on the creditor bank's own claims. Unless otherwise provided for, a guarantor has the following rights as against the debtor:

- When the creditor bank acquires a right to immediate payment of the debt, the guarantor is entitled to call upon the debtor to pay the amount of the debt guaranteed so as to relieve the guarantor of his obligation. It would be the same even though the guarantor had paid nothing under the guarantee and the creditor bank had not demanded payment from him or from the debtor. The guarantor may ask the court for a declaration that he has a right in equity to require the debtor to exonerate him from his liability under the guarantee by paying off the debt.
- After paying the creditor bank, the guarantor may claim reimbursement from the debtor. Sometimes the debtor may expressly give the guarantor the right to claim reimbursement. Where the right is not expressly given, the guarantor still has an implied right of indemnification from the debtor if the guarantee is given at the request of the debtor. If the guarantee is not given at the request of the debtor, the guarantor may not claim reimbursement.

  In most bank's guarantee forms, there is a non-competition clause whose aim is to prevent the guarantor from taking any step to claim reimbursement from the debtor, unless and until the creditor bank has been fully repaid. If such were the case, the guarantor's right to claim reimbursement from the debtor would have to wait until the creditor bank has been fully paid.
- As soon as the guarantor pays anything under his guarantee, he has an immediate right of action against the debtor. But the guarantor cannot accelerate this remedy by paying the guaranteed debt before it becomes legally due. If the debtor is bankrupt, the guarantor may present proof of debt to his estate for the amount which he has paid under the guarantee. However, this right is subject to the rule against double proof, whereby a surety cannot prove, in the bankruptcy of the debtor, upon a contract to indemnify him, whether express or implied, whilst the creditor is proving for the debt itself.

Rights of Co-Guarantors

A guarantor who has paid more than his fair share of money to the creditor is entitled to claim contribution from the co-guarantors. The right arises if guarantors are liable to the creditor jointly and severally, or severally, and by the same or different instruments. The right does not arise if the guarantors are jointly but not severally liable or if the guarantors are not liable to a common demand.

The right of contribution is not found in contract but in equity, and on the principle of equality of burden and benefit. Therefore, a co-guarantor is not liable to contribute until a guarantor has paid more than his share of the debt. For example, if three persons sign a joint and several guarantee and only one of them pays to the creditor one third of the total liability, he would have no right to claim contribution from the other co-guarantors unless the creditor has accepted the one-third payment as full and final settlement of all liability under the guarantee.

A co-guarantor's duty of contribution arises even before a guarantor pays any money to the creditor under the guarantee. When a creditor bank has obtained judgment against a guarantor, the bank may immediately bring an action against the other co-guarantors, compelling them to contribute to the common liability.

Duties of the Creditor Bank

After the foregoing discussion on the liability and rights of the guarantor, co-guarantor, and debtor, we can summarise what is expected of the creditor bank under three headings: duty with regard to securities held, duty to explain, and duty of disclosure.

Duty with Regard to Securities Held

A creditor bank is not obligated to take steps to realise the value of the securities it is holding as collateral for a guaranteed debt, even in circumstances where there is a marked decline in the security's market value. The courts have suggested that the guarantor could avoid the consequences of a creditor's failure to deal with securities that are declining in value by paying the debt and obtaining a transfer of the securities.

In cases where the creditor bank takes steps to realise a security, the bank will owe a duty to take reasonable care to obtain a proper price for the security. The guarantor will have grounds for redress if the bank acts negligently in the realisation of the property by failing to take reasonable care and skill to obtain the best price reasonably obtainable for the property.

The correct way of transferring or assigning the securities to the guarantor depends on the nature of the securities. In the case of a legal charge of land or a legal mortgage of a life policy, the bank should execute a statutory receipt acknowledging the payment of a specified sum by the guarantor. This automatically transfers to the guarantor the benefit of the mortgage.

If the security is a legal mortgage of shares or stocks that have been transferred into the names of the bank's nominees, the shares or stocks should be transferred into the name of the guarantor. The fundamental principle is that the bank must make available to the guarantor the same rights as the bank possesses in relation to the security.

Duty to Explain

At law, a bank has no duty to explain the meaning, effect, or contents of a guarantee to the guarantor, except in circumstances where there is a possibility of undue influence or misrepresentation affecting an individual guarantor. However, as previously discussed, the Code of Banking Practice requires banks to advise an individual guarantor in writing of the essential terms and conditions of the guarantee.

If the bank, through its employee or lawyer, explains the guarantee to the guarantor, it owes a duty to do so accurately and in a manner which can be understood by the guarantor. Care must be taken not to make any misstatement or misrepresentation.

Duty of Disclosure

The bank's duty of disclosure comes under two headings: disclosure as required by the Code of Banking Practice and disclosure under common law. We have previously discussed the Code's requirement on disclosure, so we will not repeat it here. To summarise, the bank is required to disclose information about the guarantee to the guarantor, but it must first obtain the debtor's consent to provide certain information relating to the debtor's affairs. If the debtor refuses consent to the disclosure, the bank should inform the guarantor so that he or she can decide whether to proceed with the guarantee.

Under common law, it has been established that a contract of guarantee, unlike an insurance contract, is not *uberrimae fidei* (i.e., of the utmost good faith). The creditor bank's duty of disclosure vis-à-vis a guarantor is therefore limited. The bank is not obliged to disclose to a guarantor excessive details relating to the debtor's affairs or accounts, owing to its duty of confidentiality to the debtor as its customer. If the guarantor insists on being provided with the extra information, it is prudent for the bank to arrange a tripartite meeting with the debtor and guarantor, where the debtor's consent is obtained in the presence of the guarantor.

Discharge of the Guarantor

There are many ways that a guarantee may come to an end, which in most cases means that the guarantor is discharged of all liability. They include the normal discharge after the guaranteed debt is fully repaid, voiding of the guarantee because of vitiating factors such as duress and undue influence, discharge by conduct prejudicial to the guarantor, and termination of the guarantee by such events as the death of the debtor and revocation of the guarantee by the guarantor.

For the bank, the best outcome is generally the natural ending of the guarantee as the guaranteed debt is repaid in the normal way. However, legal issues arising from certain events and circumstances may disrupt the process. The banking professional must be aware of what can go wrong with a guarantee such that the contract does not end as envisioned and what should be done to avert such an outcome or mitigate the effects if the guarantee, despite the bank's best efforts, is terminated or voided.

Discharge by Payment, Agreement, or Expiry

A guarantee may be discharged by:

- Payment by the debtor or guarantor of the guaranteed debt;
- Discharge of the debtor;
- Agreement between the bank and the guarantor;
- Where the guarantee is for a fixed period, the expiry of that period.

If a guarantor has paid the guaranteed debt, the bank should not return the guarantee or write 'cancelled' across it, because it may be necessary for the bank to invoke certain provisions of the guarantee after its discharge. An example is the provision that the guarantor will not enforce any right or make any claim against the debtor in competition with the bank until the whole of the debtor's liabilities has been discharged, notwithstanding that the guarantee may have been discharged.

Where the guarantee is only for part of the debtor's liabilities and the bank has to pursue the debtor for his remaining debt, the bank will have to rely on this provision in the guarantee, which makes retention after discharge necessary. Bank guarantee forms commonly provide that the guarantee is the bank's property and the bank is not obliged to return it to the guarantor after discharge.

Avoidance of Guarantee

At law, the guarantee may be set aside and the liability of the guarantor discharged if any of the following vitiating factors can be proved:

- **Duress,** which is an unlawful act, or a threat to commit an unlawful or improper act, directed against the guarantor in order to induce him or her to enter into a transaction.
- **Undue influence,** which refers to the strong influence that the debtor exercises over the guarantor, which prevents the guarantor to exercise independent judgement, as discussed earlier in this chapter.
- **Misrepresentation or omission of a material fact,** even if made innocently.
- **Mistake,** which refers to the parties committing a fundamental error relating to the subject matter of the contract, resulting in a guarantee that is essentially and radically different from what the parties believed was the case when the contract was made.
- **Non est factum,** which is Latin for "It is not [my] deed," allows a party that signed a contract to escape performance of the agreement if it is proved that:
    i. The person (e.g., a guarantor) who signed a contract (e.g., a guarantee) is under a disability such as illiteracy, blindness, or poor understanding of the language in which the document is couched, which would render that person incapable of reading and sufficiently understanding the document;

ii. The document signed is fundamentally or radically different from what the person who signed had intended;
iii. The person who signed has not been careless, but had taken reasonable precautions to ascertain the contents and significance of the document.

Discharge by Conduct Prejudicial to Guarantor

In certain circumstances, a guarantee may be discharged because of the creditor bank's prejudicial conduct in relation to equitable principles. Unless the guarantee provides otherwise or the guarantor's consent is obtained for the creditor bank actions, the guarantor will be discharged if the creditor bank:

- Releases the principal debtor, or agrees with the debtor to give him time for repayment;
- Agrees with the debtor to vary the terms of the principal contract, unless the variation is immaterial or will not cause any prejudice to the guarantor;
- Releases any co-guarantor or any security given for the guaranteed obligations.

These principles are invariably excluded in banks' guarantee forms as grounds for discharge. Whether the exclusion provisions are effective is a matter of construction of their wording. Their enforceability may also be subject to the 'reasonableness' test under the Unconscionable Contracts Ordinance.

Termination

Termination of a guarantee has the effect of discharging the guarantor from future liabilities incurred by the debtor after the date of termination, but not from liabilities already accrued as of the date of termination.

A guarantor's liability will be fixed on the date of termination, but if the debtor's loan account is a current account into which monies are paid after the termination of the guarantee, the rule in Clayton's Case (as discussed in Chapter 1) will operate. This means that the debtor's debit balance as at the date of termination, which represents the guarantor's continuing liability after termination, is reduced or eventually discharged by the monies paid in.

The effect is that the guarantor's liability will likewise be eventually discharged. There are two ways in which banks may avoid this result:

- By providing in the guarantee that the guarantor's liability for the debt due from the debtor shall remain even when the guarantee is terminated, notwithstanding any subsequent payment into or out of the debtor's account;
- By closing or ruling off the debtor's account on termination of the guarantee, and opening a new account for subsequent inward and outward payments.

A guarantee may be terminated under the following circumstances: revocation by the guarantor, termination by the bank, death or mental incapacity of the guarantor, death of the debtor, change in constitution of the parties, and revocation by co-guarantors.

- *Revocation by the guarantor.* At law, a guarantor may revoke a guarantee by giving reasonable notice, even if the guarantee provides for a fixed period. Bank guarantee forms commonly allow the guarantor to terminate the guarantee by giving a fixed period of notice, normally in writing. On expiry of the notice period, the guarantor's liability will be fixed as the amount then outstanding from the debtor. A bank will normally consider whether or not to demand repayment from the debtor before expiry of the notice period, so as to fix the guarantor's liability.
- *Termination by the bank.* Where the creditor bank demands repayment from the debtor and the debtor fails to pay, this has the effect of fixing the guarantor's liability and terminating the guarantee as a continuing obligation, unless the guarantee otherwise provides. Release of the debtor or a co-guarantor without the guarantor's consent will also release the guarantor from all obligations, although bank guarantee forms typically allow the bank to release or modify the obligations of the debtor or any co-guarantor without discharging the guarantor.
- *Death or mental incapacity of the guarantor.* At law, a guarantee terminates when the bank receives actual notice of the guarantor's death or mental incapacity. However, most bank guarantee forms provide that the liability of the guarantor's estate continues until the personal representative or (in the case of mental incapacity) committee of inspection gives a fixed period of notice of their intention to terminate the guarantee.

  In the case of a joint guarantee, the death of one joint co-guarantor will discharge the liability of his/her estate such that only the surviving co-guarantors remain liable. Where the co-guarantors' liability is joint and several and one of them dies, his/her estate will be severally liable under the guarantee.
- *Death of the debtor.* Since the debtor can no longer incur further liabilities, the guarantee is treated as terminated in that the guarantor's liability is fixed as of the date of the debtor's death.
- *Change in constitution of the parties.* If the constitution of the debtor or the creditor changes, for example, the debtor being a partnership is dissolved at law by virtue of the addition or retirement of partners, or the creditor bank merges with another institution, any guarantee given for the debtor's debts or in favour of the bank will be terminated as to future transactions, unless the guarantee otherwise provides. In the case of partnerships, Section 20 of the Partnership Ordinance provides that a continuing guarantee given either to a partnership (as creditor) or to a third person in respect of the transactions of a partnership (as debtor) is, in the absence of agreement to the contrary, revoked as to future transactions by any change in the constitution of the partnership. The partners of the original partnership will remain liable for the firm's debts up to the date of revocation.

Bank guarantee forms commonly exclude the application of these rules by, for example, providing that the guarantee remains in force notwithstanding any change in constitution of the parties, and shall ensure for the benefit of the creditor bank and 'its successors and assigns.' In the case of a partnership admitting new partners, while the guarantee may continue in force and the partners of the original partnership remain liable, any new partner will not be party to the original guarantee and must be asked to sign a new guarantee.

- *Revocation by co-guarantors.* Where one of several co-guarantors gives notice of revocation to the creditor bank, then unless otherwise agreed, this terminates the further liability of all the guarantors, although they remain liable for existing debts as at the date of revocation.

  Bank guarantee forms now provide that any co-guarantor may give a fixed period of notice to withdraw from the guarantee without affecting the liability of other co-guarantors. The liability of the withdrawing co-guarantor is fixed on expiry of the notice period. If the liability is joint, he or she is liable for the entire amount of the debt owing as of that date, unless the parties agree to apportion the debt.

Summary

- A guarantee is a promise by one person (guarantor) to another (creditor) to answer for the debt, default, or miscarriage of a third person (debtor or principal obligor) towards the creditor. The guarantor's liability is only secondary or collateral. It is dependent on the debtor's obligation, and only arises when the debtor defaults.
- A guarantee may be a single/specific guarantee, continuing guarantee, or limited/unlimited continuing guarantee. A single/specific guarantee is limited to a single transaction and is risky for banks where an active account is used for the advance because the rule in Clayton's Case (see Chapter 1) could operate to discharge the guarantee.
- A continuing guarantee covers a series of transactions over a period of time. An example is where a guarantee is given for an overdraft facility, or for all sums from time to time outstanding under general banking facilities granted by the bank to the debtor. An unlimited guarantee is one where the guarantor undertakes liability for all of the borrower's debts to the creditor without limit as to amount.
- Contracts may be voided because of undue influence. This may be the case, for example, if there is a special relationship between the guarantor and debtor, such as parent-child and husband-wife, which enables one party to exert influence over the other. If a bank accepts a guarantee and it is subsequently proved that the guarantee was obtained because of the debtor's undue influence over the guarantor, the court may rule that the guarantee should be set aside.

- To avoid allegations of undue influence or misrepresentation and to discharge its duty of ensuring that a guarantor understands the nature and effect of the transaction, it is now the practice of banks in Hong Kong to require guarantors to execute the guarantee document in the presence of a bank employee at the bank's premises or, where the bank is legally represented, in the presence of the bank's lawyer at the lawyers' office.
- A bank runs the risk of having a contract of guarantee declared void if it fails to check whether the guarantor is of age. Persons below the age of 18 cannot extend guarantees. Other types of customers such as partnerships and corporations can enter into a contract of guarantee, under different circumstances and with their own respective requirements. Two or more individuals of age can also extend a guarantee, although such joint and several guarantees give rise to special problems that the bank must address.
- A guarantor has liabilities that depend on the terms contained in the bank's guarantee forms. A guarantor also has rights against the bank as creditor, which must be respected to ensure the bank is protected in the event of a legal dispute, and against the debtor, which have implications on the creditor bank's own claims. The duties of the creditor bank with regard to guarantees can be summarised under three headings: duty with regards to securities held, duty to explain, and duty of disclosure.
- There are many ways that a guarantee may come to an end, including the normal discharge after the guaranteed debt is fully repaid, voiding of the guarantee, discharge by conduct prejudicial to the guarantor, and termination of the guarantee by such events as the death of the debtor. For the bank, the best outcome is generally the natural ending of the guarantee as the guaranteed debt is repaid in the normal way.

Key Terms

co-guarantor
continuing guarantee
creditor
debtor
discharge
guarantee
guarantee forms
guarantor
joint and several guarantee
limited/unlimited guarantee
obligor
oral guarantee
revocation
security
single/specific guarantee
surety
termination
undue influence
written guarantee

Study Guide

1. Under what circumstance is a single/specific guarantee risky for banks? Refer to Chapter 1 to explain how Clayton's Case can operate in this case.
2. From the bank's point of view, what is the best type of guarantee and why? What is the best type of guarantee from the guarantor's point of view?
3. Mrs. A agreed to stand as guarantor to her husband's loan from the bank, against which he has pledged his 20% interest in a company. Does the husband-wife relationship automatically mean there is undue influence? If the bank decides to accept the guarantee, what should it do to ensure the guarantee will not be voided?
4. What are the vitiating factors that could lead the court to set aside a guarantee and discharge the liability of the guarantor? If you were a banker tasked with making a decision on whether or not to accept a guarantee, what should you do to ensure there are no such vitiating factors?
5. What are the duties of the bank vis-à-vis the guarantor, co-guarantor, and debtor? Under the duty of disclosure, to what extent can the bank tell the guarantor about the affairs of the debtor? What should the banker do if the guarantor insists on being provided with extra information?

Further Reading

Chan Bo-ching, Simon. 2001, *Hong Kong Banking Law and Practice Volume II*. First Edition. Hong Kong: Hong Kong Institute of Bankers.

Code of Banking Practice website, http://www.info.gov.hk/hkma/eng/bank/code/code_b.htm

Companies Ordinance website, http://www.hklii.org/hk/legis/ord/32/

Ko, Sai Hong. 1998, *Law and Practice of Banking Services in Hong Kong*. Hong Kong: City University Hong Kong Press.

Law Amendment and Reform (Consolidation) Ordinance website, http://www.hklii.org/hk/legis/en/ord/23/

Unconscionable Contracts Ordinance website, http://www.hklii.org/hk/legis/en/ord/458/

Mortgage of Land

Learning objectives

After studying this chapter, you should be able to:

1. Describe the basic concepts of land ownership, property, and mortgages in Hong Kong
2. List the key provisions of the Conveyancing and Property Ordinance and the Land Registration Ordinance affecting mortgages
3. Identify the formalities and procedures for creation of mortgages in Hong Kong
4. List the fundamental rules for determining priorities between competing interests affecting land
5. Identify the rights, powers, and remedies of the parties to a mortgage

Introduction

Land is generally regarded as the most secure form of security for banking facilities. In Hong Kong, mortgages are the most popular type of security. Banking facilities secured by mortgage over land have played a key role in both commercial activities and promotion of home ownership. It is therefore critical for banks to understand the law and practice relating to mortgages. This chapter explains the basic legal concepts and relevant statutes, and examines recent legal developments affecting mortgages.

Land in Hong Kong

Before discussing the legal issues around mortgages, it is important that bankers have a foundation of knowledge about land law in Hong Kong. In the legal sense, 'land' holds a much wider meaning than in everyday speech. The general rule is that whatever is attached to the soil becomes part of land. In other words, the term "land" includes the soil, the buildings, and the chattels.

The term also encompasses land covered by water, any estate, right, interest, or easement in or over any land, and the whole or part or an undivided share in land and any estate, right, interest, or easement in or over the whole or part of an undivided share in land.

Land law is concerned with the relationship of people (including bankers) to the land. In Hong Kong, land law has certain unique features due to the special administrative region's history and colonial heritage.

Tenure

English common law does not recognise absolute ownership of land. According to common law, all land in England "must be held of the King of England, otherwise he would not be the King of all English." As a British colony until 1 July 1997, when China resumed sovereignty, Hong Kong followed the same system. The only tenure in Hong Kong under the British was leasehold tenure.

This concept of tenure continues to apply in Hong Kong even though it is now a special administrative region (SAR) of China. Under Article 7 of the Basic Law of the Hong Kong SAR, the lands within Hong Kong are declared as state property. The government of the HKSAR is responsible for their management, use, and development and for their lease or grant to individuals, legal persons, or organisations for use or development.

Articles 120–123 of the Basic Law also provides for continued recognition of crown leases (now government leases) that extend beyond 1997, in the manner agreed in the Joint Declaration between the British Government and the Government of the People's Republic of China.

Estate

While the concept of tenure deals with the terms upon which the rights to use land are given, the concept of estate explains the duration of such rights. Estates in land differ according to how long they last. Estates are divided into two main categories: estates of uncertain duration, that is, freehold estates, and estates of certain duration, that is, leasehold estates. In Hong Kong, there are only leasehold estates.

Estates and interests in land may be recognised at common law or in equity. Common law, as discussed in Chapter 1, is a body of law developed through court decisions rather than bills passed by the legislature. Equity refers to a system of justice outside of the common law system. In Hong Kong, a distinction is made between legal rights and equitable rights in respect of estates and interests in land.

A brief history is useful to explain this distinction. Before 1873 in England, there were two separate systems for the administration of justice: the common law court and the Court of Chancery. The rights recognised and enforced at common law were known as 'legal rights.' The rights recognised by the Court of Chancery were termed 'equitable rights.' Petitioners denied legal remedy under common law could go to the Court of Chancery. If the party complained against is judged guilty of unconscionable conduct, the Court of Chancery would grant the claimant the appropriate remedies and deny the legal rights of the other party.

However, the decrees of the chancellor in the Court of Chancery often conflicted with the rulings of the common law judges. Eventually, it was settled that where there is conflict between the rules of law and those of equity, the rules of equity should prevail. This was preserved in England by the Judicature Act of 1873 and the Supreme Court Act of 1981. All divisions of the Supreme Court in England are given full power to administer both common law and equitable rights and remedies.

In Hong Kong, the same court system also administers both the rules of common law and the rules of equity. As in England, equity prevails where there is conflict between the two. There are many provisions in the Conveyancing and Property Ordinance that retain the distinction between legal rights and equity rights. However, the significance of the distinction is to a large extent weakened by the Land Registration Ordinance insofar as the enforcement of such rights against a third party is concerned.

Conveyancing and Property Ordinance

The Conveyancing and Property Ordinance defines legal terms that banking professionals should know as they relate to land in Hong Kong. These terms include legal estate, easement, legal charge, and equitable interest.

- **Legal estate.** Section 2 of the Ordinance defines legal estate as 'a term of years absolute' in land. A term of years is essentially an estate granted for a fixed duration, which includes 'term for less than a year, or for a year or years and a fraction of a year or from year to year.' Therefore, any term for any fixed and certain duration is a 'term of years,' for example a term of 99 years, or a yearly or monthly tenancy which have a maximum duration of a year or a month respectively.

The Ordinance also defines legal estate as 'a legal charge' and also as 'the legal interest in any easement, right or privilege in or over land for an interest equivalent to a term of years absolute.'

From these definitions, it is clear that leasehold estates are capable of being legal estates. Easements and charges are also legal estates.

- **Easement**. According to the Ordinance, an easement is a right enjoyed over the land of another person. An easement is either a positive or negative right over the land of another. It is a right to use the land of another in a particular way or a right to prevent the owner of land from using his own land in a particular way. The person who exercises the easement is a 'dominant owner' and the person whose land is used by the dominant owner is a 'servant owner.'

  Easement must be created by deed or by statute, and it must also be created for a period equivalent to a term of years absolute, that is, for a fixed period. Thus, if X is granted by deed an easement for a fixed term, his easement is legal (that is, recognised at common law). On the other hand, if X is granted an easement for as long as he lives, then his easement must necessarily be equitable (i.e., recognised in equity) because it is not granted for a period of time equivalent to a term of years. The fact that the easement for life is granted by deed does not alter its equitable nature.
- **Legal charge**. The Ordinance defines a legal charge as 'a mortgage expressed to be a legal charge.' A legal charge is a form of security granted by the owner of land in favour of the chargee (usually an authorised institution) in return for a loan advanced by that chargee. The legal charge is a security for the loan in that, if the chargor is not able to repay the loan, the chargee can take possession and receive any income from the land or sell the land to satisfy the debt.
- **Equitable interest**. The ordinance defines equitable interest to mean any estate, interest, or charge in or over land which is not a legal estate or a freehold. Thus, an equitable interest is an interest which does not fall within the definition of 'legal estate,' for example, an interest behind a trust. If land was conveyed to A on trust for B, A would be regarded in common law as the owner and B would not be regarded as having any legal right in the land. In equity, it is against A's conscience for him to deny B's true ownership. Thus, equity treats A as the legal owner and B as the equitable owner. A is required to hold the legal estate on trust for B, who enjoys the beneficial interest in the land.

  There are three interests created in equity which have no equivalents at common law: estate contracts, restrictive covenants, and the mortgagor's equity of redemption.

  Other equitable interests are equitable charges, equitable liens, and licences by estoppel. Equity also enforces certain rights that fall short of an equitable proprietary

margin as to make it commercially viable to lend against a second mortgage. In practice in Hong Kong, second mortgages are principally accepted by deposit-taking companies and finance companies.

The disadvantages of a second mortgage include:

- The second mortgagee is, to some extent, at the mercy of the first mortgagee, who is at liberty to decide on the timing and manner of exercising his powers under the first mortgage. So long as the first mortgagee acts in good faith, he is under no duty to have regard to the interests of the second mortgagee. For example, the first mortgagee is under no duty to delay a sale of the property to obtain a better price so as to improve the position of the second mortgagee.
- The first mortgagee may elect to foreclose the property. If he succeeds, the effect of a foreclosure would be to extinguish the second mortgage. Of course, the second mortgagee can apply to join in the foreclosure proceedings to make his interest known to the court, and will have the alternative of paying off the first mortgage and being elevated to the status of a first mortgagee.
- The first mortgagee under a mortgage for a fixed amount may make further advances and assert his right to tack the further advances against the security of the first mortgage—see the above section on tacking.
- All monies advanced by the first mortgagee under an all-monies mortgage will be secured by the first mortgage. Further advances beyond the initial mortgage loan may leave the second mortgagee with no margin for securing his advance.

The first mortgage invariably prohibits the creation of subsequent encumbrances without the consent of the first mortgagee. This must be obtained before the second mortgage is approved. Notice to the first mortgagee of creation of the second mortgage will oblige him to hand over the title deeds to the second mortgagee when the first mortgage is discharged. A second mortgage may be a second legal charge or a second equitable mortgage containing an undertaking by the mortgagor to execute a legal mortgage on request. The latter is rare in banking practice.

There will usually be no deposit of title deeds as there will be with the first mortgagee. The second mortgagee can arrange for inspection of the title deeds at the premises of the first mortgagee. The remedies of a second mortgagee are substantially similar to those of a first mortgagee. In theory, the second mortgagee may sell the property without the first mortgagor's consent. However, as the property will remain subject to the first mortgage, in practice, it will be rare for any purchaser to be willing to buy a property subject to an existing mortgage.

Code of Banking Practice

The Code states that banks should endeavour to ensure that a prospective individual borrower understands the principal terms and conditions of the borrowing arrangement.

Accordingly, banks are required to provide individual customers and prospective individual customers with the following information upon application for a mortgage loan or, where relevant, in a subsequent offer:

- Rate of interest for the loan, and whether it may be varied over the period of the loan;
- Basis on which interest will be determined and when it will be payable, including, where relevant, the annualised percentage rates, and the number of days in the year (in both ordinary and leap years) that will be used for the calculation;
- All fees and charges which will apply;
- Specified period for which the loan is available;
- Details of terms of repayment, including, where relevant, the instalments payable by the customer (banks are also required to provide customers with revised particulars of instalments payable by the customer after every interest adjustment);
- Any overriding right to demand immediate repayment;
- Other significant features such as late payment penalties, and the charges or termination fees for early repayment;
- The bank's right, in case of the borrower's default, to set off any credit balance in other accounts held by the borrower (or in a joint account of the borrower) against the amount due to the bank;
- For residential mortgage loans, warning that the mortgage loan is secured on the property in question and default may result in the bank taking possession of, and selling, the property.

Priorities

Successive competing interests may be created over the same property. For example, the same property may be subject to two mortgages, or a mortgaged property may be subject to other prior or subsequent encumbrances such as a third party equitable interest. It is necessary in such cases to determine which of these interests takes precedence over the other(s), so as to entitle the holder of that interest to exercise his powers in priority to the others.

The rules on priority are based on the Land Registration Ordinance and the common law principles regarding the relationship between legal and equitable interests.

Land Registration Ordinance

Section 3 of the Land Registration Ordinance provides that deeds, conveyances, and other instruments in writing affecting land that are registered at the Land Registry shall have priority according to their respective dates of registration. Any such deed, conveyance, or instrument that is not registered shall be absolutely null and void to all intents and purposes, as against any subsequent bona fide purchaser or mortgagee for valuable consideration of the property.

Registration only affects priorities among registrable instruments that are registered, but does not affect validity. An unregistered instrument remains valid and binding between the parties to it.

Section 4 of the Ordinance provides that no notice, whether actual or constructive, of a prior unregistered deed, conveyance, or other instrument in writing shall affect the priority of a registered instrument. If any such instrument is registered (which in effect means submission to the Land Registry for registration) within one month after the date of execution, it will take effect from the date of execution for the purpose of determining priority.

However, if an instrument is registered after expiry of one month from its date of execution, it will take effect from the actual date of registration in terms of priority. This means that a mortgage must be submitted for registration within one month after execution in order to ensure priority against subsequent interests created after the date of the mortgage.

In particular, in the case of *Ho King Yim v. Lau King Mo*, it was established that where both a contract for the sale and purchase of land and an assignment pursuant to that contract have been registered, no charge created after the date of the contract (but before the date of the assignment) can rank prior to the interest of the purchaser or the purchaser's successors in title. Once completed, the assignment dates back to the agreement for sale and purchase, which ranks prior to the intervening charge by virtue of its prior registration.

A lease granted by an instrument for a term not exceeding three years is not registrable. However, if the lease is for a term not exceeding three years but contains an option to renew, the option is registrable.

The Land Registration Ordinance does not apply to an unregistrable interest, such as an equitable mortgage created by mere deposit of title deeds without a written memorandum of deposit, or an equitable interest arising at law (and therefore unwritten). The equitable principles governing the relationship between legal and equitable interests will apply.

For example, the legal interest prevails in a case between the holder of a legal interest who is a bona fide purchaser for value without notice (i.e., someone who purchased or acquired a legal interest in the property for valuable consideration and in good faith, without notice of a prior interest) and the holder of a prior equitable interest. In this context, 'notice' includes both actual and constructive notice. Constructive notice includes matters which the holder of the legal interest is deemed to know, or would have discovered if he or she had made enquiry.

Purchasers and mortgagees should therefore take precautions to guard against the existence of prior unregistrable interests, knowledge of which could be imputed to them. Precautions include making enquiries of spouses and other occupiers of the property.

Equitable Interests of Occupiers

There have been cases in Hong Kong that gave recognition to the equitable interests of an occupier as against a subsequent purchaser or mortgagee of a property. These were largely a result of application of the equitable principles governing priorities.

For an occupier to establish and assert an equitable interest as against a subsequent purchaser or mortgagee, the following should be proved:

- The occupier has a proprietary interest in the property by virtue of an implied trust, for example. This issue frequently arises between spouses or cohabitees, where the property was bought in the name of one partner with the joint intention that ownership be shared. Such intention may either be evidenced by an express agreement (written or, in most cases, verbal), or inferred by, for example, contributions to the purchase price or to household or maintenance expenses by the party not having the legal title.
- The occupier was in actual occupation of the property when the property was sold or mortgaged.
- The purchaser or mortgagee had actual or constructive notice of the occupier's interests in the property at the time of the purchase or mortgage.

In Hong Kong, it was established in the case of *Wong Chim Ying v. Cheng Kam Wing* that where the party claiming title to the property (in this case, a purchaser) had knowledge of the occupier's presence when he/she acquired an interest in the property but failed to make enquiries as to the occupier's interests, and if it turned out that the occupier had an equitable interest in the property which was unregistrable, that party would be fixed with constructive notice of the occupier's interest and be bound by it.

In the case of *Wing Hang Bank v. Tsang Sze Yin and others*, an occupier applied to set aside an order for possession obtained by the mortgagee bank against the registered owners of the property. The court held that an occupier must prove that, when the legal charge was executed, either (a) the mortgagee knew that the property was occupied by someone who may have an interest in the property, which is inconsistent with the rights asserted by the mortgagor, or (b) the mortgagee, despite having reason to make enquiry, deliberately closed his eyes as to the possibility of such a person being in occupation of the property.

These principles were further extended to cover cases where a mortgagee was held to have been put on enquiry by virtue of the suspicious circumstances of the transaction. It follows that where an occupier claiming an equitable interest knew, or must have known, of the sale or mortgage of the property by the registered owner, and failed to disclose his or her interest to the prospective purchaser or mortgagee, the occupier may be estopped from subsequently challenging the sale or mortgage so as to obtain priority.

This would be the case where, for example, a bank provides refinancing of an existing mortgage or lends money on the security of a property already owned by the borrower. The occupier of the property (such as the borrower's spouse) who otherwise would have an equitable interest and who knew or must have known of the proposed mortgage failed to disclose his or her interest to the bank. In a number of English authorities, the courts had found that such a person, by his or her conduct in remaining silent, had led the mortgagee into making the loan. As a result, such a person was estopped from asserting his or her rights against the mortgagee.

To protect purchasers and mortgagees against the risk of an occupier asserting an equitable claim to the property, it is the practice of lawyers acting for a prospective purchaser or a mortgagee financing the acquisition of a property to advise their client to carry out an inspection of the property and make enquiries of all occupants as to their interests, if any, in the property. In the case of transfer of an existing mortgage, it is also the practice of lawyers acting for the new mortgagee to send letters to the mortgagor(s) and occupants of the property informing them of the proposed transaction.

The letters state that the lawyers represent only the new mortgagee and urge the mortgagor(s) and occupants to seek independent legal advice. Some law firms also request occupants to sign a Consent to Mortgage, whereby they declare that they have no interests in the property which have not been declared to the new mortgagee or, if there are any such interests, that they agree to waive or defer them to the new mortgagee's interests.

Rights of Mortgagee/Chargee

According to the Conveyancing and Property Ordinance, the mortgagee (i.e., the bank), under a legal charge or equitable mortgage by deed, and any receiver appointed by the mortgagee have the implied powers set out in the ordinance's Fourth Schedule, unless a contrary intention is expressed in the mortgage deed. These implied powers may be varied or extended by the mortgage deed. In practice, bank mortgage forms expressly spell out the powers of the mortgagee and receiver.

The rights of the mortgagee or chargee include the following:

- Right to possession of title deeds;
- Right to take out insurance;
- Right to sue;
- Right to possess the property;
- Power of sale;
- Right to appoint receiver;
- Power to foreclose;
- Right to consolidate;
- Right to tack.

Right to Possession of Title Deeds

The first mortgagee of a legal mortgage created by way of legal charge is entitled to possession of the title deeds. Under Section 47(1) of the ordinance, the mortgagor and any subsequent mortgagee who does not have possession of the title deeds are entitled at any reasonable time to inspect and make copies of the deeds.

Section 21.8 of the Code of Banking Practice provides that a bank, on receipt of a request from a mortgagor for discharge of a mortgage, should as soon as reasonably practicable release title deeds and any relevant documents (other than the mortgage itself) to the solicitor representing the mortgagor, against the solicitor's undertaking to return the documents on demand as appropriate. Unless the bank encounters any practical difficulties, this process should normally be completed within 21 days. If a bank is unable to meet this industry standard, it should promptly inform the mortgagor.

Right to Take Out Insurance

The mortgagee is entitled to insure the property at the mortgagor's expense. The Code of Banking Practice provides that banks should provide an approved list of insurers not related to the mortgagee bank, from which customers may choose insurers that they think are fit to insure the properties. A bank should inform its customers and prospective customers whether they are allowed to employ insurers other than those on the bank's approved lists, the procedures involved, any fees charged, and any extra costs involved.

The amount and nature of risks to be insured should be reasonable and mutually agreed upon between the bank and the customer. The bank should provide an option for the customer to choose whether the insured amount should be based on the loan value (Option 1) or the cost of reinstating the property in case of fire or serious damage (Option 2). Customers should also be informed of any extra cost involved, for example, annual valuation fees for Option 2.

Right to Sue

The mortgagee's right to sue is derived from the mortgagor's personal covenant to repay in the mortgage deed.

The Code of Banking Practice seeks to protect an individual who has entered into a joint borrowing relationship with another party (or parties), whether an individual or a corporation. In the case of an 'all monies' mortgage that secures all amounts payable by more than one borrower extended on or after 4 July 2005, the amount secured should not exceed the amount of liabilities incurred by the co-borrowers jointly.

In other words, where a mortgage secures all monies owed by A and B, the payment covenant should only cover advances made to A and B jointly, but not any further facilities separately made to B (for example, in respect of a credit card account) that were not contemplated at the time the mortgage was executed and of which A is not aware.

The restriction does not preclude A from voluntarily and knowingly assuming liability for the separate facilities extended to B, for example, by providing a guarantee or further security for B's liabilities, provided this is done in a transparent manner in compliance with the requirements of the code relating to the taking of third party security.

Right to Possess the Property

A mortgagee normally would take possession of the mortgaged property for either of two reasons: 1) to take over the income of the property from the mortgagor, where the property is leased out, and 2) to be able to sell the property with vacant possession at a higher price.

Where the mortgagor is in possession of the property and refuses to surrender it to the mortgagee, the mortgagee should institute a mortgage action to sue for repayment of the advances secured by the mortgage as well as delivery of possession.

The Conveyancing and Property Ordinance excludes the power of a mortgagee at common law to enter into possession of the mortgaged property without the mortgagor having committed any default. The Fourth Schedule of the Ordinance confers on the mortgagee implied power to take possession upon occurrence of a default.

According to the Ordinance, a mortgagor is in default if he or she fails to make repayment for one month after the mortgagee has served a demand for payment or if interest payable under the mortgage has been in arrears for one month after becoming due. A breach of any provision of the mortgage deed other than the covenant to repay also means the mortgagor is in default.

In practice, it is common for bank mortgage forms to provide that the mortgagee is entitled to take possession immediately upon default by the mortgagor, as defined in the mortgage deed. Default normally includes default in payment by the mortgagor of any principal or interest on the loans secured by the mortgagor.

Where the property is leased with the mortgagee's consent, the mortgagee can only take possession subject to the tenancy, but is entitled to receive the rents under the lease. Where the mortgagor is a limited company, the Companies Ordinance requires that a mortgagee who enters into possession of the company's property (or having entered into possession then goes out of possession), should give written notice of that fact to the Registrar of Companies within seven days. Failure by the mortgagee to file the notice within the stipulated period will render him liable to a fine, and in case of continuing default after expiry of that period, a daily fine.

Power of Sale

As with the power to possess, the Fourth Schedule of the Conveyancing and Property Ordinance provides that the power of sale is only exercisable upon default. A sale by the mortgagee is subject to any prior estates, interests, and rights to which the property is subject, but free from all other estates, interests, and rights to which the mortgage has priority.

To expedite the sales process, bank mortgage forms include an irrevocable power of attorney, whereby the mortgagor appoints the mortgagee as his attorney with the power to deal with the property. Under the Powers of Attorney Ordinance, where an irrevocable power of attorney is given as security for an obligation owed to the donee (the mortgagee in this case), the power of attorney shall not be revoked by the death, incapacity, bankruptcy, or winding-up of the donor (the mortgagor in this case). This provision applies so long as the secured obligation remains undischarged.

A mortgagee is entitled to sell the property at such time, in such manner, and subject to such lawful conditions as he thinks fit, provided that he acts like a prudent vendor selling his own property and in good faith, and the interests of the mortgagor are not unfairly prejudiced.

It is now common practice for banks to sell mortgaged properties by public auction, with expert advice on the reserve price. However, sale by auction by itself is not full proof that the sale is unimpeachable. The mortgagee still has to observe the principles of good faith. In particular, a mortgagee cannot sell the mortgaged property to himself or a trustee or agent for himself, unless the sale is directed by the court and the mortgagee obtains leave from the court to bid for the property.

Where it is proved that there was irregularity in the mortgagee's exercise of its power of sale, the mortgagor's remedy would be 1) damages for any loss incurred, in case of breach of a duty of care, although the title of the purchaser would not be affected, or 2) rescission of the sale such that the mortgagor can recover his equity of redemption, in case of breach of a duty of good faith, but only if it would not be inequitable to do so.

Right to Appoint Receiver

Section 50 of the Conveyancing and Property Ordinance provides that a mortgagee under a legal charge or equitable mortgage by deed has an implied power to appoint one or more receivers of the mortgaged property, and to remove or replace any receiver(s) so appointed.

The receiver is deemed to be the mortgagor's agent, and may act in his own name or in the mortgagor's name. The appointment is made by notice in writing sent by the mortgagee to the receiver and copied to the mortgagor. The Fourth Schedule to the Ordinance sets out the implied powers of a receiver, which are identical to those of the mortgagee, and are exercisable upon occurrence of the same events of default (except for the power to insure the property). However, the mortgage deed may exclude, vary, or extend these implied powers.

The Companies Ordinance also requires the filing of a notice of appointment of receiver by the mortgagee, if the mortgagor is a limited company. The requirements and penalty for non-compliance are identical to those applicable to a mortgagee entering into possession.

Power to Foreclose

Foreclosure extinguishes the mortgagor's equity of redemption and vests his entire legal estate on the mortgagee. Section 44 of the Conveyancing and Property Ordinance expressly preserves the mortgagee's right to foreclose. This right originates from a series of English authorities towards the end of the 19th century. The courts were concerned with protecting the rights of owners of small properties who lost their right of redemption through accidental or inadvertent late payment, or where the property had some special value.

Application for foreclosure must be made to the court within 12 years from the date when the mortgage loan became due. If the court is satisfied that the foreclosure should be ordered, it will make a foreclosure order nisi that allows the mortgagor a period, normally six months, to repay the loan. If the mortgagor fails to do so, the foreclosure order will be made absolute. A mortgagee who has obtained an order nisi cannot unilaterally discontinue the foreclosure proceedings and sell the mortgaged property to a third party without first obtaining the leave of the court, because this might be prejudicial to the mortgagor.

After a foreclosure is made absolute or even after the mortgagee has sold the property, the court has discretion to re-open a foreclosure in appropriate circumstances, if the mortgagor makes application within a reasonable time. The effect of re-opening is to allow the mortgagor to redeem the property upon payment of the mortgage loan.

In the absence of fraud, there is no absolute entitlement to re-opening a foreclosure, which is entirely a matter of the court's discretion. The fact that a mortgagee that has sold the property will enjoy a profit out of the proceeds after repayment of the mortgage loan, owing to appreciation in value of the property, does not of itself entitle the mortgagor to re-opening of the foreclosure in order to claim the profit.

Right to Consolidate

A mortgagee who holds more than one mortgage from the same mortgagor may refuse a request by that mortgagor to redeem one of the mortgages, unless the mortgagor agrees to redeem all the mortgages. This right arises in equity and aims to protect the mortgagee in circumstances where, for example, the value of one mortgaged property appreciates whilst that of another depreciates. It would be unfair to allow the mortgagor to redeem the first-mentioned property while leaving the second-mentioned one under mortgage.

Right to Tack

Where a bank takes a mortgage securing advances up to a fixed amount and subsequently makes further advances to the mortgagor on the security of the initial mortgage, the law allows the mortgagee to 'tack' the further advances to the original mortgage. Tacking is relevant where a subsequent mortgage is created over the same property in favour of another mortgagee. It enables the first mortgagee to claim priority over the subsequent mortgage, in respect of both the initial and subsequent advances to the mortgagor.

Section 45(1) of the Conveyancing and Property Ordinance sets out the circumstances under which a mortgagee may tack further advances to the mortgage as against a subsequent mortgagee:

- If the subsequent mortgagee consents to the tacking;
- If the further advance, together with the outstanding advance, does not exceed the maximum amount expressed to be secured by the prior mortgage;
- If the prior mortgage is an all-monies mortgage in favour of an authorised institution.

The first two circumstances apply whether or not the prior mortgagee had notice of the subsequent mortgage at the time the further advance was made. A bank taking a second mortgage over a property should therefore ascertain whether the prior mortgagee bank had the right to tack further advances by checking details of the amount secured under the prior mortgage.

Additional Remedies for Equitable Mortgagees

The implied powers set out in the Fourth Schedule to the Conveyancing and Property Ordinance as discussed above apply to all mortgagees and chargees, including an equitable mortgage by deed. In addition, an equitable mortgagee is vested with other implied powers in relation to an equitable mortgage over the mortgagor's interest in the mortgaged property and in any agreement for purchase of the property (for example, where the equitable mortgagee is financing the sale of a unit in an uncompleted development where the mortgagor's interest is merely equitable).

The following additional powers of the equitable mortgagee are implied:

- Comply and require compliance in all respects with the agreement for purchase;
- Accept the assignment to the mortgagor;
- Execute a legal charge over the property in favour of the mortgagee in such form and containing such covenants and provisions as the mortgagee may require;
- Sign, seal, execute, deliver, perfect, and do all other deeds, instruments, acts and things which may be required or which the mortgagee shall think fit for carrying out any obligation imposed on the mortgagor under the mortgage or for carrying into effect any sale, lease, charge, or dealing by the mortgagee or for giving to the mortgagee the full benefit of that charge.

With regard to the mortgagee's power of sale under an equitable mortgage by deed, it should be noted that such power only covers the sale of the mortgaged equitable interest and not the legal estate in the property. To enable the mortgagee to deal with the legal estate, the deed should include a power of attorney authorising the mortgagee to sell the legal estate. Alternatively, the mortgagor should declare himself trustee of the legal estate for the mortgagee, and should authorise the mortgagee to replace the trustee at any time.

Where an equitable mortgage is created other than by deed, the mortgagee does not enjoy the statutory rights under the Conveyancing and Property Ordinance and his rights are much less extensive. The right to take possession, foreclose, sell, or appoint a receiver arises at common law and a court order is necessary for the mortgagee to avail himself of such remedies. Should an equitable mortgagee apply to court for foreclosure, the court may instead order a sale.

Rights of Mortgagors/Chargors

The banking professional should know not only the rights and protections owed to the bank as mortgagee or chargee, but also the rights and protections of the mortgagor and charger. In this way, the practitioner can deal with the customer and other parties in a manner that respects their rights and avoids making mistakes that may cause legal action against the bank.

A mortgagor/charger has the following protections and rights: 1) right of redemption, 2) protection against collateral advantages, 3) protection from extortionate money lending agreements, 4) protection from oppressive and unconscionable terms, 5) protection from undue influence or misrepresentation, 6) right of disposition, 7) right of possession, and 8) right to lease.

Right of Redemption

The right of redemption is regarded by equity as fundamentally important. It is not affected by the mortgagee's insolvency, and applies to security on an interest in land and a chose in action (i.e., the right to sue). Equity will not allow the right to redemption to be circumvented, and insists that no 'clogs or fetters' can be imposed on the right. Any attempt to exclude the right will be regarded as void.

In *Samuel v. Jarrah Timber and Wood Paving Corp*, it was held that a term giving the mortgagee an option to purchase the mortgaged property outright within 12 months of the mortgage was void. The reason was that the term excluded the mortgagor's right of redemption, even though on the facts it was a perfectly fair bargain. The term changed the nature of the transaction from a mortgage to a sale and it might be a result of unfair bargaining.

Collateral Advantages

Mortgagors may be required to confer collateral advantages to the mortgagee, such as a brewery requiring a public house to buy all its beer from it as a condition for extending a loan. The asking and granting of collateral advantages are legal so long as the term is reasonable. But if the term is judged to be an unreasonable restraint of trade, it may be voided.

In *Kreglinger v. New Patagonia Meat & Cold Storage Co. Ltd.*, the mortgagor agreed that it would offer its sheepskins to the mortgagee for a period of five years. The mortgage was redeemed two years later. However, the House of Lords held that the mortgagor was still liable to sell its sheepskins to the mortgagee for the full period of five years. It was held that the term was reasonable and further that such arrangements will be valid if they are not unfair and unconscionable; or in the nature of a penalty clogging the equity of the redemption, or inconsistent with or repugnant to the contractual and equitable right to redeem.

Other cases may be in the form of unreasonable restraints of trade. An arrangement preventing the mortgagor from competing with the mortgagee or restricting the mortgagor's freedom in the way he carries on his trade or profession may be void, if it is not reasonably necessary to protect the mortgagee's interest.

Extortionate Money Lending Agreement

If the mortgagee is a moneylender within the meaning of the Money Lenders Ordinance and if the court finds the transaction extortionate, it may reopen the transaction so as to do justice between the parties. A transaction is extortionate if the payments to be made under it are 'grossly exorbitant' or if it 'otherwise grossly contravenes ordinary principles of fair dealing,' taking into account:

- The interest rates prevailing at the date of the transaction;
- The debtor's personal circumstances (such as age, experience, business capacity, state of health, and degree and nature of financial pressure he had at the date of agreement);
- The degree of risk accepted by the lender having regard to the nature and value of any security provided;
- The lender's relationship to the debtor;
- Whether or not a specious cash price was quoted for any goods or services included in the transaction, whether any other transaction was required for the protection of the parties or was in the debtor's interest;
- Any other relevant considerations.

By virtue of the Money Lenders Ordinance, it is a criminal offence to charge an interest rate which exceeds 60% per annum. A loan agreement in which such an interest is charged and any security in respect of such agreement are unenforceable. There is a rebuttable presumption that a transaction is extortionate if the rate of interest exceeds 48% per annum, although the court may declare otherwise if it is satisfied that the rate is not unreasonable or unfair in the circumstances.

It should be noted that the Money Lenders Ordinance does not apply to any authorised institution under the Banking Ordinance. However, the Code of Banking Practice expects that authorised institutions should not charge customers extortionate interest rates. If the annualized percentage rates charged by them exceed the level which is presumed to be extortionate under the Money Lenders Ordinance, they should be able to justify why such high interest is not unreasonable or unfair. Unless justified by exceptional monetary conditions, the annualized percentage rates should not exceed the legal limit as stated in the Money Lenders Ordinance.

The liquidator or the corporate mortgagor may also invoke section 264B of the Companies Ordinance for setting aside or varying extortionate credit transactions. Further, the trustee in bankruptcy may also invoke section 71A of the Bankruptcy Ordinance for setting aside or varying extortionate credit transactions.

'Oppressive and Unconscionable' Terms

Equity has always been prepared to intervene where the mortgage terms are 'oppressive and unconscionable.' An important term is the rate of interest payable by the mortgagor. It is common for the rate of interest to be variable throughout the loan period and this practice is now widely thought to be valid despite its inherent uncertainty. Interest may also be linked to the Best Lending Rate or Prime Rate (e.g., 2% above the BLR) or to the fluctuation in the rate of exchange between one currency and another.

As discussed above, where the lending agreement is governed by the Money Lenders Ordinance, the rate of interest charged is also regulated. However, where the agreement is not governed by the Ordinance and the interest rate is so high that it is 'oppressive and unconscionable,' the court has occasionally been prepared to exercise its inherent equitable power to intervene.

Undue Influence or Misrepresentation

The mortgagor has the right to have a mortgage set aside if it can be proved that the mortgage was entered into under the undue influence of another party, such that the mortgagor could not exercise his or her independent judgement. This is similar to the issue of undue influence in guarantees as discussed in Chapter 5 of this book.

For example, a mortgagor (a wife) may charge a property as a surety for a debtor (her husband) in favour of the mortgagee (the bank). This typically occurs where the husband is in need of a loan for his business debts. When the business for which the loan is acquired fails, the mortgagor wife may seek to set aside the mortgage. The most common grounds upon which the mortgagor relies is the doctrine of undue influence or misrepresentation.

Right of Disposition

In theory, a mortgagor can deal with the mortgaged property in any way consistent with the rights of the mortgagee. He or she may sell the legal estate in the mortgaged property or grant a second legal mortgage on it. In practice, however, the title deeds will have been retained by the mortgagee. Without title deeds, the mortgagor will be unable to show his title before the completion of sale.

In any case, the mortgage, except an equitable mortgage by deposit of title deed, would normally have been registered at the Land Registry. Any purchaser will then know that the property has been mortgaged and would require the vendor to discharge the mortgage.

As regards the creation of a second mortgage, the first legal mortgage would normally have been registered and, if it is an equitable mortgage by the deposit of title deeds, the first mortgagee would have had possession of the title deeds. Therefore, in practice, the second mortgagee is often able to find out if there exists a first mortgage and can decide whether the land offered is sufficient security for the proposed loan.

Right of Possession

Under the Conveyancing and Property Ordinance, the mortgagor retains the legal estate on the mortgaged property. Although the mortgagee of a legal mortgage by way of a legal charge is given the same protection, powers, and remedies as if the mortgage had been created by assignment of the legal estate, the power of the mortgagee to enter into possession before any default by the mortgagor is excluded.

Where a mortgagor is given the right to be in possession, he has the right to sue for such possession or to protect his possession for example, to prevent trespass, nuisance, damage to property, or breach of restrictive covenant, and to sue for the recovery of the rents and profits.

Right to Lease

Since the mortgagor retains a legal estate in the mortgaged property, he may grant a lease even after the mortgage is created. In practice, the mortgage agreement usually prohibits the leasing of the mortgaged property without the prior written consent of the mortgagee.

The mortgagor may grant a lease on the mortgaged property before the mortgage was created to enable him to purchase the property. In such a case, although the purchaser-mortgagor has not acquired the legal estate in the mortgaged property and is therefore incapable of granting a legal lease of it, he is estopped from denying the lessee's title. The lease between the lessee and the purchaser-mortgagor subsequently acquires the legal estate in the property by reason of the mortgage. The tenancy is fed and becomes a full legal tenancy.

In theory, the mortgagor cannot grant a mortgage of a legal estate before he acquires the legal estate. The conveyance of the legal estate necessarily precedes the grant of the mortgage. Thus there is a *scintilla temporis* or a fragment of time between the acquisition by the mortgagor of the legal estate and the grant of the mortgage. It used to be thought that such a legal estate was free of the mortgage, which funded the purchase in that split second. And in that split second the tenancy by estoppel was fed by the legal estate which was free of the mortgage and, being a legal tenancy, it then bound the mortgagee.

However, in *Abbey National Building Society v. Cann*, the House of Lords conclusively rejected the idea of *scintilla temporis* where the purchase of the property and the mortgage, which wholly or partly funded the purchase, were simultaneous. There is no *scintilla temporis* in which the purchase-mortgagor would get a legal estate free of the mortgage that feeds the tenancy by estoppel. The purchaser obtains no more than an equity of redemption (i.e., a legal estate with a right of redemption subject to the mortgagee's interest).

When the equity of redemption feeds the tenancy by estoppel, the tenancy is also subject to the mortgagee's interest. Thus, a tenancy by estoppel does not bind the mortgagee who either partly or wholly funds the purchase of the legal estate which feeds the estoppel.

Discharge

A mortgage is discharged when it is redeemed by the mortgagor. It is also discharged when the mortgagee exercises his power of sale or foreclosure, or if the mortgagee's right is statute-barred under the Limitation Ordinance. A receipt written on or annexed to the mortgage deed and executed by the mortgagee will take effect as a valid discharge.

An equitable mortgage, whether created by deed or under hand, does not create any legal estate or interest in land. A formal release or written receipt is therefore not strictly necessary. Where a memorandum of deposit of title deeds was executed, the bank may simply write 'cancelled' across the memorandum and return it to the mortgagor together with the title deeds. If the mortgagor insists, a receipt may still be written on or annexed to the memorandum of deposit.

Summary

- The concept of tenure deals with the terms upon which the rights to use land are given. In Hong Kong, the only tenure is leasehold tenure, which rests on the declaration in the Basic Law that all land within Hong Kong is the property of the state. The government of Hong Kong is responsible for the management, use, and development of land, and for their lease or grant to individuals, legal persons, or organisations.
- The concept of estate explains the duration of tenure rights over land. Estates are divided into two main categories: estates of uncertain duration, that is, freehold estates, and estates of certain duration, that is, leasehold estates. In Hong Kong, there are only leasehold estates.
- Land in Hong Kong, meaning the soil, buildings, chattels, rights, interest, and easement, can be used as security to support borrowings from a bank. This security is known as a mortgage, which the Conveyancing and Property Ordinance defines as "a security over land for securing money or money's worth." This security can be a legal mortgage or an equitable mortgage.

- The same property may be subject to two mortgages, or a mortgaged property may be subject to other prior or subsequent encumbrances such as a third party equitable interest. It is necessary in such cases to determine which of these interests takes precedence. The rules on priority are based on the Land Registration Ordinance and the common law principles regarding the relationship between legal and equitable interests.
- As a mortgagee, the bank's rights include the right to possession of title deeds, take out insurance, sue, possess the property, appoint a receiver, foreclose, and consolidate. If the bank is an equitable mortgagee, it will have additional implied powers such as requiring compliance in all respects with the agreement for purchase, acceptance of the assignment to the mortgagor, and execution of a legal charge over the property.
- The banking professional should know not only the rights and protections owed to the bank as mortgagee, but also the rights and protections of the mortgagor. In this way, the practitioner can deal with the customer and other parties in a manner that respects their rights and avoids making mistakes that may cause legal action against the bank.
- The rights of the mortgagor include the following: 1) right of redemption, 2) protection against collateral advantages, 3) protection from extortionate money lending agreements, 4) protection from oppressive and unconscionable terms, 5) protection from undue influence or misrepresentation, 6) right of disposition, 7) right of possession, and 8) right to lease.
- A mortgage is discharged when it is redeemed by the mortgagor. It is also discharged when the mortgagee exercises his power of sale or foreclosure, or if the mortgagee's right is statute-barred under the Limitation Ordinance. A receipt written on or annexed to the mortgage deed and executed by the mortgagee will take effect as a valid discharge.

Key Terms

charge
chargee
charger
easement
equitable interest
equitable mortgage
estate
freehold estate
land
leasehold estate
legal charge
legal estate
legal mortgage
mortgage
mortgagee
mortgagor
property
tenure
title deed

Study Guide

1. Differentiate between freehold and leasehold. What is the only kind of estate that exists in Hong Kong?
2. Distinguish between estates and interest in land that is recognised at common law and in equity. If there is conflict between the two, which one will prevail?
3. Before accepting a legal mortgage as security, what steps should a bank undertake?
4. What are the four ways to create an equitable mortgage in Hong Kong? Explain how a bank can finance the purchase by a customer of an uncompleted housing unit from a developer that has only an equitable interest in the land. What do you think are the risks for the bank in financing such an equitable mortgage?
5. Why is it important for the bank to know and respect the protections and rights of mortgagors? What are these protections and rights?

Further Reading

Chan Bo-ching, Simon. 2001, *Hong Kong Banking Law and Practice Volume II*. First Edition. Hong Kong: Hong Kong Institute of Bankers.

Code of Banking Practice Website, http://www.hkma.gov.hk/media/eng/doc/code_eng.pdf

Conveyancing and Property Ordinance website, http://www.hklii.org/hk/legis/en/ord/219/

Ko, Sai Hong. 1998, *Law and Practice of Banking Services in Hong Kong*. Hong Kong: City University Hong Kong Press.

Land Registration Ordinance website, http://www.hklii.org/hk/legis/en/ord/128/

Money Lenders Ordinance website, http://www.hklii.org/hk/legis/en/ord/163/

CHAPTER 7

7

Other Security Interests

Learning objectives

After studying this chapter, you should be able to:

1. Discuss the key concepts, nature, and characteristics relating to the use of charges, shares and stocks, goods, and life assurance policies as security
2. List the formal requirements for the creation of each type of security
3. Identify the rights and duties of the parties to the taking of a security, in particular the powers and remedies available to a bank as the security holder
4. List the basic rules for determining priority between competing securities and other interests

Introduction

While guarantees and mortgages over land are among the most popular forms of security, it is also common for banks to take security over other types of assets. This chapter explains the legal concepts and issues in relation to taking security given by companies, the most widely used being the company charge. We also discuss the use of shares and stocks, goods, and life assurance policies as security by both a company and an individual. This chapter also gives a brief overview of the banker's common law lien.

Company Charge

The security used most widely to secure bank advances made to a company is the charge. A charge is the appropriation of real or personal property for the discharge of a debt or other obligation, without giving the creditor a general or special property in, or possession of, the property. In case of default in payment of the debt or discharge of the obligation, the creditor has a right to realise the security through legal proceedings.

A charge differs from a mortgage, which transfers property to the creditor. A charge also differs from a pledge, which confers on the creditor the actual or constructive possession. At common law, a charge is regarded as a mere agreement to confer some security title, but equity treats the security as being effected at the time of the execution of the agreement. There are three conditions that must be fulfilled for equity to intervene:

- It must be shown that the advance has been made;
- It must be established that the parties intend to confer on the creditor an equitable interest in the property and not a mere contractual right;
- The parties have to manifest an intention that the interests attach immediately or, if the property is to be acquired by the debtor at a later date, as soon as he acquires the title.

When a company creates a charge over its assets, it may grant either a fixed charge or a floating charge.

Fixed Charge

A fixed charge is sometimes described as a 'specific' charge. It is a charge on fixed or specific assets of the company which are identified when the charge is created and do not change during the duration of the charge. A fixed charge encumbers the property when it is created.

A fixed charge can be a fixed legal charge or a fixed equitable charge.

- **Fixed legal charge.** A legal charge is created by a formal charge document, usually a deed. An equitable fixed charge may be created by deed or by the mere deposit of title deeds or other documents of title. A deposit of documents is usually accompanied by an agreement setting out the terms of the security arrangements.

- **Fixed equitable charge.** An example of a fixed equitable charge is a charge over future assets which are yet to exist or which the company has not yet acquired. It is not necessary for the property to exist when the charge is created or for the company to own it. It is sufficient that the property or the class of assets to which it belongs is sufficiently defined in the instrument creating the charge so that there can be no doubt whether the property will be caught by the charge when it comes into existence or when the company acquires it.

  In other cases, whether a fixed charge is legal or equitable will depend on the intention of the parties, the actual working of their agreement, and the form of the charge.

Whether a fixed charge is legal or equitable is important for two reasons. The first is that it may affect the priority of the charge. In the event that a receiver is appointed or a company is wound up, and the chargor has granted more than one charge over the same assets, the nature of the charge may determine who is to be paid first. The second reason is that it determines the powers of the chargee (i.e., the creditor bank).

Floating Charge

A floating charge is a form of equitable charge that is not intended to be put into immediate operation. A company may offer as security a certain class of its assets, such as stock or book debts, on terms that the charge does not attach to any particular assets and allows the company to continue to use those assets in the ordinary course of its business.

A floating charge would be valueless if the lender or creditor secured by it could not convert it into a specific charge. In certain circumstances he can do this; the process is called 'crystallization.' The Companies Ordinance itself does not define a floating charge, and no particular form of words is necessary in order to create such a charge.

A floating charge has the following characteristics:

- The charge is on a class of assets, both present and future, such as book debts or stocks.
- The assets charged change from time to time during the ordinary course of business and includes assets acquired after the charge is created. A fixed charge normally prohibits disposition of or dealing with the specific assets subject to the charge.
- The company may continue to use the assets subject to the floating charge in its ordinary course of business, until the creditor takes action on the charge.

Describing a charge as a fixed charge does not necessarily make it so. If the company is allowed to freely deal with, or continue to use, the charged assets in the ordinary course of business, the charge will be treated as a floating charge. In general, it is preferable to make a company charge a fixed charge rather than a floating charge because a fixed charge has priority over a floating charge.

In practice, bankers usually take a fixed charge over all fixed assets and book debts (both present and future) and a floating charge over the company's undertaking, which includes all remaining assets. A debenture (a document that evidences the creation of a debt) is commonly used to create the fixed or floating charges and will include the company's covenant to repay its liabilities to the creditor.

Crystallization

Crystallization is the term used to describe the process by which a floating charge is converted into a normal fixed charge. From the company's point of view, the advantage of the floating charge is that the company can give security for a loan and still continue to deal with the property charged. The company can use and even sell the assets, provided it is acting in the usual course of business, until something occurs which causes the charge to crystallize.

These events commonly include: the chargee giving notice of crystallization, or automatic crystallization (without any action by the chargee) upon default by the company in repayment of the advances, or breach by the company of the terms of the charge. In practice, chargees rely on automatic crystallization so that the fixed charge arising on crystallization takes effect immediately when the specified event occurs. However, they will normally notify the company in writing that crystallization has occurred.

Upon crystallization, the charge is converted into an equitable fixed charge and the company's powers to deal with the charged assets cease.

Priority of Charges

The registration of particulars of a charge at the Companies Registry does not determine priority. It serves as notice of the existence of a charge and, as such, affects the determination of priorities at common law. Non-registration renders a charge void against the company's liquidator and creditors and therefore may defeat an existing priority.

At common law, priority is determined by the order of creation of competing charges and the nature of the charge (whether fixed or floating, legal or equitable).

- Generally, between charges of the same kind (i.e., both fixed, or both floating, and both registered in time), the first in time prevails.
- Generally, a fixed charge, whether legal or equitable, ranks in priority to a floating charge, a subsequent fixed charge, and preferential creditors in a winding-up.
- A subsequent fixed charge ranks in priority to a prior floating charge, unless the fixed charge was created outside the ordinary course of the company's business and the chargee had notice of the prior charge (registration of which constitutes constructive notice).

- Between a legal charge and a prior equitable charge, the legal charge has priority if the legal charge was taken in good faith, for value and without notice of the prior charge. While registration of the prior charge constitutes notice, if the subsequent charge is created during the five-week time lag between creation and registration of the prior charge, the subsequent legal chargee will not have notice of the prior equitable charge and will have priority.
- An exception to the above rules is where successive charges are created over a chose in action (i.e., a right of action to enforce payment of money or recover damages, hence includes book debts) and the subsequent chargee has no notice of the prior charge. The rule in *Dearle v. Hall (1828)* applies such that priority is determined by the order in which notice of the charge is given to the debtor.

Date of Creation

Section 80 of the Companies Ordinance requires registration of certain charges (such as a charge on land, book debts, goodwill, patent, or trademark) granted by a company within five weeks of being created. Failure to have the charge registered with the Registrar of Companies within the stipulated period will make the charge void against the liquidator and every creditor of the company.

However, this requirement does not provide any assurance to a potential chargee that the company in question has not, in the previous five weeks, created other charges. The time lag between creation and registration of charges can have significant legal consequences.

For example, a bank conducts a search of the Companies Registry on 1 February and discovers that SC Co. Ltd. has not registered any charge. The bank therefore agrees to grant the SC Co. Ltd. a loan secured on its general undertaking. On 20 February, documents for registration of the charge are submitted to the registry. However, in the interim between 1 February and 20 February, it is possible that a charge created in January had been registered and would have priority over the new charge.

Another issue lies where the court grants an extension of time for registration under Section 86. The order is usually made on condition that registration will not prejudice the rights of other persons acquired before the late registration is actually effected. However, it does not cover the five-week period after the date when the charge (i.e., the charge which was not registered) was created. Within that period it is possible that some other charge which was created first will be registered.

Nature of the Charge

Priority is affected not only by the date of creation of a charge, but also the nature of the charge, that is, whether it is fixed or floating and whether it is legal or equitable.

Priority in a Fixed Charge

If the charge is a fixed charge, whether legal or equitable, a lender (banker) who lends on the security of such a charge is always entitled to repayment of his advances, provided the fixed charge is registered in accordance with Section 80. This lender is entitled to be repaid from the proceeds of the sale of the security before any other creditor of the company, except a creditor who has a charge over the same property that ranks first in priority to the lender's charge.

If a second fixed charge is created before the first one is registered, the second charge will have priority if two conditions are met:

- The first fixed charge is equitable and the second legal.
- The second chargee has no notice of the first or if the first chargee induces the second to believe that there is no first charge.

The general rule is that 'the first in time prevails,' that is, the first fixed charge to be created has priority. There is one exception. If the property in question is a debt which has been charged more than once and there are competing claims to the proceeds, the priority goes to the first to give notice to the debtor (provided he has no notice of any pre-existing charge). It does not matter whether the fixed charge is legal or equitable.

Priority in a Floating Charge

The rules relating to a floating charge are more complex because the chargor has freedom to deal with the charged assets in the ordinary course of business. Thus, a chargee who takes a floating charge is not in as secure a position as a chargee of a fixed charge. Priority therefore depends in part on the terms on which the charge was granted and whether the charge reserves priority or includes a negative pledge clause.

- **Reserving priority.** On granting a floating charge, the chargor may expressly reserve the right to create a second floating charge in priority to a registered floating charge.
- **Negative pledge clause.** A chargee may insist on a clause in the floating charge which provides that the chargee will not create any later fixed charges (legal or equitable) over specific assets ranking in priority or *pari passu* to the floating charge. Such a provision is termed a negative pledge clause and is commonly used in banking practice.

There is no constructive notice of reserving priority or negative pledge clause, so a chargee may not be aware that a previous floating charge, for example, may in fact rank higher in priority than his own floating charge because of these prohibitions. Although registration of the charge under Section 80 is constructive notice of the charge, it is not a notice that the charge contains a provision prohibiting the creation of subsequent charges with priority over the floating charge.

Furthermore, although a company is required by Section 88 to keep a copy of all the charges it creates at its registered office or at some other office in Hong Kong, such copies are only available for inspection by existing members and creditors. There is no way in which a potential chargee can discover the actual terms of previous charges.

Subordination Agreement

A company's chargees may enter into an agreement that overturns the general rules which govern priority and provides for a different order of payment. Such an agreement is described as a 'subordination agreement' because the party who would have had priority agrees to be paid after the party/parties who, but for the agreement, would not have had priority.

Requirement to Register

Registration of charges provides a picture of the state of the encumbrances on a company's property, something which is obviously of interest to those contemplating entering into a secured lending transaction with the company. Registration is also of interest to credit analysts, liquidators, receivers, shareholders, and prospective investors. Further, registration operates to protect the security-holder, by providing him with a certain degree of protection as to the validity and priority of his charge once it is registered; this in turn benefits the company by enabling it to give the charge the guarantee of such protection.

Charges Requiring Registration

Bankers should note that not all charges created by a company require registration. The question whether a charge is one requiring registration is sometimes debatable. Section 90(2) of the Companies Ordinance specifies the following charges as requiring registration:

- A charge for the purpose of securing any issue of debentures.
- A charge on uncalled share capital of the company. Shares may be issued partly paid and this fact needs to be disclosed in the company's return of allotments and annual return. The remaining uncalled amount is a reserve of capital and, rather than calling on it, a company may seek a loan and offer that reserve as security for the loan.
- A charge created or evidenced by an instrument which, if executed by an individual, would require registration as a bill of sale. The Bills of Sale Ordinance generally requires registration of a fixed charge granted by an individual over goods. An individual cannot grant a floating charge, but a company can generally avoid the bills of sale legislation by granting a floating charge over a class of assets (e.g., the goods) or by using some other form of security device.
- A charge on land or any interest in land. The banker must bear in mind that any fixed charge on land must be registered in the Land Registry in accordance with the Land Registration Ordinance.

- A charge on book debts. A book debt is money due to the company but not yet received. A company may offer a specific present or future debt as security or may regard book debts as a class of assets and create a floating charge as security.
- A floating charge on the undertaking or property of the company.
- A charge on calls made but not paid.
- A charge on a ship or any share in a ship.
- A charge on goodwill, on a patent or licence under a patent, on a trademark, or on a copyright or licence under a copyright.

Particulars to be Registered

Where a charge is created by a company for the benefit of the holders of a series of debentures, who are entitled *pari passu*, the registration must include:

- The total amount secured by the whole series;
- The date of the resolution authorising the issue of the series and the date of the deed, if any, by which the security is created or defined;
- A general description of the property charged;
- The names of the trustees, if any, for the debenture holders;
- The deed containing the charge or, if there is no such deed, one of the debentures of the series.

In the case of other charges, the registration must include:

- The date and description of the instrument creating the charge;
- The amount secured by the charge;
- Short particulars of the property charged;
- The names, addresses, and description of the charges (or the persons entitled to the charge);
- Details of any commission, discount, or allowance payable to any person in consideration of his agreeing to subscribe to any debenture.

Where any commission, allowance, or discount is paid by a company to any person in consideration of his procuring subscriptions, the percentage rate of commission, discount, or allowance must also be included in the registration details. The particulars must be submitted together with the deed containing the charge.

Duty to Register

It is the duty of the company (i.e., the charger) to register the charge, although registration may be effected on the application of any person who has an interest. That person is entitled to recover any fees he has paid from the company. If a company fails to register particulars of a charge then, unless some other person registers the charge, the company and every officer in default is liable on summary conviction. In practice, bankers will register charges for any advances granted to companies.

Validity of Charges in Winding-Up

Under Section 266 of the Companies Ordinance, fixed and floating charges will be invalid if created within six months before the commencement of winding-up and if such charges are an unfair preference. Unfair preference is defined in the Bankruptcy Ordinance as a debtor giving an unfair preference to a creditor (or a surety or guarantor for any of his debts or other liabilities) by doing anything that puts that creditor in a better position in the event of the debtor's bankruptcy or winding-up, compared to that creditor's position if that thing had not been done.

The Companies Ordinance further provides that if a floating charge is created within 12 months of the commencement of winding-up, it is invalid except to the extent of any cash paid to the company at the time or subsequent to the creation of, and in consideration of, the charge, unless it can be proved that the company was solvent (i.e., able to pay all its debts) immediately after creating the charge. Some creditors have attempted to avoid this provision by advancing cash to the company against the security of a floating charge, on the understanding that the new 'loan' will be applied to discharge the company's existing debt to the creditor. The court is likely to look upon the transaction as a sham and invalid.

Chargee's Powers and Remedies

The methods of enforcing a security's interest depends on the nature of the rights conferred on the chargee and are often in no way peculiar to general company law. However, the Companies Ordinance does provide a distinct procedure for the enforcement of a floating charge through the appointment of a receiver.

Appointment of Receiver

A receiver may be appointed to enforce a floating charge under a power contained in the debenture or by the court.

- Section 21L of the High Court Ordinance empowers the court to appoint a receiver where it appears just or convenient to do so. Generally, the court will appoint a receiver when the loan or interest payable by the company to the debenture holder is in arrears, the company is in liquidation, or the security is in jeopardy (i.e., at risk of being seized to discharge claims which have no priority over the debenture holder's rights).
- Where a debenture creates a charge over the company's business or undertaking and property, a manager may be appointed to carry on the business with the object of selling it as a going concern. Normally the same person(s) is/are appointed receiver(s) and manager(s).
- Section 87 of the Companies Ordinance requires a notice of appointment of receiver or manager to be given to the Registrar of Companies within seven days of the appointment or court order.
- A corporation is not qualified for appointment as a receiver.

Powers and Duties of Receiver

The power of a receiver is determined by the debenture or court order under which he is appointed. A receiver is appointed primarily:

- To collect, preserve, and realize the company's assets charged under the debenture;
- To distribute the proceeds of sale to the debenture holder in satisfaction of its claim;
- To return any surplus or unrealised assets to the company.

A receiver is not appointed with a view to winding up the company. That is left to the liquidator. Where a receiver is appointed by debenture holders, the debenture will normally provide that the receiver is the agent of the company. As agent, the receiver owes fiduciary duties to his principal, being the company. In this way, if the receiver is found guilty of any wrongful act, the company will have recourse against him, instead of the debenture holder appointing him, for breach of fiduciary duty. The debenture holder is thus protected from liability for the receiver's wrongdoing, but may become liable for the receiver's acts if it interfered with the receiver's conduct during the receivership.

The receiver also owes fiduciary duties to the debenture holder to take reasonable steps to realise the secured assets. Where a receiver is appointed by the court, he is not an agent of the company. It is now established law that a receiver owes no general duty of care in tort (i.e., negligence) to the company or subsequent encumbrancers to exercise reasonable care in exercising his powers. However, equity imposes specific duties on a receiver, including the duty to exercise his powers in good faith for the purpose of obtaining repayment. If he exercises the power of sale, he must take reasonable care to obtain a proper price.

Liabilities of Receiver

Under section 298A(2) of the Companies Ordinance, a receiver or manager is personally liable on any contract entered into by him in performance of his functions, except to the extent that the contract provides otherwise. He is entitled to be indemnified out of the company's assets for personal liabilities so incurred.

Pledge

A pledge is the characteristic mode of taking goods as security. The Factors Ordinance defines the term as 'any contract pledging, or giving a lien or security on goods, whether in consideration of an original advance, or of any further or continuing advance, or of any pecuniary liability.'

Section 4 of the Ordinance provides that a pledge of the documents of title to goods is deemed to be a pledge of the goods. A document of title is defined as including (a) any bill of lading, dock warrant, warehouse keeper's certificate, and warrant or order for the delivery of goods; (b) any other document used in the ordinary course of business as proof of the possession or control of goods, or authorising or purporting to authorise, either by indorsement or by delivery, the possessor of the document to transfer or receive goods thereby represented.

A pledge is created when a creditor (the pledgee) is given possession of goods or documents of title to goods belonging to another person (the pledgor) as security for payment of a debt or discharge of some other obligation. The express or implied understanding is that the goods (or documents of title) will be restored to the pledgor when the debt or obligation is discharged. Title to the goods does not pass, but remains with the pledgor. The pledgee acquires possession of the goods and some special right or interest in them that enables him to sell the goods upon default by the pledgor.

Delivery of Possession

In a pledge, the delivery of possession may either be actual delivery or constructive delivery.

- *Actual delivery*. If the pledgor has the goods in his physical possession, he can effect a pledge by actual delivery. For example, A may borrow money from B and hand over his watch by way of pledge. Lending of this type is usually regarded as the province of a pawnbroker rather than of a banker. In practice, bankers are not willing to take such security.
- *Constructive delivery*. This may take place in various ways. Constructive delivery may be made not by handing over the goods themselves, but by some symbolic act, such as handing over the key of the store in which the goods are deposited. Where goods are represented by a bill of lading, the transfer of the bill of lading operates as a transfer of the possession of, as well as the property in, the goods.

  Possession may be delivered while the goods are in the custody of a third person (e.g., a warehousekeeper), by the agreement of the pledgor and the pledgee, with the assent of that third person, that they are to be held in the name or on the account of the pledgee. The third party is said to 'attorn' to the pledgee, and the transaction is sometimes referred to as 'delivery by attornment.'

General Letter of Pledge

Strictly speaking, there is no necessity for any written evidence of a pledge. However, in practice, a banker usually obtains his customer's signature to a document. Some banks require their customers to sign a document of this nature in respect of each transaction, in which case the documents of title to the goods are listed in a schedule. Other banks obtain the customer's signature to a document which covers all transactions.

A document of the second type is commonly called a 'general letter of pledge,' which usually includes the following provisions:

- The customer agrees that the bank is to have a pledge upon all goods now and/or in the future that are delivered by the customer or by his agents, into the possession of the bank or of its agents, upon all bills of lading and other documents to title deposited by the customer or by his agents, with the bank or with its agents.
- The customer agrees that the goods and documents of title are pledged as a continuing security for the payment of all sums owed by the customer, either solely or jointly with any other person or persons, whether on balance of account or on guarantees or in respect of bills of exchange, and including interest and other banking charges (to overcome the operation of the Rule in Clayton's Case).
- The customer agrees that in case of default in repayment of such sum or sums on demand, the bank may sell the goods or any part thereof.
- The customer agrees to keep the goods fully insured in such office as the bank may approve.
- The customer undertakes to pay all rent and other expenses of and incidental to the warehousing of the goods.
- The customer agrees that the bank is not to be responsible for the default of any broker employed to sell the goods.
- The customer agrees that the pledge shall cover the customer's past, present, and future liability to the bank, whether actual or contingent, and will cover the bank's interest charges and expenses associated with the conduct of the account, and the costs involved in relation to the protection of the security at any time.
- The customer agrees that the bank shall not be responsible for any loss which might arise in any dealing with the goods at any time, whether such loss arises before or after the bank intervenes to sell on its own behalf.

The formalities of taking the general letter of pledge and perfecting it are simple. The bank's standard document is dated, signed by the customer, and witnessed by a bank officer. In practice, the goods will be located in a warehouse and will be retained there, but in the bank's name, with a warehouse warrant issued in favour of the bank or a warehouse receipt indorsed in the bank's favour.

The bank should give attention to the insurance question and the policy should be examined and will need to cover the risks associated with the particular goods. The bank should look for the last premium receipt to assure itself that the cover is adequate. In practice, the banker will input the diary notes on the customer's file in order to ensure that any future premiums due are properly paid without delay and the premium receipt at that time is again exhibited to the bank.

The bank will give notice to the insurance company of its interest and an acknowledgement in writing will be obtained. Of course, the banker must ensure that the warehouse keeper is reputable. The bank will wish to ensure that any charge due to the warehouseman has been paid to date and receipts must be exhibited.

Trust Receipts

Bankers must note that despite the wide terms of the letter of pledge, it is the actual or constructive possession of the goods that is the most important factor. Accordingly, when it is necessary for the goods to be released by the bank so that a sale can go ahead, the customer will be asked to execute a further document, known as the 'trust receipt' or 'trust letter.'

By signing this document, the customer gives certain undertakings to the bank. He undertakes to hold the documents, the goods represented thereby, and the net proceeds thereof as trustee for the bank. If the intention is to warehouse the goods, the customer undertakes to deliver the warehousekeeper's warrants to the bank and to insure the goods. If the goods are to be sold, the customer undertakes to pay the proceeds of all sales to the bank, and to give to the bank on request authority to receive from the buyers the purchase moneys for the goods.

However, there are risks to the bank in permitting a customer to deal with the goods in this way. If the customer is dishonest, he may sell the goods and divert the proceeds of sale. He may pledge the goods to some other lender, who will thereby obtain priority over the pledge.

To minimise the risk, the bank should keep in close touch with the position. If the bills of lading are released in order that the goods may be warehoused in the bank's name, the bank will expect to receive a warehousekeeper's warrant within a reasonable period. When documents are released in order that the goods may be sold, inquiry should be made if the proceeds are not presently forthcoming.

In practice, the bank should permit the system of trust receipts to be used only by customers whose integrity is not in doubt.

Rights at Common Law

A pledgee has the following rights at common law:

- Right to possess the goods until the debt is discharged.
- Right to sell the goods upon the debtor's default.
- Right to assign his interest in the goods as pledgee or to sub-pledge the goods by delivering possession to the assignee or sub-pledgee. The pledgee remains responsible to the pledgor for return of the goods when the debt or obligation secured by the original pledge is discharged.
- A pledgee is obliged to use the goods if usage is necessary to preserve the goods, and may use them where usage enhances their quality or increases their value. However, if usage results in a deterioration or wastage of the goods, the pledgee should not use them, otherwise he may be liable to compensate the pledgor for the loss or loss in value of the goods.

For his part, a pledgor has the following rights at common law:

- Right to sell before redemption.
- Right to redeem upon payment of the debt of discharge of the obligation secured by the pledge.

Hypothecation

The term 'hypothecation' has no precise meaning at law. It is a legal transaction whereby goods are made available as security for a debt, without transfer of title or possession to the creditor. In effect, it is an equitable charge on goods as security without transfer of title or delivery of actual or constructive possession.

Hypothecation is considered only where the owner of goods is for some reason unable to deliver actual or constructive possession to the creditor by way of pledge. The risks of lending against the hypothecation of goods include the following:

- The creditor does not have actual or constructive possession of the goods. This leaves ample opportunity for the debtor to deal with them fraudulently.
- An instrument creating a right of hypothecation over goods may fall within the definition of a bill of sale. If executed by an individual, it requires registration under the Bills of Sale Ordinance. If executed by a company, it is required to be registered by Section 80 of the Companies Ordinance.

It is not to the bank's advantage to have an instrument of hypothecation construed as a bill of sale because the holder of the bill has power, with or without notice, to seize or take possession of the chattels subject to the bill. However, Section 2 of the Bills of Sale Ordinance provides for certain exceptions where instruments that would otherwise be a bill of sale are exempted. These include:

- Charges over imported goods in transit, being instruments charging or creating any security on, or declaring trusts of, imported goods that are given or executed at any time prior to their deposit in a warehouse, godown, factory, or store, or to their being re-shipped for export, or delivered to a purchaser
- Bills of sale of goods in any place outside Hong Kong or at sea
- Transfers of goods in the ordinary course of business of any trade or calling, and documents used in the ordinary course of business as proof of the possession or control of the goods

The risk of an instrument creating a hypothecation over goods being construed as a bill of sale makes hypothecation a questionable security for banks. The safest course is to obtain a pledge by gaining constructive possession of the goods intended as security, for example, by procuring attornment by the third party having custody of the goods, or by obtaining a full set of the bills of lading where the goods are shipped by ocean-going vessels. The rationale is that if at the time the letter of pledge or hypothecation is executed, the pledgor is no longer in possession of the goods (although constructively), and the letter is unlikely to be construed as a bill of sale.

Letter of Hypothecation

It is the practice of most banks to obtain a letter of hypothecation, which may be in respect of a single transaction or of all transactions between the bank and its customers. Some banks incorporate a pledge or hypothecation clause in their general agreement with lending customers. Generally, the letter or clause will include the following provisions:

- Pledge of all goods from time to time delivered by the customer to the bank, and pledge over all bills of lading and other documents of title deposited by the customer with the bank, as continuing security for customer's liabilities to the bank.
- Power of the bank to sell the goods upon customer's default.
- Customer's undertaking to keep goods fully insured, and pay all warehousing expenses.
- The bank has no responsibility for default of broker employed to sell goods, for any loss arising in dealing with the goods.

The term 'hypothecation' is often used loosely in bank forms, where in fact what the bank contemplates obtaining is a pledge. It is therefore necessary to look behind the wording of each document to construe the intention of the parties.

Risk of Hypothecation

The risk of lending against the hypothecation of goods is two-fold. First, the lender does not obtain actual or constructive possession of goods so his control over the goods is often very limited. The borrower potentially has ample opportunity for fraud.

The second type of risk arises from the extraordinary complexity of the Bills of Sale Ordinance. Many instruments used in connection with transactions of this sort require registration under the Ordinance and, if not registered, are void. If one knew precisely when an instrument requires registration, the position would be easier but, in fact, it is difficult to ascertain whether any particular instrument does or does not fall within the Ordinance.

In *National Provincial and Union Bank of England v. Lindsell*, a charge obtained by the bank was judged invalid because it had not been registered as a bill of sale. A customer of the bank was the owner of a car, which he delivered to Mr. Lindsell, who was a motor engineer, for the purpose of being repaired. The customer wrote a letter authorising Mr. Lindsell to hold the car to the order of the National Provincial and Union Bank of England Ltd. and also forwarded a copy of the letter to the bank.

Later, Mr. Lindsell sold the car on the customer's instructions and, after his own repair charges had been satisfied, had a balance of £235, which he ought to have paid over to the bank under the terms of the agreement. However, the customer falsely represented to him 'he had made it all right with the bank' and that the bank was content to receive £135 out of the proceeds. Mr. Lindsell, therefore, remitted this sum to the bank and handed the balance of £100 to the customer.

The bank thereupon brought an action against Mr. Lindsell claiming that they were assignees of the proceeds of sale of the car and claiming payment from him of the £100 which he had paid to the customer. It was held that the letter signed by the customer was void, so far as it constituted a charge on the car, being an unregistered bill of sale. Although the car had been sold and was represented by the proceeds in the repairer's hands, the invalid charge on the car could not be separated from the charge on the proceeds so as to make the latter valid.

The above case stands as a good warning to bankers. In order to perfect its security without the necessity of registering a bill of sale, the bank should have obtained a pledge of the car by arranging for the repairer to attorn to the bank. This would have given to the bank the constructive possession of the vehicle. Thereafter, the customer could have signed a letter addressed to the bank setting out the terms of the transaction, and this letter would not have required registration as a bill of sale. The rule is that if goods have already passed out of the possession of the pledgor, documents subsequently executed evidencing the transaction are not bills of sale.

Company Shares

A share is defined as the interest of a shareholder in the company measured by a sum of money, for the purpose of liability in the first place, and of interest in the second, but also consisting of a series of mutual covenants entered into by all shareholders in accordance with the Companies Ordinance.

Except in the case of private companies within the meaning of Section 29 of the Companies Ordinance, a shareholder can usually transfer his shares to a purchaser without any restriction. In most cases a shareholder will have acquired his shares either by having had them allotted to him by the company or by having bought them from someone else.

An owner of shares can create a legal mortgage of them by transferring them to a mortgagee; or he can retain the legal title to the shares and create an equitable mortgage. However, if the shares are in bearer form, they may only be made available as security by way of pledge.

Quoted Shares as Security

Shares listed on a recognised stock exchange are known as quoted shares. They are typically easy to value and sell, requiring relatively few formalities and no complicated investigations of title, as is the case with mortgages of land, for example.

However, there are also disadvantages in taking quoted shares as security. Their price can be volatile. In times of abnormal price movements, a bank holding shares as security may be forced to call in margin facilities, which is bound to further aggravate the customer's financial position as well as adversely impact the financial markets.

Unquoted Shares as Security

Because unquoted shares are not listed on a stock exchange, valuing them poses a problem for the creditor. He or she will have to work out a valuation from various sources such as recent valuations made, the prices at which the shares have changed hands during the past 12 months, dividends paid over the past two or three years, valuation of the company's assets, and so on.

The articles of association of private companies typically contain restrictions on transfer of shares. This has two consequences:

- It may be impossible for the bank to obtain a legal mortgage of shares by way of immediate transfer into the name of a bank's nominee, unless the directors agree to register the transfer. Normally a legal mortgage is possible only where the mortgagors also control the board of directors. In the absence of board consensus to the transfer, the bank can take only an equitable mortgage.
- Should it become necessary to realise the security, it will often be difficult for the mortgagee to find a purchaser willing to buy shares in a private company. Even if a purchaser is found, the company directors may decline to register the transfer. Normally a bank will either offer the shares to existing shareholders, who are in a position to procure board approval of the transfer, or sell to a purchaser of the company's entire undertaking with the consensus and cooperation of the existing shareholders.

Mortgage of Company Shares

A mortgage of shares may be legal or equitable. If it is a legal mortgage, the mortgagor (the borrower) transfers the legal title to the shares to the mortgagee (the lender) and the transfer is registered in the company's register of members. This makes the mortgagee personally liable for calls or instalments of the issue price if the shares are only partly paid, even though the company is aware when it registers the transfer to the mortgagee that the mortgagee is interested in the shares only as security. In practice, the banks as a lender would ask the mortgagor of the shares to transfer the shares to the bank's nominee companies.

If the mortgage is equitable, the mortgagor remains the registered holder of the shares or stocks, thereby retaining the legal title. The mortgagor normally effects the mortgage by depositing his share certificates with the mortgagee. A form of transfer of the shares is executed by the mortgagor, with the name of the transferee and the consideration for the transfer left blank. This implies an agreement to create a legal mortgage. The mortgagee can then convert the mortgage into a legal one by completing the blank transfer with his own name as transferee and procuring its registration by the company.

Creation of a Legal Mortgage

It is necessary for the creation of a legal mortgage of shares that the transfer of shares be completed in accordance with the Companies Ordinance and the articles of the company. Section 66 of the Companies Ordinance provides that "notwithstanding anything in articles of a company, it shall not be lawful for the company to register a transfer of shares in or debentures of the company unless a proper instrument of transfer has been delivered to the company."

The articles of a company usually require that the instrument of transfer shall be executed by or on behalf of the transferor and transferee. The lack of the signature of the transferee is an irregularity which, after a lapse of several years and intervening recognition of the transferee as a shareholder, does not invalidate the transfer of fully paid shares.

The articles also usually provide that the directors may decline to recognise any instrument of transfer unless the instrument is accompanied by the certificate of shares to which it relates, and such evidence as the directors may reasonably require showing the right of the transferor to make the transfer. Where the transferor claims the certificate of shares has been lost, the usual practice is to register the transfer against an indemnity.

Where executed transfers are delivered by way of mortgage, they are often executed in blank. The mortgagee has implied authority to fill in the name of the transferee. If all that the articles require is a transfer executed under hand, the completion and subsequent registration would complete the transferee's legal title. However, if the articles require a transfer executed by deed, the instrument executed in blank and subsequently completed by the transferee is ineffective and the registration so procured may be set aside unless the authority to complete the transfer was granted by deed.

In some cases, a legal mortgage of shares cannot be created without the approval of a third party. Articles 24 and 25 of Table A in the First Schedule to the Companies Ordinance contain restrictions on transfers. A company may modify or exclude these articles, but in fact, many private companies prescribe additional restrictions in their articles. Where a company declines to register a transfer, the mortgagee cannot acquire a legal title. The company cannot be compelled to waive its restrictions.

A legal title is not acquired until the transferee is placed on the register of members as the owner of the shares or at the earliest when the person seeking to register has a present absolute and unconditional right to have the transfer registered. The company is justified in refusing to register a transfer on receipt of notification of adverse interest.

Most banks prefer a legal mortgage in taking company shares as security over an equitable mortgage. However, there are disadvantages to a legal mortgage.

- **Partly paid shares.** Where the mortgaged shares are partly paid and transferred into the name of the bank's nominee company, that company may be liable for any calls made by the company on the shares.
- **Restriction on share transfer to company.** The articles of some companies prohibit registration of a company as member. The mortgaged shares therefore cannot be transferred to the bank's nominee company. The bank will have to accept either a transfer

into its officials' personal names (which will pose additional risk to the bank) or settle for an equitable mortgage.

- **Directors' qualification shares.** Some company's articles require directors to hold share qualifications. If a director offers his shares in the company as security, a transfer of the shares to the bank's nominee company will result in the director losing his directorship.
- **Forged transfers.** A person who sends to a company a forged instrument of transfer for registration is obliged to indemnify the company in respect of any loss incurred, notwithstanding that he may have been an innocent party acting in good faith.

Creation of an Equitable Mortgage

There are various ways of creating an equitable mortgage:

- **Deposit of share certificates with a 'blank' transfer form.** A 'blank' transfer is a proper instrument of transfer signed by the registered holder of the shares (the borrower or equitable mortgagor), but otherwise not complete. If the borrower defaults in repaying the loan, the lender will convert the equitable mortgage into a legal mortgage by completing the transfer form and sending it to the company for registration. A mortgagee who wrongly completes the transfer will be liable for the tort of conversion.
- **Pending for registration.** Because of the potential liability that may be attracted by registering as a shareholder, a creditor may decide to keep the share certificate and the transfer without tendering it to the company for registration. He will then have an equitable mortgage. An equitable mortgage is also created when the share certificate is deposited with an executed transfer without any accompanying security document. In such cases, the creditor has an inchoate legal title which is completed on registration.
- **Mere deposit of share certificates.** A common way of creating an equitable mortgage is by mere deposit of share certificates. Where the deposit is unaccompanied by any document, it is not easy to determine whether a mortgage or a charge is created. The characterisation of the deposit would depend on the intention of the parties, which is not easy to establish given that such parties are usually ignorant of the difference between a mortgage and a charge.
- **Failure of legal mortgage.** A transfer that fails to confer a legal title because of non-compliance with restrictions on transfer or with requirements for a deed nevertheless confers an equitable interest in the transferee.

As noted earlier, banks typically prefer to enter into a legal mortgage in taking company shares as security, rather than an equitable mortgage. This is because of the disadvantages of equitable mortgages, which are set out below:

- **Legal mortgage.** An equitable mortgage is subordinate to a legal mortgage of the shares taken in good faith and for value, even if the legal mortgage is created after the equitable mortgage where, for example, the mortgagor fraudulently obtains a new share certificate by declaring loss of his original. To guard against this risk, the equitable mortgagee may notify the company of its interest in the shares.

- **Prior equitable interest.** The equitable principle that 'where the equities are equal, the first in time prevails' applies, such that the bank's equitable mortgage will be postponed to a prior equitable interest.
- **Bona fide purchaser.** An equitable mortgage does not defeat the title of a bona fide purchaser for value of the shares.
- **Difficulty in realising the security.** If blank transfers are obtained, there may be difficulty in procuring a registration of the transfer with a private company. Without blank transfers, the shares cannot be realised without a court order or the mortgagor's cooperation.
- **Issue of bonus shares without the mortgagor's knowledge.** Because the holder of an equitable mortgage is not registered as a shareholder, he will not be informed or eligible to vote on the issue of new shares. In certain cases, such new issues can have a serious adverse impact on the value of the security.

Mortgage of Shares Held by CCASS

Hong Kong has a dual system of share custody for private investors. Share certificates can be issued in the name of the registered owner and held in his or her own custody. Shares can also be registered in the name of a common nominee, the Hong Kong Securities Central Clearing Ltd. (HKSCC), for the account of a market participant (being a licensed broker) and held under the Central Clearing and Settlement System (CCASS). The broker acts as agent of the private investor with regard to the securities. Dividends, bonus shares, or warrants derived from the shares will be distributed to the broker for onward transmission to the investor as the beneficial owner.

For legal mortgage of shares deposited with CCASS, the mortgagor will execute the legal mortgage and sign a Settlement Instruction Form, instructing CCASS or the CCASS participant acting for the mortgagor, to transfer the relevant share entitlement held in the participant's stock account to the CCASS account of the bank's nominee. On release of the share mortgage, the relevant share entitlement will be transferred back to the mortgagor via CCASS.

There are advantages of mortgage over CCAS-held securities. Where a mortgagee bank requests a company to register a transfer of shares and delivers completed instruments of transfer, it may be held as making an implied warranty to the company that the signatures on the instruments of transfer are genuine, and may be held liable to the true owners of the shares if the signatures turn out to have been forged. For CCASS-held securities, since the request for transfer originates from the mortgagor and not the mortgagee, the mortgagee does not carry the same risk.

Powers and Remedies of Mortgagees

In both a legal mortgage and an equitable mortgage, the mortgagee enjoys the power of sale. In a legal mortgage, no special formalities need be observed when it is desired to realise company shares that have been transferred into the name of the bank's nominee company. The memorandum which the customer signs when the mortgage is executed normally confers upon the bank an express power of sale at any time if the customer fails to repay upon demand.

However, bankers should ensure that the demand is still effective at the time the bank realises the shares. If the bank demands repayment and then accepts further security in lieu of repayment, the right to sell the shares ceases to exist because there is no longer any default in payment. If the bank then proceeds to sell the shares without making a fresh demand, the court will intervene at the instance of the mortgagor. Bankers should also note that when they exercise the power of sale for the pledge of shares, they have to give reasonable notice to the borrowing customers.

Aside from the power of sale, mortgagees of a legal mortgage have the right to vote on the mortgaged shares. This means that the mortgagee can be informed and have a say on company decisions such as the issue of new shares, which can have a negative effect on the value of the mortgaged shares.

In an equitable mortgage created with the deposit of share certificates with blank transfers, an implied power of sale is conferred, which may be exercised after reasonable notice. In practice, the memorandum of deposit evidencing the equitable mortgage confers express power to complete and register the share transfer to the bank's nominee or directly to a purchaser.

Where blank transfers have not been obtained, the bank needs to call on the mortgagor to give instructions for sale pursuant to his agreement in the memorandum of deposit to execute transfers when called upon to do so. If the mortgagor refuses to comply or can no longer be traced, the bank may apply to court for an order for sale, or an order for transfer and foreclosure.

An equitable mortgagee does not have a right to vote on the mortgaged shares, unlike the legal mortgagee. The right to vote remains with the mortgagor.

Insurance Policies

The contract of insurance is basically governed by the general rules of the law of contract, but it has attracted many principles of its own due to its special features. A contract of insurance is a contract *uberrimae fidei*, that is, a contract in which the utmost good faith must be observed. There must be full disclosure of all facts and circumstances affecting the risk.

As such, an insurance policy may be vitiated by non-disclosure, whether innocent or fraudulent. This is a key consideration for a bank taking an insurance policy as security.

The banker must make sure that the borrower has observed and continues to observe good faith with regard to the contract of insurance.

Insurance policies may be grouped under two categories: life assurance policies and insurance relating to goods. Bankers should note that the term 'life assurance,' as it refers to life policies, should be used in preference to life insurance. This is because insurance refers exclusively to property risks, for example, fire insurance and marine insurance. However, in practice, this distinction is not strictly observed.

Life Assurance Policies

In Hong Kong, the two types of life assurance policies usually offered as security are the 'endowment policy' and the 'whole-life policy.' Either type may have been issued 'with profit' or 'without profit.' Life policies can provide security against two events:

- Loss that the creditor may incur upon the debtor's demise;
- Loss from the debtor's insolvency or default.

As security against the debtor's debt, a life assurance policy represents a good security for bankers. As security against insolvency or default, a life policy is security only for the amount that it yields at the time of the default or insolvency.

In a whole-life policy, the insured person's main object is to protect his family against his own death. The amount of the policy is therefore payable on his death. In an endowment policy, the amount involved is payable either on the insured person's death or when he reaches an agreed age. This policy therefore provides protection for old age.

In general, the amount yielded by an endowment policy is smaller than the amount for which the policy would give cover, on payment of the same premiums, in a whole-life policy. However, the surrendered value of a whole-life policy is usually lower than that of an endowment policy. In the premises, an endowment policy is a better security for a bank advance.

Advantages and Disadvantages

Life policies have advantages as security. They are simple and cheap to charge, and their value can easily be ascertained. A life policy is also easy to realise and it is usually stable in value. The surrender value continually increases provided the premiums are paid, so there is no need for the bank to allow for depreciation.

However, the banker must be aware of a number of risks with regard to taking life policies as security. They include the following:

- The customer may be unable to pay future premiums. This is the most important defect of a life policy as a security, particularly in cases where the banker has been unwise to allow the customer to overdraw to the full amount of the surrender value. The bank may pay the premiums and debit the amounts from the customer's account. This keeps the policy alive and automatically increases the surrender value.

- The policy may be vitiated by the assured's non-disclosure of all facts and circumstances affecting the risk, or by actions that violate conditions of the insurance coverage, such as engaging in certain specified occupations such as aviation or mining.
- The customer may die in circumstances that will not involve the insurance company in liability, for example, if he commits a capital offense and is executed. Although suicide is no longer a crime in Hong Kong, the assured's estate would not be allowed to recover from the insurance company any loss occasioned intentionally by the assured's own hand.

Examination of a Life Policy

When a banker is offered a life policy as security, he should make a careful examination of its terms and conditions. The bank will expect the amount assured to be stated in Hong Kong dollars and to be payable in Hong Kong dollars so that there is no added risk of exchange rate fluctuations.

The name of the company that issued the policy should be noted. Policies issued by companies domiciled abroad and having no office in Hong Kong are not usually accepted. In practice, most banks have a list of approved insurance companies. If the potential borrower's insurer is not on that list, the banker either refuses to take the life policy as security or refers the case to senior management for special approval.

The number of years during which the policy has been in force and the amount of the annual premium should be noted. As a general rule, a policy acquires a surrender value after two or three annual premiums have been paid, with the amount of the surrender value a percentage of the sums so paid. In most cases, the policy itself indicates how the surrender value is to be calculated.

Any special conditions attached to the policy should be examined. The banker should also ensure that the last premium receipt is with the policy and that the policy is properly stamped.

Some insurance companies do not require the assured to furnish proof of age before the policy is issued, but will do so before paying any sum claimed under the policy. The banker should therefore make sure that the life assured has stated his age correctly. If cases where age has not been admitted, the bank should help the customer do so. Age is usually proved through the birth certificate or Hong Kong Identity Card. If the life assured is a woman who has married since the policy was issued, a copy of her marriage license should be obtained and registered with the insurance company.

Insurance Relating to Goods

In providing import and export finance, banks will normally take the goods involved as primary security and the insurance policy relating to the goods in transit as supporting security. Where goods are shipped at sea and covered by a marine insurance policy, the Marine Insurance Ordinance provides that such policy is assignable unless it contains terms expressly prohibiting assignment.

Other types of insurance are unregulated and therefore legally assignable, unless the terms of the contract specifically prohibit assignment.

Creation of Security Interest

The usual form of security interest in an insurance policy is a legal mortgage, which is effected by an assignment by way of security. The assignment is not of the policy itself, but only the right to receive or recover insurance moneys under the policy. Assignment of the entire policy to include both the benefit and the burden is rare because it leaves the policyholder without cover, makes the bank assumes liability to pay the premium, and violates a prohibition against assignment without the insurance company's consent.

An insurance policy is a chose in action (a right of action to enforce payment of money or recover damages) and is assignable as such. The Law Amendment and Reform (Consolidation) Ordinance requires assignment of a chose in action or debt to be in writing and signed by the assignor, and written notice of the assignment must be given to the debtor. Normally the policyholder will execute an assignment of insurance policy in favour of the bank.

No particular formality is necessary to create an equitable mortgage of a life policy, which is not common in practice. Mere deposit of the policy with the creditor, normally accompanied by a memorandum of deposit, is not considered an equitable assignment of the policy, but it does create an equitable charge on the proceeds. The customer's signature on a memorandum of deposit should be obtained, containing clauses whereby the customer agrees that the security is to be a continuing security, that he will pay the premiums when they become due, and that he will execute a legal mortgage if called upon.

After execution of the assignment in favour of the bank, the bank will give notice of the assignment to the insurer, for the following reasons:

- The bank will be able to claim and sue on the policy in its own name.
- It binds the insurer in that if the insurer pays the insurance money to another person, the insurer will be liable to the bank.
- The bank will have priority over any prior assignee who has not given notice of assignment to the insurer, provided that the bank did not have actual or constructive notice of the earlier assignment when it took the insurance policy as security. The policyholder's failure to produce the original policy may constitute constructive notice of a prior encumbrance. It is always prudent for the bank to insist on production of the original policy before taking the security. (Another reason for doing so is that life policies often require the delivery of the policy as a prerequisite to payment of the insurance money.) When giving notice to the insurer, the bank may also inquire whether the insurer has been notified of a prior encumbrance and whether the insurer itself has any charge on the policy.

While there is no statutory requirement that notice be given to the insurer of an equitable mortgage, notice should be given anyway to bestow priority to the mortgagee bank.

To ensure that the policy is maintained on the same terms throughout the term of the secured debt, a bank will usually ask the insurer to provide (or the policyholder to procure from the insurer) the following undertakings:

- To advise the bank of proposed changes to the terms of the policy;
- To notify the bank if instructions for renewal are not received by a certain date before expiry;
- To inform the bank if the policy is terminated for any reason;
- To deliver fresh undertakings on each renewal of the policy (or that the same undertakings are deemed to have been given afresh on each renewal).

Creditors often require the policyholder to name them as loss payees in the policy. It is not advisable to rely solely on such a designation because policies often include the clause 'gives no rights to the loss payee unless it also constitutes or evidences an assignment of the assured's rights under the policy or evidences the fact that the designated person is an original assured.' At the least, the loss payable clause should designate the creditor bank as the mortgagee, if such is the case.

The terms of a life policy may give the insurer a right to require the delivery of the policy before making payment. Secured parties should therefore require the assured offering life policies as security to deliver up the original policy.

Common Provisions of a Security Document

An assignment of a life policy by way of mortgage normally includes the following provisions:

- **Assignment.** The mortgagor's right to receive the insurance money is absolutely assigned to the bank as a continuing security.
- **Redemption.** The bank will re-assign the right to the mortgagor on full repayment of the debt.
- **Mortgagor's covenants.** These include the requirement for the policy holder to disclose all relevant facts to the insurance company and to pay all premiums duly and punctually and produce the receipts to the mortgagee.

As noted, there are no particular formalities that must be observed to create an equitable mortgage from an insurance policy. However, a common provision in the memorandum of deposit is an undertaking by the mortgagor to execute a legal mortgage when called on to do so.

Powers and Remedies of Mortgagees

Upon occurrence of an event of default as defined in the mortgage deed or memorandum of deposit, the mortgagee has the following powers and remedies.

- **Receive insurance moneys payable.** Where the policy moneys are already payable because the life assured has died or the policy has matured, the mortgagee may simply claim the insurance moneys payable by delivering to the insurance company the policy and the mortgage deed together with the insurer's claim form and form of receipt, signed by the bank. In the case of a legal mortgage, it is not necessary for the assured's personal representatives to join in the receipt. However, this is necessary in an equitable mortgage, where the legal title remains with the assured and, on his death, vests on his personal representatives.
- **Surrender policy to insurer without the assured's consent.** The bank can deliver the policy and the mortgage deed or memorandum of deposit of policy to the insurance company. The insurer will pay the bank, as mortgagee, the surrender value of the policy. This is applicable only to a legal mortgage.
- **Sell the policy.** This is in effect an assignment of the benefit (being the assured's right to receive the policy moneys) and burden (to pay future premiums) of the policy, and is applicable only to a legal mortgage. There are companies that specialise in the purchase of life policies and reversionary interests as an investment. Since normally the purchase price far exceeds the surrender value, this is a much more profitable manner of enforcing the security, provided a purchaser can be found.
- **Convert policy into paid-up policy.** Where the mortgagor defaults in payment of the premium, the mortgagee may agree with the insurer to convert the policy into a paid-up one with a lesser value, in replacement of the existing one that has not been paid-up. The surrender value is usually not affected. This is applicable only to a legal mortgage.
- **Receive loan by insurer against policy.** The assured applies to the insurer for a loan against the security of the policy and authorises the insurer to pay the loan proceeds directly to the bank to discharge his debt to the bank, against the bank's undertaking to release its mortgage and deliver the policy to the insurer as the new mortgagee. This is workable if the amount that the insurer is prepared to advance is sufficient to repay the bank, and is preferable to surrender as the policy is kept alive for the assured's benefit. This applies only to a legal mortgage.
- **Foreclose an equitable mortgage.** The bank will call on the mortgagor to execute a legal mortgage, or consent to a surrender or sale of the policy. If the mortgagor fails to comply, the bank may apply to court for a foreclosure order or order for sale. When a foreclosure order is made absolute, the mortgagor's rights are extinguished and the mortgagee becomes the owner of the policy, subject to any prior charges binding on it.

Release of Security

A legal mortgage may be discharged by the mortgagee endorsing a receipt on the mortgage deed and returning it to the mortgagor together with the policy. For an equitable mortgage, it is sufficient to write 'cancelled' across the memorandum of deposit and return it to the mortgagor with the policy. In either case, the insurance company should be notified of the release.

Bankers' Lien

A lien is a right to retain possession of a debtor's goods until the debt is paid. In general law, a bank has a lien over securities deposited by the customer with the bank to the extent of the customer's indebtedness to the bank. The banker's lien is a useful last recourse for the bank in the event the security it has taken from a borrower cannot be realised or is insufficient to cover repayment of the debt.

The types of assets subject to a banker's lien are the following:

- Share certificates;
- Negotiable instruments;
- Insurance policies;
- Credit balances in bank accounts (which strictly should be subject to the banker's right of set-off).

The bank has the right to retain the asset subject to its lien. The bank has an implied power to sell the asset subject to the lien if the debtor defaults in repayment, after giving notice to the debtor of its intention to sell. Where the lien is asserted on instruments deposited with the bank for collection or presentment, the bank is not relieved of its duty to collect or make presentment; hence, there is no need for the bank to rely on a power of sale. The bank cannot use the asset under lien unless the debtor has defaulted and the bank seeks to enforce its lien.

It is now the practice of banks to either obtain from customers a letter of lien that expressly sets out the rights of the bank in relation to assets subject to the lien, or to incorporate a provision to such effect in its general agreement for lending customers. A genuine lien coupled with a contractual power of sale is not a charge.

A banker's lien can only be exercised in relation to an actual liability. It is doubtful whether a mere contingent liability can support a banker's lien. The lien may be excluded by an express or implied agreement between the bank and the debtor, which is inconsistent with a lien. Such a situation may arise when the assets are deposited for safe custody only or when the assets are deposited as security for a specific advance.

However, if after discharge of the security the assets are left in the hands of the bank, or the security is realised and the surplus proceeds of sale are held by the bank, these may be subject to the bank's lien for other existing or subsequent advances made to the same debtor.

The banker's lien is excluded if, at the time the assets are deposited, the bank is aware that they belong to a third party, for example, that they are held by the customer on trust. However, if the bank receives the assets in good faith and without notice that they belong to a third party, the lien is not excluded.

Summary

- The security used most widely to secure bank advances made to a company is the charge. A charge is the appropriation of real or personal property for the discharge of a debt or other obligation, without giving the creditor (i.e., the bank) a general or special property in, or possession of, the property. When a company creates a charge over its assets, it may grant either a fixed charge or a floating charge.
- A fixed charge encumbers the property when it is created. A floating charge, on the other hand, is not intended to be put into immediate operation. A company may offer as security a certain class of its assets, such as stock or book debts, on terms that the charge does not attach to any particular assets and the company is allowed to continue to use those assets in the ordinary course of its business. Crystallization is the term used to describe the process by which a floating charge is converted into a normal fixed charge.
- A pledge is the characteristic mode of taking goods as security. The Factors Ordinance defines the term as 'any contract pledging, or giving a lien or security on goods, whether in consideration of an original advance, or of any further or continuing advance, or of any pecuniary liability.'
- Hypothecation is a legal transaction whereby goods are made available as security for a debt, without transfer of title or possession to the creditor. In effect, it is an equitable charge on goods as security without transfer of title or delivery of actual or constructive possession. Hypothecation is considered only where the owner of goods is for some reason unable to deliver actual or constructive possession to the creditor by way of pledge.
- Quoted shares are listed on a recognised stock exchange and are typically easy to value and sell. But there are disadvantages for the bank in taking quoted shares as security because their price can be volatile. Unquoted shares are not listed on a stock exchange so valuing them poses a problem for the creditor bank. A valuation must be worked out from various sources such as recent valuations made, the prices at which the shares have changed hands during the past 12 months, dividends paid over the past two or three years, and valuation of the company's assets.
- Insurance policies may be grouped under two categories: life assurance policies and insurance relating to goods. In Hong Kong, the two types of life assurance

policies usually offered as security are the 'endowment policy' and the 'whole-life policy.' In providing import and export finance, banks will normally take the goods involved as primary security and the insurance policy relating to the goods in transit as supporting security.

- A banker's lien is a right to retain possession of a debtor's goods until the debt is paid. In general law, a bank has a lien over securities deposited by the customer to the extent of the customer's indebtedness to the bank. The banker's lien is a useful last recourse for the bank in the event the security it has taken from a borrower cannot be realised or is insufficient to cover repayment of the debt.

Key Terms

banker's lien
chargee
charger
company charge
crystallization
fixed charge
fixed equitable charge
fixed legal charge
floating charge
general letter of pledge
hypothecation
insurance policy
letter of hypothecation
life assurance policy
negative pledge
pledge
pledgee
pledgor
quoted shares
trust receipt
unquoted shares

Study Guide

1. Distinguish a fixed charge from a floating charge. If you have a choice as a banker, is it better to have a fixed charge as security rather than a floating charge? Explain your answer.
2. When is a pledge created? Distinguish between a pledge and a hypothecation. From the point of view of the banker, which of these two instruments presents the better security? Explain your answer.
3. How would you differentiate between a mortgage of land, as discussed in Chapter 6, a mortgage of company shares, and a mortgage of a life insurance policy? In general, which of these three instruments do you think is the better security for a lending bank? Explain your answer.
4. In taking a life insurance policy as security, why is it important for the banker to remember that such a contract is *uberrimae fidei*? In practical terms, what does this

characteristic mean for the banker in terms of vetting a particular life insurance policy as a security?

5. When can a bank exercise a banker's lien in relation to the taking of security? What are the types of assets that are subject to a banker's lien? What assets cannot be subjected to a banker's lien?

Further Reading

Bankruptcy Ordinance website, http://www.hklii.org/hk/legis/ord/6/

Bills of Sale Ordinance website, http://www.hklii.org/hk/legis/en/ord/20/

Chan Bo-ching, Simon. 2001, *Hong Kong Banking Law and Practice Volume II*. First Edition. Hong Kong: Hong Kong Institute of Bankers.

Companies Ordinance website, http://www.hklii.org/hk/legis/ord/32/

Factors Ordinance website, http://www.hklii.org/hk/legis/en/ord/48/

High Court Ordinance website, http://www.hklii.org/hk/legis/ord/4/

Land Registration Ordinance website, http://www.hklii.org/hk/legis/en/ord/128/

Law Amendment and Reform (Consolidation) Ordinance website, http://www.hklii.org/hk/legis/en/ord/23/

Marine Insurance Ordinance website, http://www.hklii.org/hk/legis/en/ord/329/

PART 4

4

INSOLVENCY

CHAPTER 8

8

Bankruptcy

Learning objectives

After studying this chapter, you should be able to:

1. Explain the concept of bankruptcy and who can be made bankrupt in Hong Kong
2. Describe the process of bankruptcy and the implications of the various stages of the proceedings on the bank as creditor
3. Understand the implications of a bankruptcy proceeding against a bank depositor or customer on the bank

Introduction

Bankruptcy occurs when a person (an individual, not a legal person such as a corporation) becomes insolvent—that is, the person is unable to pay or has no reasonable prospect of being able to pay his or her debts as they become due. As a result, the individual's estate is compulsorily administered by the Court of First Instance of the High Court of the Hong Kong Special Administrative Region for the benefit of his or her creditors.

This chapter focuses on the concept of bankruptcy and the legal issues around it that have implications for banks and bankers. If a bank borrower becomes bankrupt, the bank as creditor will obviously be affected by the bankruptcy. The bankruptcy of a depositor (who is not a debtor to the bank) has implications on the bank as well, since the assets of that client deposited with the bank could become subject to legal action.

Bankruptcy

After the implementation of the Bankruptcy (Amendment) Ordinance of 1996 and the related Bankruptcy (Amendment) Rules of 1998, the primary objectives of the bankruptcy laws in Hong Kong are now threefold.

- The Bankruptcy Ordinance enables a debtor who needs a moratorium to negotiate a settlement with his creditors to apply to the court for an interim that will stay all legal proceedings against him, except with leave of the court.
- If a debtor is in a hopeless financial position, the Bankruptcy Ordinance provides relief to the debtor to free him as expeditiously and inexpensively as possible from his debts and liabilities so that he can make a fresh start.
- The Banking Ordinance ensures that the assets of the debtor are equitably used to pay genuine creditors rateably according to the amount owed to each.

Bankruptcy Petition

Under Section 4(1) of the Bankruptcy Law, a bankruptcy petition shall not be presented to the court unless the debtor:

- Is domiciled in Hong Kong;
- Is personally present in Hong Kong on the day on which the petition is presented; or
- At any time in the period of three years ending with that day has been ordinarily resident, or has had a place of residence, in Hong Kong or has carried on business in Hong Kong.

The debtor is usually an individual, not a legal person such as a corporation (whose insolvency takes the form of a winding up, as discussed in Chapter 9 of this book). However, a bankruptcy petition can be presented to the court against a firm or the partners of a firm trading in partnership. A court may also make out a bankruptcy order against a person who is convicted of an offence, and it appears to the court that one or more persons have suffered loss or damage exceeding HK$150,000 due to the crime. The purpose of the order is to recover the assets from the convicted person for compensating the persons suffering the loss or damage.

The debtor himself, a creditor, a nominee under a voluntary arrangement, or the Official Petitioner can present a bankruptcy petition to the court. The petitioner is required to pay a deposit to the Official Receiver when he presents the bankruptcy petition. A debtor's self-petition should be accompanied by a deposit as well, along with a statement of his affairs.

Creditor's Petition

The bank is a creditor and so the banker must know the grounds for the creditor's petition, as provided in Section 6 of the Bankruptcy Ordinance. In order to present a creditor's petition, the following conditions must be met:

- The amount of the debt is at least HK$10,000 or more (or as prescribed from time to time by the Financial Secretary). 'Debt' means any liquidated sum that is provable in bankruptcy and which would have been recoverable by legal process. The debt due to the petition creditor/s must have existed as a liquidated sum at the date the petition is presented. It should be noted that a debt is not to be regarded as a debt for a liquidated sum by reason only that the amount of the debt is specified in a criminal bankruptcy order.
- The debt is unsecured and is a liquidated sum payable immediately, or at a certain time. However, a secured creditor can still file a bankruptcy petition against a debtor if the secured creditor is prepared to give up his security for the benefit of all creditors or if the petition is expressed as applicable only to the unsecured part of the debt.
- The debtor appears to be unable to pay. A debtor appears to be *'unable to pay'* if:
    i. The debt is immediately repayable.
    ii. Statutory demand of payment of the debt is served in the prescribed form, but at least three weeks have elapsed and the demand has been neither complied with nor set aside.
    iii. Execution or other process in respect of a judgment debt has been returned unsatisfied in whole or in part.
- The debtor appears to have no reasonable prospect of being able to pay. A debtor appears to *'have no reasonable prospect of being able to pay'* if:
    i. The debt is not immediately repayable.
    ii. Statutory demand in the prescribed form requiring the debtor to establish to the creditor's satisfaction that he has reasonable prospect of being able to pay the debt as it falls due, but at least three weeks have elapsed and the demand has been neither complied with nor set aside.

- There is no outstanding application to set aside a demand in the prescribed form, requiring the debtor to pay the debt or to secure or compound for it to the satisfaction of the creditor.
- There are reasonable grounds to believe that the debtor intends to depart, or has departed, from Hong Kong, and that the debtor knows or ought reasonably to know that his departure would result in defeat or delay for his creditors.

A creditor's petition can be filed earlier than the three-week grace period allowed for the debtor to respond to a statutory demand if the petition states that there is a serious possibility that the debtor's property or the value of any of his property will be significantly diminished in the interim.

Debtor's Petition

The debtor can take the initiative and file a self-petition for bankruptcy. This decision may be taken if the debtor needs time to negotiate a settlement with the creditor or if the debtor wants to extricate himself from all his debts quickly and with the least cost in order to start afresh.

Unlike a creditor's petition, there is no requirement in a debtor's petition as to the amount of debt. The debtor needs to show only that he or she is not able to pay the debt. The debtor's petition must therefore be accompanied by a statement of the debtor's affairs, containing particulars about his or her creditors, debts, and other assets and liabilities.

Interim Receiver

After a bankruptcy petition is presented to the court but before the court issues a bankruptcy order, the petitioner may apply for the appointment of the Official Receiver (who is appointed as such by the Chief Executive of Hong Kong, along with other assisting officers) as interim receiver of the debtor's property. This may be done if the debtor's assets are in jeopardy. The appointment of the Official Receiver as interim receiver will remain valid until it is set aside, such as when the bankruptcy petition is dismissed or when a bankruptcy order is issued.

Bankruptcy Order

The court may dismiss the bankruptcy petition if it is not satisfied with the proof of the debt owing to the petitioning creditor or with the service of the petition, or if it judges that the debtor is able to pay his debts or has a reasonable prospect of doing so, or for other sufficient cause.

On the other hand, the court may accept the bankruptcy petition. If it does, it will issue a bankruptcy order that will come into effect at once. The consequences of a bankruptcy order are as follows:

- The debtor will immediately become bankrupt and will continue to be so until discharged.
- No proceedings can be commenced or proceeded with against the property or person without the leave of the court.
- The bankrupt individual's property is to vest in a trustee for distribution amongst his creditors.
- No creditor with a debt provable in bankruptcy can pursue any remedy against the bankrupt individual (except that secured creditors may exercise their power to realize their securities).
- The court may order a stay of pending proceedings against the bankrupt individual.
- The bankrupt individual is disqualified from holding certain public offices, acting as a company director or taking part in the management of a company without leave of the court.
- It is a criminal offence if the bankrupt individual, without disclosing that he is an undischarged bankrupt individual, obtains credit of HK$100 or more, or engages in any business under a different name and obtains credit in the course of such business.

Official Receiver

After the making of the bankruptcy order, the Official Receiver takes control of all the assets of the bankrupt individual, pending the appointment of a trustee in bankruptcy. The Official Receiver seizes the assets, including accounting books and documents of the bankrupt's firm (if the bankrupt individual is a sole proprietor or partner in a partnership), particularly the wage records of employees.

The Official Receiver investigates the conduct of the bankrupt individual and reports to the court whether there is reason to believe that the bankrupt individual has committed any act that constitutes an indictable offence under the Bankruptcy Ordinance or that there is cause for the court to refuse, suspend, or qualify an order for the bankrupt individual's discharge.

The Official Receiver also has discretion whether or not to conduct a public examination of the bankrupt individual, which entails the bankrupt individual being put under oath and being questioned by the Official Receiver, or the trustee in bankruptcy or the bankrupt individual's creditors. If a request by notice is made to the Official Receiver by any creditor with the concurrence of not less than one-fourth in value of the debt held by creditors (including the creditor giving notice), the Official Receiver is duty bound to apply to the court to authorise a public examination of the bankrupt individual.

Where the total value of all the property of the bankrupt individual is not likely to exceed HK$200,000, the Official Receiver may apply to the High Court for an order that the bankrupt individual's estate be administered in a summary manner. If the court agrees, the general meeting of creditors will be dispensed with and the Official Receiver becomes the trustee of the property of the bankrupt individual without a creditor committee.

The Official Receiver will decide whether to summon a general meeting of creditors for the purpose of appointing a trustee in bankruptcy within 12 weeks from the date of the bankruptcy order. If he calls for such a meeting, the creditors will appoint a trustee in bankruptcy, who will report to a creditor committee also appointed by the creditors. The quorum for a general meeting is at least one creditor entitled to vote, either present in person or by proxy (including the chairman, if he holds a valid proxy).

If the Official Receiver decides not to summon a general meeting of the creditors, he will give notice of this decision to the court and to every known creditor before the end of the 12 weeks. The Official Receiver will become the trustee on the date of his giving such notice to the court. However, a creditor may compel the Official Receiver to summon a meeting provided that creditor has the support of not less than one-fourth of the value of the debt held by all the creditors.

Trustee in Bankruptcy

The trustee in bankruptcy appointed by the creditors (and the Official Receiver, if he also acts as the trustee—the term "trustee" in this section refers to both the trustee appointed by creditors and the Official Receiver acting as the trustee) is vested with the property of the bankrupt individual. These assets will eventually be realised by the trustee and applied to repay creditors by way of dividends.

The trustee's task becomes more complex if he discovers cases of the bankrupt's property having been disposed of contrary to the interests of the bankrupt individual's estate. There are several antecedent transaction avoidance provisions that allow the trustee to recover assets of the bankrupt individual for the benefit of his estate. These can be grouped under three headings: 1) transactions at an undervalue, 2) unfair preferences, and 3) extortionate credit transactions.

Transactions at Undervalue

Section 49 of the Bankruptcy Ordinance contains provisions that enable the trustee in bankruptcy to recover for the benefit of the creditors any property that the bankrupt individual had given away for nothing or at undervalue during the period of five years prior to the presentation of the bankruptcy petition, by permitting the trustee to apply to the court for an order to redress the transaction.

A debtor may have entered into a transaction with another person at an undervalue if:

- He makes a gift to that person or he otherwise enters into a transaction with that person on terms that provide for him to receive no consideration.
- He enters into a transaction with that person in consideration of marriage.
- He enters into a transaction with that person for a consideration, the value of which, in money or money's worth, is significantly less than the value, in money or money's worth, of the consideration provided by the debtor.

If the transaction was entered into any time more than two years but not more than five years before the day the bankruptcy petition was presented, the trustee must establish that that the debtor was either insolvent at the time the transaction was entered into or that the debtor became insolvent in consequence of the transaction itself. This applies to a transferee that is an associate of the debtor, who is defined as a spouse, relative, spouse of a relative of the debtor, or the debtor's spouse and other persons with close ties to the debtor, as enumerated in Section 51B of the Bankruptcy Ordinance.

Unfair Preferences

If the trustee believes that the bankrupt individual has given unfair preferences to another party, the trustee may apply to the court to redress that transaction. This applies to transactions completed within a period of six months ending with the day of the presentation of the bankruptcy order. If the person given unfair preference is an associate, as defined by Section 51B of the Bankruptcy Ordinance, the trustee may ask for redress for transactions that go back two years.

There is no need to prove any fraudulent elements in an unfair preference. Upon the application being made by the trustee, the court shall make such order as it thinks fit for restoring the position to what it would have been if the debtor had not given that unfair preference. A debtor is said to have extended an unfair preference to another person if:

- That person is one of the debtor's creditors or a surety or guarantor for any of his debts or other liabilities; and
- The debtor does anything or suffers anything to be done which (in either case) has the effect of putting that person into a position which, in the event of the debtor's bankruptcy, will be better than the position he would have been in if that thing had not been done.

Extortionate Credit Transactions

The trustee is empowered to apply to the court to make an order in respect of an extortionate credit transaction, provided that transaction was entered into by the bankrupt individual no more than three years before the commencement of the bankruptcy. A transaction is extortionate if, having regard to the risk accepted by the person providing the credit:

- The terms of it are or were such as to require grossly exorbitant payments to be made (whether unconditionally or in certain contingencies) in respect of the provision of the credit; or
- It otherwise grossly contravened ordinary principles of fair dealing.

The burden of proof in this case is on the provider of the credit. It is presumed that unless the contrary is shown the transaction is extortionate. The court may set aside or vary the terms of the whole or part of any obligation created by the transaction, or the terms of any security held, or order payments to be made to the trustee. It may require any person to surrender property held as security to the trustee or direct accounts to be taken between any persons.

Discharge From Bankruptcy

A bankrupt individual is automatically discharged from bankruptcy after a period of four years, provided there is no valid objection. The bankrupt individual should also have been in Hong Kong at the time the bankruptcy order was made against him and had not since then left Hong Kong without notifying the trustee.

If the bankrupt individual does not cooperate fully with the trustee or fails to comply with other requirements under the Bankruptcy Ordinance, the period of his bankruptcy can be extended up to eight years, depending on the severity of the matter. A bankrupt individual may also apply to the court for an early discharge after he has fully accounted for his affairs, dealings, and property, and the causes of his failure to the Official Receiver or the trustee.

Voluntary Arrangements

If a debtor wishes to avoid bankruptcy proceedings against him, he may make use of the voluntary arrangement procedure provided in the Bankruptcy Ordinance. A voluntary arrangement involves a formal proposal made by a debtor to his creditors for repayment of his debt and a statutory moratorium against individual debt enforcement. The voluntary arrangement procedure may be used either by a debtor whose insolvency is imminent and predictable or by a bankrupt individual after a bankruptcy order has been made.

Nominee

The debtor must find a nominee who is prepared to act for him in relation to the voluntary arrangement. Under Section 2 of the Banking Ordinance, the nominee means the Official Receiver or some person who by reason of his experience and qualifications is, in the opinion of the court, a suitable person to perform the duties relating to voluntary arrangements.

In general, the nominee's principal tasks are to prepare the report, chair the meeting of creditors, and file his report with the court. Thereafter, his task as nominee has ended, although in the majority of cases he continues to act in the role of supervisor.

Proposal

Every candidate for a voluntary arrangement must be, or be about to become, insolvent but able to put forward a proposal, the outcome of which will place creditors in a better position than would result from bankruptcy. In other words, the proposal is the key document in any voluntary arrangement.

In a proposal the debt sets out the precise manner in which he will pay or compromise with his creditors. The nominee is able to use this proposal to report to the court. Due to technical matters which are required to be dealt with within the proposal, the debtor will almost invariably consult the intended nominee in drafting his proposal.

The proposal must provide a short explanation as to why, in the debtor's opinion, a voluntary arrangement is desirable and give reasons why the creditors may be expected to concur therewith. Further, the proposal must provide for a nominee to act in relation to the voluntary arrangement either as trustee or otherwise for the purpose of supervising its implementation.

Statement of Affairs

The debtor must submit a statement of his affairs, which should be made up to a date not earlier than two weeks before the date of the written notice of the proposal to the nominee. If the debtor is an undischarged bankrupt individual and has already lodged a statement of affairs in the bankruptcy proceedings, he need not deliver a further statement of affairs unless required to do so by the nominee.

Interim Order

At an early stage in the procedure, the debtor should seek an interim order from the court, the effect of which is that no bankruptcy petition relating to the debtor may be presented or proceeded with. No other proceedings, no execution or other legal process, and no distress may be commenced or continued against the debtor or his property except with the leave of the court.

The interim order gives to the individual debtor a moratorium early in the proceedings. It also gives the debtor an opportunity to negotiate an amicable settlement with his creditors and thereby avoid bankruptcy proceedings.

Whilst the interim order provides some protection to the debtor's estate until the creditors have an opportunity to consider the proposal, this protection has some limitations. The interim order will not debar a landlord from enforcing his right of distress for non-payment of rent.

Where the debtor is an undischarged bankrupt individual, the interim order may contain provisions as to the conduct of the bankruptcy and the administration of the bankrupt individual's estate during the period for which the order is in force. Further, the application may alternatively be made by the trustee in bankruptcy or by the Official Receiver.

Nominee's Report

At least three days before the expiry of the interim order, the nominee shall submit a report to the court stating whether in his opinion a meeting of the debtor's creditors should be summoned to consider the proposal, and if such a meeting should be summoned, the date, time, and place of the meeting.

After receiving the nominee's report, if the court is satisfied that a meeting should be summoned, the court can extend the interim order for a further period so that the proposal can be considered by the creditors.

Creditors' Meeting

As soon as the nominee's report has been considered by the court, and assuming that there is no court direction to the contrary, the nominee should hold a creditors' meeting. The meeting is held to decide whether or not to approve the proposal in relation to the voluntary arrangement, with or without modifications. The debtor should attend the creditors' meeting, since modifications may involve substantive negotiations between the debtor and the creditors.

The approval or modifications of a proposal at a creditors' meeting requires a majority in excess of three-quarters in value of the creditors present, in person or by proxy and voting on the resolution. Where a creditors' meeting approves the proposal, it will bind every creditor, who in accordance with the rules had notice of and was entitled to vote at the meeting, whether or not he was present or represented at it.

Approved Voluntary Arrangement

The approved proposal for a voluntary arrangement is deemed to be in force and effective from the date of the creditors' meeting. The nominee appointed at the creditors' meeting will implement the arrangement and pay the creditors in accordance with the accepted proposal.

Any bankruptcy petition which has been stayed by the interim order, will be deemed dismissed on the interim order, ceasing to have effect 28 days after the meeting approving the proposal has been reported to the court.

The court may annul the bankruptcy order made against a bankrupt individual with or without conditions if his proposal is approved by the creditors' meeting.

Legal Issues for the Banker

The various stages of bankruptcy and voluntary arrangements can give rise to legal issues for the bank as creditor and as holder of a bankrupt individual's assets (e.g., his or her bank accounts). The preparation and submission of the creditor's petition is one obvious area that concerns the banker, if his bank decides to initiate bankruptcy proceedings against a bank borrower. But other stages in the process also give rise to legal issues involving bankers, among them the bankruptcy order and discharge from bankruptcy.

if the company is solvent, in which case it is the company's members (shareholders) that appoint the liquidators.

If the company is not solvent, its creditors have the power to determine who the liquidator shall be.

In practice, if the company is solvent and the directors of the company make a statutory declaration of solvency, the liquidation will be a members' voluntary liquidation. If no declaration of solvency is sworn or it is discovered later that the company cannot meet its liabilities in full within the period specified in the declaration of solvency, the liquidation will become a creditors' voluntary liquidation.

In all these cases, the aim of the winding-up process is not exclusively the realisation of the assets and distribution of the net proceeds to the creditors (and if anything is left, to the members, in accordance with their respective priorities under the law). The voluntary winding up also opens the way for the conduct of the company's management to be examined. Such investigation can result in civil and criminal proceedings being taken against those who have engaged in any malpractices under the law and in the adjustment or avoidance of various transactions.

In Hong Kong, most liquidations are carried out as a voluntary winding up. This is because a voluntary winding up has many advantages over a compulsory winding up, including the fact that that the formalities to be complied with are not as many as the formalities in a compulsory winding up.

Members' Voluntary Winding Up

When a voluntary liquidation is proposed, the directors (or a majority of them, if there are more than two directors) may, at a meeting of the directors, make a statutory declaration that:

- They have made a full inquiry into the affairs of the company; and
- They have formed the opinion that the company will be able to pay its debts in full within a maximum of 12 months, starting from the day the resolution for voluntary winding up is passed.

The statutory declaration should be made within five weeks preceding the resolution, or on the day of the resolution, but before the resolution is passed. The declaration must be delivered to the Registrar of Companies for registration not later than the time the copy of the resolution to wind up is delivered, and it must contain a statement of the company's assets and liabilities as at the latest practicable date before the declaration is made.

If a director makes a statutory declaration without having reasonable grounds, he commits an offence. If the company's debts are not paid as stated in the declaration, it is presumed that the directors did not have 'reasonable grounds' for their opinion, until the contrary is proved.

Creditors' Voluntary Winding Up

In a creditors' voluntary winding up, the company arranges a meeting of creditors for the day of or day after the meeting. The resolution to wind up is proposed in that meeting. Notice of the meeting of creditors should be sent out simultaneously with the notice to shareholders of the proposed resolution to wind up the company.

The notice of the meeting of the creditors should be advertised once in *The Government of the Hong Kong Special Administration Gazette* and at least once in both an English-language newspaper and a Chinese-language newspaper in circulation in Hong Kong. The agenda of the meeting will include the appointment of a liquidator and a committee of inspection.

The directors should compile a full statement of the company's affairs for discussion at the meeting. The statement should include a list of the company's creditors and the estimated amount of their claims. The directors should appoint one of their members to preside over the meeting.

In winding up a company that is insolvent, bankruptcy rules that concern set-off and contingent liabilities are applicable. The bank should therefore combine all bank accounts in the name of the company to determine the net amount owing to or from the company. Any remaining credit balance may be retained against any contingent liability of the company to the bank, such as bills discounted but not yet matured.

Special Procedure for Voluntary Winding Up

Section 228(A) of the Companies Ordinance provides a special procedure for a voluntary winding up. If the directors of a company or a majority of them believe that the company's existence should be terminated, they should resolve that:

- The company can no longer continue its business because of its liabilities; and
- The directors consider it necessary that the company be wound up and they believe that there are good and sufficient reasons for the winding up to be commenced under section 228(A); and
- The company's shareholders and creditors will be summoned to a meeting that will be held no later than 28 days from the filing of the statutory declaration that verifies the directors' resolution.

The directors must also appoint a person to be the provisional liquidator and to deliver evidence of the appointment to the registrar, together with the statutory declaration. This provisional liquidator must either be a solicitor or a professional accountant under the Professional Accountants Ordinance. He must also give his written consent to the appointment.

A Section 228(A) winding up can potentially protect whatever remains of the company's assets more speedily than a members' or a creditors' voluntary winding up, because the liquidation starts when the statutory declaration is filed and a provisional liquidator is immediately appointed.

However, this special procedure is also open to abuse. Unscrupulous directors may take advantage of the period (which can last up to five weeks) between the date of the resolution and the meeting of creditors and contributors to draw off the company's assets. This will be possible if the provisional liquidator is negligent or unscrupulous himself.

Petition for Winding Up

The Companies Ordinance provides that a petition to wind up a company may be presented to the court by the company itself, its creditors (including its bankers) or contributories, the Financial Secretary, the Registrar, or the Official Receiver. The Securities and Futures Commission (SFC), the Office of the Commissioner of Insurance, and the Hong Kong Monetary Authority may also present a winding up petition to the court.

Regardless of who petitioned to wind up a company, the court's order operates in favour of all the creditors and contributories, as if the order were made on a joint petition of a creditor and a contributory.

Once the order is issued, no action or proceeding against the company can be started or continued without the court's permission. The liquidator is also empowered to take into his custody or place under his control all the property and choses in action (such as the right to launch legal proceedings to enforce payment of a debt).

In Hong Kong, a creditor's petition is the most common way to ask the court to wind up a company. The creditor is usually unsecured and the usual reason for the winding up petition is because the company is unable to pay its debts.

A secured creditor may also present a petition without being deemed as having surrendered the security. Bankers should note that such a secured creditor may be constrained from selling the security pending the hearing of the petition. The court will dismiss a secured creditor's petition if the company has adequate assets to meet the amount due and the charge against the property is registered properly. In this case, the best remedy for the secured creditor (which may be a bank) is to realise the security and not go through the winding up process.

The Liquidator

When the court makes a winding-up order, it may appoint a liquidator under Section 192 of the Companies Ordinance. If the order does not name a liquidator, the Official Receiver will act as the provisional liquidator until such time as another person has become the liquidator. The Official Receiver may ask the court at any time for a person to be appointed liquidator in his place.

In a members' voluntary winding up, the liquidator is appointed by the members. In a creditors' voluntary winding up, the creditors and the company may nominate a liquidator during their respective meetings. If the creditors and the company nominate different persons, the creditors' nominee will be the one appointed.

However, a director, member, or creditor has the right to apply to the court within seven days of the creditors' nomination to have the company's nominee named as the liquidator or for an entirely different person to be so named. The court will then settle the dispute. If the creditors do not name a nominee, the company's nominee becomes the liquidator.

Liquidator in Compulsory Winding Up

The liquidator in a winding up by the court exercises powers on his own, without asking for the sanction of either the court or the committee of inspection, which is a committee of up to ten members, half of whom are appointed by creditors and the other half by the company. (The court may also appoint other persons to the committee of inspection.)

Powers Exercisable Without Sanction

Under section 199(2) of the Companies Ordinance, the liquidator in a winding up by the court shall have the following powers without the sanction of either the court or the committee of inspection:

- To sell the real and personal property and things in action of the company by public auction or private contract, with power to transfer the whole of it to any person or company, or to sell the same in parcel;
- To do all acts and to execute, in the name and on behalf of the company, all deeds, receipts, and other documents, and for that purpose to use, when necessary, the company's seal;
- To prove, rank, and claim in the bankruptcy, insolvency, or sequestration of any contributory, for any balance against his estate, and to receive dividends in the bankruptcy, insolvency, or sequestration, in respect of that balance as a separate debt due from the bankrupt or insolvent party, and rateably with the other separate creditors;
- To draw, accept, make, and indorse any bill of exchange or promissory note in the name and on behalf of the company, with the same effect with respect to the company's liability as if the bill or note had been drawn, accepted, made, or indorsed by or on behalf of the company;
- To raise on the security of the company's assets any money requisite;
- To take out in his official name letters of administration to any deceased contributory, and to do in his official name any other act necessary for obtaining payment of any money due from a contributory or his estate which cannot conveniently be done in the name of the company;

the shareholders who appoint the liquidator, provided that the directors are able to prove that the company is solvent. If the company is insolvent, it is the creditors (which may include the banks) that have the power to appoint the liquidator. The creditors also exercise general control over the liquidation.

In some circumstances, the company's shareholders or creditors can voluntarily wind up the company:

- When the period, if any, fixed for the duration of the company by its articles expires and the company in general meeting passes a resolution requiring the company to be wound up voluntarily;
- If an event occurs that, under the memorandum or articles, require that the company be dissolved;
- If the company resolves by special resolution that the company be wound up voluntarily;
- If the company resolves by special resolution that it cannot, by reason of its liabilities, continue its business, and that it is advisable to wind up;
- If the majority of the company's directors make and deliver to the Registrar of Companies a winding up statement under Section 228 of the Companies Ordinance.

Compulsory Winding Up

The process of the compulsory winding up of a company begins with a winding up petition lodged with the Court of First Instance of the High Court of Hong Kong. The court will examine the petition for correctness in form and substance. If it judges that the petition has merit, the court will issue a winding up order that will ultimately end with the company's dissolution.

The court may order that the company be wound up in a summary manner. Alternatively, it may direct that the winding up of the company be regulated specially by the court. This is known as a regulating order issue, and may be included in the winding up order, or made after the winding up order is issued.

Summary Procedure

Under Section 227 of the Companies Ordinance, the court has the option to order that the company be wound up in a summary manner if, in its opinion, the value of the property of the company is not likely to exceed HK$200,000.

This means that there will be no meetings of creditors and contributories (that is, current shareholders and former shareholders of partly paid shares who have transferred their shares in the preceding year), nor will there be a committee of inspection. The liquidator will be the Official Receiver, and he may act on all matters that normally could only be done with the sanction of a committee of inspection.

The court may also modify the winding up procedures, towards the end of saving on expenditures and simplifying the process.

Regulating Order

The court may order that the winding up be done under its direction if the company has large numbers of creditors and/or contributories or if the interests of the creditors require it, in its judgment. For example, winding up a bank with a large number of depositors may require a regulating order to facilitate the process. In such cases, any creditor who is a depositor shall, unless and until formal proof of debt is demanded from the liquidator, be deemed to have proved his debt.

Under a regulating order, the court may do away with the step of summoning creditors and contributories to a first meeting. The wishes of the creditors and contributors will still be ascertained, but it will be done in a manner directed by the court. The court may also appoint persons who it believes are fit to become members of the committee of inspection.

Grounds for Compulsory Winding Up

The court may liquidate a company in a compulsory winding up if one of the following circumstances applies:

- The company has by special resolution resolved that the company be wound by the court.
- The company has not commenced business within a year from incorporation, or it has suspended business for a whole year.
- The number of members in the company is reduced below the statutory minimum.
- The company is unable to pay its debts.
- An event comes to pass upon whose occurrence the company is to be dissolved under its memorandum or articles.
- The court is of the opinion that it is just and equitable that the company should be wound up.

The winding up is normally governed by the Companies Ordinance. However, a winding up order may also be made under other legislation, including Section 122 of the Banking Ordinance, Sections 44 to 49 of the Insurance Companies Ordinance, and Section 37A(2) of the Securities and Futures Commission Ordinance.

Inability to Pay Debts

As noted above, a company that is unable to pay its debts can be subjected to compulsory winding up. Section 178 of the Companies Ordinance considers a company to be unable to pay its debts if:

- The company neglects to pay, secure, or compound a sum exceeding HK$5,000 due to a creditor three weeks after the creditor served a statutory demand at the company's registered office; or

- The company returned, unsatisfied, in whole or in part, the execution or other process issued on a judgement, decree, or order of any court in favour of a creditor; or
- It is proved to the satisfaction of the court that the company is unable to pay its debts by taking into account the contingent and prospective liabilities of the company.

Note that if the petitioning creditor has evidence that the debtor company will be unable to pay its debts, the creditor does not need to serve the statutory demand or wait for the three weeks in order to present the petition. This is because Section 178 is only a deeming provision, meaning that it deems what should be taken to be the case only if the actual situation is unclear. If the situation is clear, then Section 178 need not apply.

Even though a company is apparently solvent, the court may judge that it is unable to pay its debts if it persists in non-payment.

Meaning of Just and Equitable

What may constitute 'just and equitable' grounds, which as noted above is one of the circumstances that may induce a court to order a compulsory winding up? These situations include but are not limited to the following:

- **Loss of substratum of the company.** This refers to a situation where it is proved that it has become impossible for the company to achieve the main objectives for which it was formed or that the company has abandoned these objectives. This ground had become less important since a company's objectives can be altered by a vote of the directors and shareholders.
- **The company was formed to carry out a fraudulent or illegal business.** In *Re TE Brinsmead and Sons [1897]*, some former employees of well-known piano makers John Brinsmead and Sons formed their own company, intending to make pianos that were to be branded as Brinsmead products. An injunction was obtained to prevent their selling the pianos. It was held that the company should be wound up because it was formed for fraudulent purposes.
- **Quasi-partnership cases.** The court may dissolve a partnership whenever circumstances have arisen which, in the opinion of the court, render it just and equitable that the partnership be dissolved. Section 177 of the Companies Ordinance applies a similar principle in winding up registered companies.

  Thus, loss of mutual confidence based on lack of probity in the conduct of the company's affairs may be a reason for winding up a company on just and equitable grounds. For example, in a small company where the 'profits' were taken out by way of directors' remuneration (a common practice in partnerships) and no dividends were paid, one of the directors was voted out of office. It was held that it was just and equitable that the company then be wound up on just and equitable grounds.

  Another example is where the position of one of the directors/shareholders is diluted by a share issue, in circumstances in which it is known that this director cannot take up any new shares. In *Re Quality International Ltd.* [*1964*], it was held that this was a small company in the nature of a partnership and that the evidence showed that there existed the sort of deadlock which can best be resolved by winding up.

- **Justice or equity.** Equity enables the court to subject the exercise of legal rights to equitable consideration. This ground covers cases of oppression of minority shareholders in situations other than a quasi-partnership. Subject to the court's reluctance to wind up a company if alternative remedy is available, unfair prejudice will generally be sufficient for winding up a company.
- **Other considerations.** The petitioner who relies on the just and equitable ground must come to the courts with 'clean hands.' In *Re Shiu Fook Company Ltd.* [*1989*], it was held that as the company in question was a quasi-partnership, it was established that a state of deadlock had been reached, but that the deadlock was brought about by the petitioners' own conduct. A winding-up order was not granted.

The court cannot refuse to make a winding-up order on the ground only that the company's assets have been mortgaged to an amount equal to or greater than their value, or that the company has no assets. Other matters including the wishes of the creditors and contributories—the latter of which would attract less weight and generally become material only if the debts were not likely to exhaust the assets—must all be taken into account.

In general, the court may not order a winding up on the just and equitable ground if the company is solvent and the majority shareholders have made a fair offer to buy out the shares of the expelled directors. However, where the mutual trust and confidence of those owning and running the company no longer exist, the court would order the appointment of a provisional liquidator prior to winding up.

There are two principal tests for solvency: the cash flow test and balance sheet test. Under the cash flow test (also called the liquidity test), a company is solvent if it is able to pay its debts as they fall due. The company's assets or prospective assets are not considered. In the balance sheet test (also called the assets test), a company is solvent if its liabilities exceed its realisable assets. In most cases, the company will be solvent under both tests, but there are rare cases where one test might produce a different result from the other test.

Voluntary Winding Up

The key difference between voluntary winding up and a compulsory winding up by the court is that the compulsory winding up does not necessarily involve action taken by any unit of the company itself. In a voluntary winding up, the initiative is taken by shareholders or by creditors.

Voluntary winding up is subdivided into two types—members' voluntary winding up and creditors' voluntary winding up. A members' voluntary winding up is possible only

- If the court issues a bankruptcy order in response to a petition, the debtor immediately becomes bankrupt and no proceedings can be launched or continued against the person or his property without the court's permission. The Official Receiver initially takes control of the bankrupt individual's property and may investigate or hold a public examination of the conduct of the bankrupt individual. The bankrupt individual's property may then be vested on a trustee appointed by the creditors.
- A debtor may avoid bankruptcy proceedings by making use of the voluntary arrangement procedure in the Bankruptcy Ordinance. This involves a formal proposal made by a debtor to his creditors for repayment of his debt and a statutory moratorium against individual debt enforcement. The voluntary arrangement procedure may be used either by a debtor whose insolvency is imminent and predictable or by a bankrupt individual after a bankruptcy order has been made.
- The various stages of bankruptcy and voluntary arrangements can give rise to legal issues for the bank as creditor and as holder of a bankrupt individual's assets. In filing a creditor's petition to the court, the bank must make sure that the statutory demand is correct in form and content as provided by Rule 44 of the Bankruptcy (Amendment) Rules.
- As soon as the bank learns that a bankruptcy order has been made against a customer, it should not allow any cheque to be drawn against that customer's account. Where one account holder in a joint account is adjudicated bankrupt individual, the bank is best advised to dishonour any further cheques drawn on the account, regardless of whether they are drawn by both holders jointly or by one of them entitled to sign on his own.
- If the bank discovers that a customer is an undischarged bankrupt individual, it should notify the trustee in bankruptcy of the existence of the account(s) the bankrupt individual maintains with the bank. The bankrupt individual's salaries or wages paid into a bank account is considered 'after-acquired property,' which the trustee is entitled to claim by notice.
- Like the other creditors, the bank must present proof of debt to satisfy the trustee and the court that it has a legitimate claim on the bankrupt individual's property. It must complete and return a proof of debt form that includes documentary evidence in support of its claim. The bank is entitled to set off against the amount due to the customer any amount due to the bank from him, such as a sum accrued on an overdraft or outstanding personal loan. The balance which remains payable to the customer must be paid over by the bank to the trustee in bankruptcy.
- A bankrupt individual's estate comprises all property belonging to or vested in the bankrupt individual at the commencement of the bankruptcy, excluding such items as tools, books, clothing, furniture, and other equipment necessary for the bankrupt individual's employment, business, vocation, and satisfaction of the basic domestic needs of the bankrupt individual and his family. The bank as creditor may apply to the trustee for a particular item to be included or excluded from the bankrupt individual's property available for payment to creditors.

Key Terms

bankrupt
bankruptcy
bankruptcy order
bankruptcy petition
creditor
creditor's petition
debtor
discharge
extortionate credit transaction
interim receiver
nominee
Official Receiver
proof of debt
set-off
transaction at an undervalue
trustee in bankruptcy
unfair preference
voluntary arrangement

Study Guide

1. What are the three primary objectives of Hong Kong's Bankruptcy Ordinance? Frame your answer in terms of the legal persons that are most affected and explain how the mechanisms that a debtor can use to move towards bankruptcy work.
2. Under what circumstances will a court dismiss a bankruptcy petition? Explain the consequences, for the debtor, of the court accepting a bankruptcy petition.
3. What is the role of the trustee in bankruptcy? What role, if any, does a bank play in determining who the trustee will be?
4. A bankruptcy order is issued for Mr. Leung, a customer of the bank. What should the bank do upon learning of the bankruptcy order?
5. What conditions have to be met for the bank to present a creditor's petition in the case of Mr. Leung's bankruptcy?

Further Reading

Bankruptcy Ordinance website, http://www.hklii.org/hk/legis/ord/6/

Chan Bo-ching, Simon. 2000, *Hong Kong Banking Law and Practice Volume 1*. First Edition. Hong Kong: Hong Kong Institute of Bankers.

Chan Bo-ching, Simon. 2001. *Hong Kong Banking Law and Practice Volume II*. First Edition. Hong Kong: Hong Kong Institute of Bankers.

Ko, Sai Hong. 1998. *Law and Practice of Banking Services in Hong Kong*. Hong Kong: City University Hong Kong Press.

Winding Up

Learning objectives

After studying this chapter, you should be able to:

1. Discuss the nature and types of winding up and the consequences on the company and the bank
2. Explain the duties and powers of a liquidator
3. Understand the legal issues for the banker around the process of winding up

Introduction

When lawyers and bankers talk about winding up, they refer to the process of ending the life of a company. Winding up involves the sale of the company's assets and repayment of its debts. Funds that are left over, if any, are distributed to the shareholders or otherwise disposed of in accordance with the company's articles of incorporation and other rules and regulations.

In this chapter,[1] we discuss the concept and practice of winding up and the legal issues that arise, which may involve the bank. We look at the main legislation that governs winding up in Hong Kong, namely Part V of the Companies Ordinance, and the implementing regulations in the companies (winding up) rules. This chapter also discusses the appointment of a liquidator, who assumes the functions of the board of directors and oversees the formal act of dissolution after the completion of the winding up process.

Winding Up

A company that has been wound up ceases to have any legal existence. All its contractual relationships, including those with its bankers, are terminated.

The process of winding up is complicated and complex, and can take months or even years to complete. In the interim, the company will continue to exist. Subject to the relevant provisions of the Companies Ordinance, its relationship with banks also continues. At some point, however, control of the company and of its bank accounts will be transferred from the board of directors to the liquidator (including the provisional liquidator).

The liquidator is equivalent to the trustee in a bankruptcy, as discussed in Chapter 8. In both cases, these two practitioners collect and realise the assets of the insolvent person or company, and distribute dividends following a statutory order of priority. Both must observe the same underlying principles that govern preferential debts, *pari passu* distribution among ordinary unsecured creditors, and avoidance of transactions conducted as preferences or transactions at an undervalue.

However, a bankruptcy and a winding up have different objectives. The ultimate goal of the bankruptcy process is to discharge the bankrupt individual from his liabilities so that he can restart his life with a clean slate, free from the burden of his debts, and thus can begin to rehabilitate and reintegrate himself into the community. In contrast, the ultimate fate of a company in a winding up is dissolution, that is, the complete termination of its existence.

Liquidating a company can be through a compulsory winding up by the court or through a voluntary winding up. The legal position between the company and the banks will depend on the mode of the winding up.

When it is the court that orders a winding up, the court appoints the liquidator, who can act only under the court's direction and control. In a voluntary winding up, it is

---

[1]This chapter uses draws from *Hong Kong Banking Law and Practice, Volume Two*, by Chan Bo-ching Simon, with permission from the publisher, the Hong Kong Institute of Bankers.

- To appoint an agent to do any business which the liquidator is unable to do himself; and
- To do all such other things as may be necessary for winding up the affairs of the company and distributing its assets.

Powers Exercisable With Sanction

Under section 199(1) of the Companies Ordinance, the liquidator in a winding up by the court shall have the following powers, provided the liquidator has the sanction of either the court or the committee of inspection:

- To bring or defend any action or other legal proceeding in the name and on behalf of the company;
- To carry on the business of the company, so far as may be necessary for its beneficial winding up;
- To appoint a solicitor to assist him in the performance of his duties;
- To pay any classes of creditors in full;
- To make any compromise or arrangement with creditors, or persons claiming to be creditors, or having or alleging themselves to have any claim, present or future, certain or contingent, ascertained or sounding only in damages against the company, or whereby the company may be rendered liable;
- To compromise on such terms as may be agreed:
    i. All calls and liabilities to call, debts and liabilities capable of resulting in debts, and all claims, present or future, certain or contingent, ascertained or sounding only in damages, subsisting or supposed to subsist between the company and a contributory or alleged contributory or other debtor or person apprehending liability to the company; and
    ii. All questions in any way relating to or affecting the assets or the winding up of the company, and to take any security for the discharge of any such call, debt, liability or claim, and give a complete discharge in respect thereof.

Books, Accounts, and Audit

The liquidator in a compulsory winding up is required to maintain proper books and keep a record of entries or minutes of all proceedings and resolutions passed at any meeting of creditors or contributories or of the committee of inspection. The liquidator must also record all matters needed to give a correct view of how he is administering the company's affairs.

If the process of winding up by the court is not completed within one year, the liquidator must send to the Registrar a statement containing particulars on the proceedings and position of the liquidation. These particulars are prescribed in Section 284(1) of the Companies Ordinance. A creditor or contributory of the company is entitled at all reasonable times to inspect the statement.

Bank Accounts

In a compulsory winding up, the Official Receiver is required to keep a bank account styled as the 'Companies Liquidation Account.' The company's committee of inspection may also apply to the Official Receiver for authorisation to open a special bank account.

- **Companies Liquidation Account.** This account should be maintained in a bank that the Chief Executive of the HKSAR may from time to time direct to be used. All monies received by the Official Receiver in respect of proceedings in connection with the winding up of companies must be paid into this account. All payments out of this bank account must be made following the manner that the Director of Accounting Services prescribes from time to time.

  A liquidator other than the Official Receiver must also pay all monies he receives in the process of winding up into the Companies Liquidation Account.
- **Special bank account.** The committee of inspection may apply to the Official Receiver for the liquidator to be authorised to open a special bank account, and the Official Receiver may authorise the liquidator to pay all moneys received by him into that account to his credit as liquidator of the company. The Official Receiver may grant such authorisation for such time and on such terms as he may think fit, and he may at any time order the account to be closed if he is of the opinion that the account is no longer required for the purposes mentioned in the application.

All payments out of the special bank account must be made by cheque payable to order, and every cheque must have marked or written on the face of it the name of the company, and must be signed by the liquidator, and must be countersigned by at least one member of the committee of inspection, and by such other person, if any, as the committee of inspection may appoint.

Liquidator in Voluntary Winding Up

In general, the liquidator in a voluntary winding up may exercise any of the powers which a liquidator in a compulsory winding up may exercise, as explained in the preceding section.

He may summon general meetings of the company to obtain its sanction or for any other purpose. The liquidator may also exercise the power of the court relating to settlement of the list of contributories and making calls. He must pay the debts of the company, adjust the rights of the contributories among themselves, and keep account of his receipts and payments. The account must be audited, unless the committee of inspection or the company decides in a general meeting that an audit is not required.

The liquidator in a voluntary winding up can exercise certain powers only with the sanction of those who appointed him. These are:

- Pay any class of creditors in full;
- Make any compromise or arrangement with creditors or persons having any claim for which the company may be liable; and
- Enter into a compromise on all calls, debts, and claims between the company and any person, and take security to discharge such liabilities and give a complete discharge of liability.

Under Section 255(1) of the Companies Ordinance, the liquidator or any contributory or creditor may apply to the court:

- To determine any question arising in the course of the winding up; or
- To exercise its powers with respect to enforcing calls; or
- To exercise all or any of the powers which it might exercise if the company was being wound up by the court.

The court, if satisfied that the determination of the question or the required exercise of power will be just and beneficial, may accede wholly or partially to the application on such terms and conditions as it thinks fit, or may make such other order on the application as it thinks just.

In the event of the voluntary winding up continuing for more than one year, the liquidator must summon a meeting of the company within three months of the end of the year (and each succeeding year) and lay before the members an account of his acts, dealings, and of the conduct of the winding up. In a creditors' voluntary winding up, a meeting of creditors will also be summoned for this purpose.

Liquidator in a Members' Voluntary Winding Up

The liquidator in a members' voluntary winding up is an agent for the company, not an officer of the court as in the case of a liquidator in a winding up by the court. No person who is an undischarged bankrupt and no corporate body are qualified for appointment as a liquidator of a company, whether in a compulsory or voluntary liquidation.

Appointment. The company in a general meeting appoints one or more liquidators for the purpose of winding up the affairs and distributing the effects of the company. The appointment may be made at the meeting, at which the resolution of voluntary winding up is passed. Within 21 days, the liquidator must give notice of his appointment to the registrar for registration and publish the appointment in the Gazette.

On the appointment of a liquidator, the powers of the directors cease, unless the company in general meeting or the liquidator permits the continuance of such powers.

Removal. The company in general meeting may also remove the liquidator by special resolution. Any contributory may convene such a meeting for this purpose. A notice specifying the intention to propose such a resolution must be given to the creditors and to the liquidator. However, on the application of any contributory or creditor, the court may order that the liquidator whom it is proposed to remove from his office shall not be so removed.

The court may, on cause shown, remove a liquidator and appoint another liquidator in his place. 'On cause shown' is not the same as 'if the court thinks fit.' In the 1987 case *Re Keypak Homecare Ltd.*, the court ruled that the burden of proof is on the applicant to show due cause why the liquidator should be removed.

'Due cause' does not require anything amounting to misconduct or personal unfitness. In the *Keypak Homecare* case, the liquidator was proved to have failed to show sufficient vigour in carrying out his duties. The court ruled that he had displayed a relaxed and complacent attitude to the possibility of wrongdoing on the part of the directors and it was appropriate that he should be removed. If bankers wish to apply to the court to remove the liquidator, they should bear in mind that it is for them to show cause.

Vacancy. If a vacancy in the office of the liquidator occurs by reason of death, resignation, or otherwise, subject to any arrangement with creditors, the company in general meeting may fill that vacancy. The general meeting may be convened by any contributory or by the continuing liquidator (if there were more than one liquidator) and they may apply to the court to determine the manner of conducting such meeting. If for any reason what so ever there is no liquidator acting, the court may appoint one.

If the liquidator at any time is of the opinion that the company will not be able to pay its debts in full within the period stated in the declaration under Section 233 of the Companies Ordinance, that is, that the company is insolvent, he must summon a meeting of creditors and present a statement of the assets and liabilities of the company. At that meeting, the creditors may appoint another liquidator, fix his remuneration, and appoint a committee of inspection, and the winding up will continue as a creditors' voluntary winding up.

Liquidator in a Creditors' Voluntary Winding Up

The creditors and the company at their respective meetings may nominate a person to be liquidator. If they nominate different persons, the person nominated by the creditors will be appointed, unless a director, member, or creditor applies to the court within seven days of the creditors' nomination for an order appointing the company's nominee, or appointing some other person entirely.

If no person is nominated by the creditors, the company's nominee will be the liquidator. If no person is nominated by the creditors, the shareholders' nominee will be the liquidator. If there is no committee of inspection, the creditors will decide on the liquidator's remuneration.

As in a members' voluntary winding up, the liquidator must publish notice of it in the Gazette and deliver a copy to the registrar for registration within 21 days of his appointment. If a vacancy in the office of the liquidator occurs by reason of death, resignation, or otherwise, the creditors may fill the vacancy. However, if the liquidator was appointed by the court, the court may appoint another liquidator to the vacancy.

Upon the appointment of the liquidator, all the powers of the directors cease unless the committee of inspection or the creditors sanction otherwise.

Unregistered Companies

Part X of the Companies Ordinance regulates the winding up of unregistered companies. An 'unregistered company' includes any partnership, whether limited to not, any association, and any company. The exceptions are companies registered under the Companies Ordinance; a partnership, association, or company with fewer than eight members and is not formed or established outside Hong Kong; and a partnership registered in Hong Kong under the Limited Partnership Ordinance.

Any unregistered company may be wound up if it has been dissolved, has ceased to carry on business, is carrying on business only for the purpose of winding up, or is unable to pay its debts.

An unregistered company is deemed to be unable to pay its debts if:

- A creditor is owed HK$5,000 and serves notice on the company requiring it to pay within the following three weeks and it neglects to pay, or secure, or compound it to the creditor's satisfaction;
- An action is brought against any member for any debt due from the company or from him in his character of member, and notice of the action is served on the company and it does not respond within the following ten days by paying, securing, or compounding the debt, or staying the proceedings, or indemnifying the defendant to his reasonable satisfaction;
- Any execution or order, ordained in any court in favour of a creditor against the company or any member, is returned unsatisfied; or
- It is proved to the court's satisfaction that the company is unable to pay its debts; or
- The court is of the opinion that it is just and equitable that the company should be wound up.

A company incorporated outside Hong Kong which had carried on business in Hong Kong but had stopped doing so may be wound up as an unregistered company, even if it has been dissolved or otherwise ceased to exist as a company under the laws of its place of incorporation.

Assets Available for Distribution

When a company is wound up, all its assets (except for those it holds as trustee) are collected and realised and used to repay its debts. When the debts have been repaid, the remaining money is returned to the company's members in proportion to the sums that they have contributed to the company, or according to what is due them following their classification of membership.

The liquidator is duty bound to realise the assets of the company. If those assets are insufficient to cover the company's debts, the liquidator may call upon the members of the company to contribute to the extent that their shares are not fully paid.

Subject to the rights of the secured creditors and of certain creditors to be paid in priority, the assets in winding up are subject to a statutory trust for the benefit of all the creditors to the extent of their debts, and shall be distributed upon the footing of equality.

Members' Liability to Contribute

In the event of a company being wound up, every past and present member is liable to contribute to the assets of the company up to a sum that is sufficient to pay:

- The company's debts and liabilities;
- The costs, charges, and expenses of winding up; and
- The adjustment of rights between the members.

However, the liability to contribute is qualified if the company is incorporated with limited liability:

- In the case of a company limited by shares, no contribution is required from any past or present member which exceeds the amount, if any, that is unpaid on his shares;
- In the case of a company limited by guarantee, no contribution is required which exceeds the amount which was undertaken to be contributed in the event of the company being wound up;
- In the winding up of a company limited by guarantee which has a share capital in addition to the amount undertaken to be contributed in the event of a winding up, the members are liable to contribute to the extent of any sums unpaid on any shares they hold.

A past member will also not be liable if he ceased to be a member one year or more before the commencement of the winding up; or in respect of the debts and liabilities of the company contracted after he ceased to be a member. Past members will only be liable if it appears to the court that the existing members are unable to satisfy the contribution required to be made by them.

When a company is registered as unlimited and then re-registers as limited, special provisions apply to the liability of the members of the company:

- A past member who was a member at the time of re-registration is liable to contribute to the assets of the company to satisfy debts and liabilities contracted before re-registration, if the winding up commences within three years or within re-registration.
- If none of the existing members was a member at the time of re-registration, a person who was a past or is a present member may be liable to contribute.
- There is no limit on the amount which a person who was a past or is a present member at the time of re-registration is liable to contribute.

Directors' Liability to Contribute

Where any director of a limited liability company has undertaken to be personally liable for the debts of the company to an unlimited amount, he is liable to make a further contribution as if he were a member of un unlimited liability company. This is in addition to his liability (if any) to contribute as an ordinary member.

In such circumstances, a director is regarded as a contributory. However, a past director is not liable to make such a further contribution if he had stopped holding office for one year or more before the commencement of the winding up, or in respect of any debt or liability of the company contracted after he ceased to hold office.

Subject to the company's articles, a director is not liable to make such further contribution unless the court deems it necessary.

Liability of the Contributory

The term 'contributory' means a person who is liable to contribute to the assets of a company in the event of it being wound up, and includes any person alleged to be a contributory. The holder of fully paid shares is a contributory because all members are liable to contribute. However, since the holder of fully paid shares is no longer liable to make any contribution to the assets, he will not be placed on the list of contributories unless he requests that this be done or if there is a likelihood of surplus assets being returned to contributories.

A person who is just a debtor of the company, or who is liable to indemnify a trustee on the register, is not a contributory.

The liability of a contributory shall create a debt of the nature of a specialty accruing due from him at the time when his liability commenced, but payable at those times when calls are made for enforcing the liability. Thus, any action for the debt must be commenced within 12 years of the liability starting (this is because the debt is treated as a contract of speciality).

If a contributory dies before or after he has been placed on the list of contributories, his personal representative is liable in the course of administering the contributory's estate and he is regarded as a contributory.

If a contributory becomes bankrupt before or after being placed on the list of contributories, his trustee in bankruptcy will represent him for the purposes of the winding up and he will also be regarded as a contributory.

Collection of the Company's Assets

The court has the power to cause the assets of the company to be collected. It may order any purchases or the company's debtors to pay the amount due into a specified bank account.

These powers may be delegated to the liquidator. Provisions in the Companies Ordinance enable the liquidator to add to the company's assets and thus increase the sum available to repay creditors or to return to members.

- **Personal liability in the event of fraudulent trading.** If in the course of a winding up it appears that the business of the company has been carried on with an intent to defraud its creditors, any person who knows that the business has been carried on in that manner may be personally liable for the debts or other liabilities of the company, as the court may direct.
- **Damages assessed against delinquent officers of the company.** If in the course of a winding up it appears than any person who has taken part in the formation or promotion of the company, or that any past or present officer, liquidator, or receiver has misapplied, retained, or become accountable for the money or property of the company or been guilty of any misfeasance or breach of duty which is actionable by the company, he may be compelled to repay or restore the money or property or otherwise contribute towards the assets of the company by way of compensation, as the court thinks just.
- **Restrictions on execution orders.** Where a company has been sued for debt, a judgment creditor has issued execution against its property, and it is subsequently wound up, the creditor is not entitled to retain the benefit of the execution against the liquidator unless it is completed before the commencement of the winding up or before the creditor receives notice of a proposed resolution for voluntary winding up.

Ranking of Claims

In a winding up, there is a requirement to lodge proofs of debt. In general, all claims by creditors are provable as debts against the company, whether they are present and future, certain or contingent, ascertained or sounding only in damages.

A debt may be proved in any winding up by delivering or sending through the post a proof of debt in the prescribed form to the Official Receiver or, if a liquidator has been appointed, to the liquidator. The court may fix a date on or before which creditors are to prove their debts or claims.

Claims against the company that rank in equal priority should be treated equal, without preference for one or the other *(pari passu)*. However, certain creditors of the insolvent estate may claim preferential treatment. This means that, although ranking equally between themselves, their claims must be provided for in full in priority to any claim made by the general body of unsecured creditors.

Preferential Payments

Preferential payments operate to the disadvantage of ordinary unsecured creditors, including banks. In a winding up, the relevant ordinance specifies which preferential payments must be paid ahead of all other debts. They include but are not limited to the following:

- Payments to a clerk, servant, labourer, or workman in respect of wages and salary owed for services rendered to the company, provided the payment was made during a period of four months before the commencement of the winding up. Other employee preferential payments include severance payments, accrued holiday remuneration, and long service payments;
- Statutory debts due from the company to the government of the HKSAR at the relevant date and which became due and payable within 12 months next before that date;
- Sums payable to a person in respect of any claim (other than a claim for a refund of premium) made under or in accordance with a contract of insurance (but not a contract of reinsurance);
- Sums payable (after offsetting the amount of any sums owning from the claimant) to a person in respect of any claim (other than a claim for a refund of premium) made under or in accordance with a contract of reinsurance effected by the company, as reinsurer, as part of its general business carried on in or from Hong Kong.

A banker may be owed money by the company being wound up for wage advances and for other advances that are not classed as preferential payments. The banks may so arrange matters that it retains higher priority. In *William Hall (Contractors) Ltd.* [*1969*], the creditor had a security which he realised but which did not cover the whole indebtedness. He was held entitled to appropriate the proceeds of the realisation of his security primarily to the unpreferred debt, so as to retain priority as much as possible.

Secured Creditors

A secured creditor is a person who held a mortgage, charge, or lien on the company's property, or any part of it, as security for a debt due to him from the company. A secured creditor (including a banker) need not prove debts at all; he may rely only on his security. However, he may also pursue the remedies which he possessed before the winding up.

If a secured creditor has realised his security, he may prove for the balance of the debt owed him, after deducting the amount realised. He may appropriate the proceeds of realisation as he thinks fit between preferential and other claims. The net proceeds of the realisation shall not be applied to interest accrued thereafter. However, profits made from an unrealised security thereafter may be so applied.

If it is found at any time that the proof made by or on behalf of a secured creditor has omitted to state that he is a secured creditor, he must surrender his security to the Official Receiver or to the liquidator. The surrendered security will be used for the general benefit of creditors. However, the court on application may rule that the omission by the secured creditor was inadvertent. In this case, the court may allow the proof to be amended upon such terms as to the repayment of any dividends or otherwise as the court may consider just.

Unsecured Creditors

The property of the company being wound up must be applied to satisfy its liabilities *pari passu*. As discussed earlier, however, this basic principle of insolvency law has been eroded by the extension of the list of preferential debts.

In most cases, the secured creditors take all or most of the assets of the company in the winding up after the preferential payments. If anything is left over, the unsecured creditors will be paid in accordance with the principle of *pari passu*. Debts due to a member of the company in his capacity as a member must be deferred until the ordinary creditors have been paid in full.

When the creditor is also a member of the company, the payment of certain debts will be deferred. Sums due to a member 'in his character of member' by way of dividends or profits are deferred to the claims of other creditors.

Antecedent Transactions

As in cases of bankruptcy as discussed in Chapter 8, there are transactions entered into before the winding up that are judged invalid and therefore can be reclaimed and the proceeds used to satisfy the liabilities owed to creditors and members. Such transactions may show fraudulent preference (unfair preference after 1 April 1998), be judged as extortionate credit transactions, or involve floating charges.

Fraudulent Preference

Any conveyance, mortgage, delivery of goods, payment, execution, or other act relating to property made or done by or against a company within six months before the commencement of its winding up will be deemed a fraudulent preference of its creditors if it is established:

- That the payment was made by a person unable to meet his debts as they became due from his own resources;
- That the transaction in fact preferred one creditor to another; and
- That the dominant intent with which the payment was made was a desire to prefer the creditor to whom payment was made.

Where any payment was void as a fraudulent preference, misfeasance proceedings can be taken against the directors causing or procuring the payment to be made to recover the amount paid.

Where the winding up of a company commenced on or after the day on which the provision relating to unfair preference came into operation (1 April 1998), any reference to a fraudulent preference in the provisions already mentioned is deemed to be a reference to an unfair preference.

The unfair preference provisions apply to any transactions by the company 1) within two years in the case of an associate; or 2) within six months in the case of any other person. They do not apply to a winding up which commences before 1 April 1998, to which the old provisions above would apply.

Under the unfair preference provisions, it is no longer necessary to establish a dominant intention to prefer; it is sufficient that the decision was influenced by the desire to put the creditor into a position which, in the event of the company going into insolvent liquidation, would be better than the position he would have been in if preference had not been made.

Extortionate Credit Transactions

A transaction is extortionate if, having regard to the risk accepted by the person providing the credit:

- The terms of it require grossly exorbitant payments to be made (whether unconditionally or in certain contingencies) in respect of the provision of credit; or
- It otherwise grossly contravenes ordinary principles of fair dealing, and it is to be presumed that a transaction with respect to which an application is made was extortionate.

Credit is not defined in the Companies Ordinance. However, since Section 264B was introduced in the context of interest on debts of the company, credit is generally taken as referring to loan facilities granted to the company at interest.

On the application of the liquidator, the court may issue an order, with respect to a transaction that it judges to be extortionate, that contains one or more of the following:

- Provision setting aside the whole or part of any obligation created by the transaction;
- Provision otherwise varying the terms of the transaction or varying the terms on which any security for the purposes of the transaction is held;
- Provision requiring any person who is or was a party to the transaction to pay to the liquidator any sums paid to that person, by virtue of the transaction, by the company;
- Provision requiring any person to surrender to the liquidator any property held by him as security for the purposes of the transaction; or
- Provision directing accounts to be taken between any persons.

Effect of Floating Charge

We discussed the definition and nature of the floating charge in Chapter 7. In the case of a company that is being wound up, a charge is invalid if it was created as a floating charge on the undertaking or property of the company within 12 months of the commencement of the winding up. However, such a charge is valid if it can be proved that the company was solvent immediately after the creation of the charge.

A charge is created when it is executed. The question of whether or not the payment of money was effected at the time of the creation of the charge is one of fact. Where a payment is made before and in anticipation of the creation of the charge, and in reliance on a promise to execute it, a distinction is to be made between two classes of case:

- An agreement to give security; and
- An agreement to give security which was so expressed as to be merely an agreement that, in some future circumstances, a security will be created.

Where the floating charge is given to a bank to secure an overdraft on a current account, cash is advanced subsequent to and in consideration of the charge whenever the bank honours a cheque drawn by the company, on that bank account, in favour of a third party.

Legal Issues for the Banker

The many types of winding up and bankruptcy and the various stages of the process can give rise to legal issues for the bank as the banker, creditor, and holder of assets (for example, bank accounts) of the company being wound up. We have alluded to some of these issues in the preceding discussions.

The legal issues to follow are by no means exhaustive. The bank's legal department can give the banker more details and explanations about them, and also update the information in this book, since laws and regulations change over time. In any case, when it comes to banking law and practice, it is prudent for the banker to always consult with the bank's lawyers.

In general, the winding up or bankruptcy of a customer will have a deep impact on the relationship with the bank.

When a company is wound up, it no longer exists legally. Problems for the bank may arise in the often-long period before the winding up process is complete. At some point, control of the company passes to a liquidator but the relationship with the bank continues.

It is important for the bank to distinguish between winding up and bankruptcy. Although both rely on similar principles in dealing with debts, the distribution of assets, and avoiding undervalued transactions, there are some differences between the two. The goal of a bankruptcy process is to discharge the liabilities of the bankrupt entity, to start again later on a clean slate, while the ultimate goal of a winding up is to terminate an entity. This section deals with winding up.

Winding Up Petition

When a bank becomes aware that a winding up petition has been presented against one of its customers, it should take the following courses of action:

- Freeze the company's account;
- Stop lending to the company;
- Refrain from paying cheques drawn on the account;
- Hold any money paid into the company's account in a separate account;
- Review guarantee and security if the bank's lending to the company is guaranteed or secured.

Notice of the resolution for voluntary winding up must be published in the *Government Gazette*, so the bank should know whether a company is being wound up even if the directors fail to inform it. In practice, bank staff are designated to review the *Government Gazette* to make sure the bank is so informed. It is also the case that if the company's account is overdrawn, the bank will receive notice of the creditors' meeting.

As soon as the banker learns that a resolution for winding up has been passed, the mandate relating to operations on that company's accounts should be treated as determined. Thereafter, no cheques drawn pursuant to the mandate should be paid without the consent of the liquidator, unless the directors have been allowed to continue exercising those powers. Cheques should be returned unpaid with the answer 'Refer to drawer, resolution to wind up passed.'

Where a company is being wound up, every invoice, order for goods, or business letter issued by or on behalf of a company or a liquidator, or a receiver or manager of the company's property, must contain a statement that the company is being wound up. This gives the bank another chance to learn of the winding up, if it had overlooked the announcement in the *Government Gazette*, for example, or if it is not notified by the directors. The company's bank accounts should then be frozen and other appropriate action should be taken.

Commencement of Winding Up

Under Section 184 (2) of the Companies Ordinance, a winding up is deemed to commence at the time the petition is presented to the court. For the bank, this date is important because any disposition of the company's property, any transfer of shares, or alteration in status of the members of the company made after the commencement of the winding up is void.

In the *Bank of East Asia Ltd. v. Rogerio Sou Fung Lam & Anor [1988]*, the bank debited the company's account with HK$600,000, having honoured a cheque in that sum drawn in favour of the defendant on 8 February 1984. After the winding up order made on 16 February 1984, the liquidator sought recovery of that HK$600,000 from the bank for reimbursement. The bank then sued the defendant, Rogerio Sou Fung Lam & Anor, to recover the HK$600,000.

The Court of Appeal held that:

- The validity of the payment by the bank continued until the winding up order was made on 16 February 1984, when by virtue of Section 184(2), the winding up was deemed to commence after the petition was presented on 20 August 1983. The combined effect of Sections 182 and 184(2) on or after 16 February 1984 was to render the payment void with effect from 8 February 1984, unless validated by an order of the court.
- The fact that Sections 182 and 184(2) had the combined effect of reaching back and rendering the payment void retrospectively did not mean that the bank had no mandate from the company at the time it honoured the cheque in favour of the defendant, nor was there any question of any mistake concerning the existence of the mandate.
- There were two distinct dispositions of the company's property involved. Section 182 rendered both dispositions void. As between the bank and the company, the bank remained in receipt of the company's property, to which it was not entitled on or after 16 February 1984, the date of the winding up order. As between the company and its agent, the bank, on the one hand, and the defendant on the other hand, the defendant remained in receipt of the company's property to which he was not entitled.
- As the defendant held the company's property without entitlement it was the party primarily or ultimately liable to repay the company. The bank had discharged this liability under threat of legal action and had thereby become entitled to recoup itself from the defendant as payee upon the common law principle of recoupment.
- The combined effect of Sections 182 and 184(2) had been to render void the payment of the company's money by the bank, as the company's agent, to the defendant to discharge the company's obligation to the defendant. The defendant was left to prove in the liquidation in respect of that obligation.
- It followed that there was a total failure of consideration for the bank's payment to the defendant, which entitled the bank to recover the payment. The payment was made by the bank as the company's agent in consideration of the discharge of the company's obligation. The elimination of the discharge and of the bank's entitlement to debit the company's account, with the consequential failure of consideration for the bank's payment, entitled the bank to recover the payment from the defendant under the law of restitution.

Court Validation Order

If the company has successfully obtained a validation order from the court under Section 182 of the Companies Ordinance, the banker then can act in accordance with the court order. The banker may also apply to the court for a validation order, which is an order that all dealings in the ordinary course of business on the company's account(s) pending an order to the winding up of the company should be valid.

In *Re Gray's Inn Construction Company Ltd.* [*1980*], a company had a current account with its bank, which was overdrawn to the extent of £5,332. A winding up petition was presented by one of the company's creditors. The bank followed its usual practice, which was to permit the company to continue operating its account until the date on which the petition was granted.

Between these two dates (presentation of the petition and the granting of the petition), an amount of £4,824 was paid out to creditors for goods and services supplied before the commencement of winding up and, in addition, the company sustained an extra trading loss of £5,000.

The English Court of Appeal held that any payment made into the account during the relevant period as well as any sum paid out of it constituted a disposition under Section 127 of the Insolvency Act 1986 (which in Hong Kong is equivalent to Section 182 of the Companies Ordinance). Cheques should therefore not have been honoured without the sanction of a validation order by the court.

The fact that the bank had acted after obtaining some information about the nature of each payment involved did not absolve it from liability.

Void Transactions Under Section 183

Section 183 of the Companies Ordinance voids any execution put into force against the company's assets after the commencement of the winding up. Accordingly, the liquidator is entitled to recover from a creditor or bailiff sums received by way of execution, unless the execution is completed before the commencement of the winding up by the court (the date of the presentation of the petition).

In *Re Union (V-Tex) Shirts Factory Ltd.* [*1997*], a petition presented to wind up V-Tex was presented by a bank, which held a floating charge over the company's assets. A winding up order was made.

Before and after presentation of the petition, the landlords of premises occupied by V-Tex, who were owed rent, obtained warrants of distress enabling them to take and sell property possessed by V-Tex. The proceeds of the distress were given to the Official Receiver, who sought the court's direction as to disposal.

It was held that, in so far as the distraints levied after the commencement of the winding up proceedings were concerned, Section 183 of the Companies Ordinance rendered the whole proceedings void. The proceeds were to be regarded as part of the assets of the company available for payment to creditors in the process of liquidation generally.

It was further held that, where distraint was levied prior to the commencement of the winding proceedings but sale of the goods occurred after such commencement without legal sanction, the court may void the sale under Section 182 or Section 186, or both.

Since there were ample funds available to satisfy the claims of preferred creditors and no special reasons had been shown which would render the sale inequitable, the landlords should be permitted to complete their proceedings in distress by appropriating the amounts of the outstanding rents from the funds in the hands of the Official Receiver.

Set-Off and Contingent Liabilities

Bankruptcy rules regarding set-off and contingent liabilities (as discussed in Chapter 8 of this book) are applicable in winding up a company that is insolvent. If this is the case, the bank should combine all bank accounts in the name of the company to determine the net amount owing to or from that company. Any remaining credit balance may be retained against any contingent liability of the company to the bank, such as bills discounted but not yet matured.

Summary

This section summarises the issues and topics discussed in this chapter:

- A company that has been wound up ceases to have any legal existence. All its contractual relationships, including those with its bankers, are terminated. The process of winding up can take months or even years to complete. In the interim, the company will continue to exist and its relationship with banks also continues, subject to the relevant provisions of the Companies Ordinance.
- At some point, control of the company and of its bank accounts will be transferred from the board of directors to the liquidator. The liquidator collects and realises the assets of the company, and distributes dividends following a statutory order of priority.
- Liquidating a company can be through a compulsory winding up by the court or through a voluntary winding up. The legal position between the company and the banks will depend on the mode of the winding up.
- The process of the compulsory winding up of a company begins with a winding up petition lodged with the Court of First Instance of the High Court of Hong Kong. The court will examine the petition for correctness in form and substance. If it judges that the petition has merit, the court will issue a winding-up order that will ultimately end with the company's dissolution.
- In a voluntary winding up, the initiative to liquidate the company is taken by shareholders or by creditors. A members' voluntary winding up is possible only if the company is solvent, in which case it is the company's members (shareholders) that appoint the liquidators. If the company is not solvent, its creditors have the power to determine who the liquidator shall be in a creditors' voluntary winding up.
- A petition to wind up a company may be presented to the court by the company itself, its creditors (including its bankers) or contributories, the Financial Secretary, the

Registrar, or the Official Receiver. The Securities and Futures Commission (SFC), the Office of the Commissioner of Insurance, and the Hong Kong Monetary Authority may also present a winding up petition to the court.

- A winding up is deemed to commence at the time the petition is presented to the court. For the bank, this date is important because any disposition of the company's property, any transfer of shares, or alteration in status of the members of the company made after the commencement of the winding up is void. The bank's actions should include freezing the company's account and refraining from paying cheques drawn on the account.
- Other legal issues that the banker must be aware of in cases involving companies being wound up include validation orders obtained by the company or the bank itself from the court, void transactions, and set-offs and contingent liabilities.

Key Terms

compulsory winding up
contingent liabilities
contributory
creditors' voluntary winding up
extortionate credit transactions
fraudulent preference
liquidator
members' voluntary winding up
Official Receiver
pari passu
preferential payments
provisional liquidator
ranking of claims
regulating order
set-off
summary procedure
unfair preference
validation order
voluntary winding up
winding up
winding up order
winding up petition

Study Guide

1. Differentiate between a winding up and a bankruptcy. In what ways are the two processes similar?
2. What is a compulsory winding up and how does it differ from a voluntary winding up? When may the court order a compulsory winding up and a summary procedure for a compulsory winding up?
3. A petition for winding up was lodged in a court against Company A. The court issued a winding up order two weeks later. When should the bank freeze the company's bank accounts? Why is it important for the bank to know the commencement of a winding up?

4. Explain the principle of *pari passu* with regard to the payment of claims by a company being wound up. Do you agree that this principle has been eroded in Hong Kong? Why or why not?
5. What is a validation order issued by the court? What may be the circumstances under which a bank may ask the court to issue a validation order in connection with a company that is being wound up?

Further Reading

Banking Ordinance website at http://www.hklii.org/hk/legis/ord/155/

Bankruptcy Ordinance website at http://www.hklii.org/hk/legis/ord/6/

Chan Bo-ching, Simon. 2000, *Hong Kong Banking Law and Practice Volume 1*. First Edition. Hong Kong: Hong Kong Institute of Bankers.

____________________. 2001. *Hong Kong Banking Law and Practice Volume II*. First Edition. Hong Kong: Hong Kong Institute of Bankers.

Companies (Amendment) Ordinance website at http://www.gld.gov.hk/egazette/pdf/20030728/es12003072828–1.pdf

Companies Ordinance website at http://www.hklii.org/hk/legis/ord/32/

Ko, Sai Hong. 1998. *Law and Practice of Banking Services in Hong Kong*. Hong Kong: City University Hong Kong Press.

Index

Items followed by an * indicate ordinances and laws.

Printed and bound by CPI Group (UK) Ltd, Croydon, CR0 4YY
18/09/2026
14964998-0001